Project Cool™ Guide to XML for Web Designers

Teresa A. Martin

Wiley Computer Publishing

John Wiley & Sons, Inc.
NEW YORK • CHICHESTER • WEINHEIM • BRISBANE • SINGAPORE • TORONTO

This book is dedicated to the little brick building on Cummington Street.

It is gone—demolished several years ago by a wrecking ball—but its spirit lives on. And, if you listen very carefully, you can still hear the sounds of late nights, ill-fitting headlines, balky photo processors, a monster horizontal camera forever rooted in place, and the B52's Rock Lobster. I didn't know what I had then.

That little building made this book—and much, much more—possible.

Designations used by companies to distinguish their products are often claimed as trademarks. In all instances where John Wiley & Sons, Inc., is aware of a claim, the product names appear in initial capital or ALL CAPITAL letters. Readers, however, should contact the appropriate companies for more complete information regarding trademarks and registration.

This book is printed on acid-free paper. ∞

Copyright © 1999 by Teresa A. Martin. All rights reserved.

Published by John Wiley & Sons, Inc.

Published simultaneously in Canada.

No part of this publication may be reproduced, stored in a retrieval system or transmitted in any form or by any means, electronic, mechanical, photocopying, recording, scanning or otherwise, except as permitted under Sections 107 or 108 of the 1976 United States Copyright Act, without either the prior written permission of the Publisher, or authorization through payment of the appropriate per-copy fee to the Copyright Clearance Center, 222 Rosewood Drive, Danvers, MA 01923, (978) 750-8400, fax (978) 750-4744. Requests to the Publisher for permission should be addressed to the Permissions Department, John Wiley & Sons, Inc., 605 Third Avenue, New York, NY 10158-0012, (212) 850-6011, fax (212) 850-6008, E-Mail: PERMREQ @ WILEY.COM.

This publication is designed to provide accurate and authoritative information in regard to the subject matter covered. It is sold with the understanding that the publisher is not engaged in professional services. If professional advice or other expert assistance is required, the services of a competent professional person should be sought.

Library of Congress Cataloging-in-Publication Data:

Martin, Teresa A., 1961–
    Project cool guide to XML for Web designers / Teresa Martin.
       p.   cm.
    Includes index.
    ISBN 0-471-34401-X (pbk./website : alk. paper)
    1. XML (Document markup language)   2. Web sites—Design.
QA76.76.H94M277   1999
005.7'2—dc21   99-18992
                                                                                                         CIP

Printed in the United States of America.

10 9 8 7 6 5 4 3 2 1

Contents

Foreword		**xi**
Acknowledgments		**xiii**
Introduction		**xv**
Chapter 1	**The Structured Document**	**1**
	HTML Past	1
	Documents	2
	Structure	4
	Structure versus Format	5
	Enter SGML	6
	Exit SGML	9
	The Structured Model	10
	Exploring Structure	11
	Example: Rigid Structure	12
	Example: Internal Structure	16
	Structure Benefits	19
	Customized Meaning	20
	Getting to Structure	21
	Step 1: Planning and Analysis	21
	Step 2: DTD Writing	23
	Step 3: Marking up Your Documents	24
	Tying Structure to Display	25
	Summary	26

Chapter 2	**What Is XML?**	**29**
	Data about Data	29
	EXtensible	30
	Markup	33
	Language	37
	Nouns and Adjectives	38
	Syntax	39
	XML versus HTML	41
	A Brief History of XML	43
	But What Does XML Actually Do?	46
	Summary	48
Chapter 3	**The Document Object Model**	**49**
	Document Object Model	50
	The Pizza Analogy	50
	Objects	51
	API	52
	DOM and DHTML	53
	DOM and JavaScript	56
	DOM and XML	58
	DOM and CSS	60
	Interaction	60
	The DOM Specification	62
	A Brief History of the DOM	64
	Using the DOM	66
	Summary	67
Chapter 4	**The Standards Process**	**69**
	Standards Fill a Need	70
	Standards Come from People	72
	Lauren Wood	72
	Jean Paoli	73
	Tim Bray	74
	Mary Fernandez	74
	Jeffrey Veen	75
	The W3C	76
	The W3C Process (or How an Idea Becomes a Standard)	77
	Submissions to Notes	78
	Working Groups and Working Drafts	78
	Proposed Recommendations to W3C Recommendations	80
	Standards Support	80
	What Say Do I Have?	81
	Summary	81
Chapter 5	**Alphabet Soup**	**83**
	Extensions	84

A Word about Status	84
Guide to the Proposals	85
Markup	85
SGML	89
HTML	92
XML	92
Style	92
CSS1 and CSS2	93
XSL	95
DSSSL	97
HTC	97
DHTML	97
Structure Rule Sets	98
Structure Rules in SGML, XML, and HTML	99
Schemas	100
DTD	100
DDML	101
XML Data	103
DCD	103
Processing	103
DOM	104
XML NS	104
Linking	106
XPointer	106
XLink	107
Querying	108
XML-QL	108
XQL	109
Metadata	109
RDF	110
Application-Specific XML	111
XFDL	112
SMIL	112
Ad Markup	112
ICE	112
Math ML	112
Summary	113

Chapter 6   XML Document Basics   115

XML Alone Does Nothing	115
XML Is Not about Display	117
Well-Formed versus Valid Files	117
Before You Create a Document	118
Know Your Data	118
Know Your DTD	119
Elements	120

	Attributes	121
	What Exactly Is and XML Document?	122
	Declarations	122
	Marked-Up Text	123
	Comments	123
	XML Syntax	123
	XML Tags Begin with < and End with >, Just Like HTML	123
	XML Tags Surround the Elements They Mark Up	124
	All Tags Must Close	124
	Empty Tags Must Close, Too	124
	XML Is Case Sensitive	125
	Nest Tags Properly	125
	Quote Attribute Values	125
	XML Tools	126
	Summary	127
Chapter 7	**Creating Well-Formed and Valid XML Documents**	**129**
	Parsers	129
	Well-Formed XML	130
	Creating a Well-Formed XML Document	131
	The Full XML Declaration	132
	Valid XML	132
	More about DTDs	133
	Creating a Valid XML Document	134
	The Full XML Declaration	134
	The DOCTYPE Declaration	135
	Putting DTD Data into the DOCTYPE Definition	136
	Types of Element Data	139
	Attribute Lists	141
	Parsing an XML File	143
	Summary	147
Chapter 8	**Other Pieces of an XML Document**	**149**
	Comments	149
	CDATA	150
	CDATA in an Attribute List	150
	CDATA Sections in a Document	150
	Entities	153
	Entities Save Typing for Repeated Content	154
	Entities Minimize Potential Errors	154
	Entities Are Easy to Update	154
	Entities Can Be Placeholders	155
	Predefined Entities	155
	Internal Entities	155
	External Entities	156
	Nontext Entities	156

	Defining Entities	156
	Using Entities	157
	Namespaces	158
	Declaring Namespaces	159
	Using Namespaces	160
	Summary	160
Chapter 9	**Understanding a DTD**	**163**
	Document Trees	163
	Parsers and Applications	166
	Parts of a DTD	166
	To DTD or Not to DTD?	167
	Large Document Set?	168
	Very Specific Needs?	168
	Industry Needs?	168
	Small Set, Single Creator?	168
	Finding a DTD	169
	Share Existing DTDs	169
	Roll Your Own	169
	Internalize	170
	Reading a DTD	170
	Read the Comments	170
	Look for Basic Elements	171
	Read the Element Declarations	171
	Look for Parent/Child Relationships	172
	Look for the Element's Data	172
	Look for Element Attributes	177
	Read the Attribute Lists	178
	Explore an Example	181
	Check for Entities	185
	Check for Notations	186
	Summary	187
Chapter 10	**Creating a DTD**	**189**
	The DTD Process	190
	Sketch Out Your Structure	190
	Start the File	190
	Use Comments	191
	Set the Doctype Declaration	191
	Create Elements	192
	Element Rules	192
	Free-Form Elements	193
	Textual Elements	193
	Elements within Elements	194
	Element within Element Rules	194
	Mixing Text and Specific Elements	201

	Empty Elements	202
	Create Attribute Lists	202
	Attribute Values	203
	Attribute Defaults	205
Entities		207
	Declaring Entities	207
	Using Entities	208
Notations		209
Ignore and Include Sections		209
Creating an Internal DTD		210
	Example	210
	Using the DOCTYPE Declaration	211
Summary		211

Chapter 11 Under the Hood: A Simple XML Example — 213

Our Example		213
Understanding Your Data		213
	What Top-Level Pieces Appear?	215
	What Smaller Pieces Appear?	215
	Do Similar Subelements Appear?	216
	What Information Do You Want to Know about the Element?	217
	Do You Want to Require That the Element Be Used?	217
	How Many Times Do You Want This Piece to Appear?	217
DTD Building		218
	Understand the People	218
	Learning Curve	219
	Document What You've Done	221
	Our Example DTD	221
Making the XML Document		223
Parsing the Document		224
Displaying the Document		227
Summary		231

Chapter 12 Displaying an XML Document — 233

A Tiny Taste		234
Style Options		236
	XSL	237
	CSS1 and CSS2	237
	HTC	237
XSL versus CSS		238
	CSS Is in Use Today; XSL Will Be Used Tomorrow	238
	XSL Goes Further than CSS	239
	CSS Defines Style; XSL Adds Transformation Powers	239
	CSS Works with HTML and XML; XSL Focuses on XML	239
	CSS Isn't Contextual; XSL Is	240
Cascading Style Sheet Concepts		240
	What Is a Style?	240

	What Is Cascading?	240
	What Are Style Sheets?	242
	A Style Sheet Example	242
	Creating a CSS Style Sheet	244
	ASCII Text File	245
	Style Properties	245
	Style Rules	247
	Style Declarations	247
	Property Values	249
	The Display Property	250
	Connecting an XML File to a Style Sheet	252
	A Few Practical Pointers	252
	Start with a Checklist	252
	Start at the Top	252
	Remember the Display Property	253
	Test, Test, Test	253
	Summary	253
Chapter 13	**HTC Behaviors**	**255**
	What a Behavior Does	255
	Support for Behaviors	257
	HTC Behavior Concepts	260
	Separate Content from Display	260
	Separate Skill Sets	262
	Custom Tags	262
	Creating an HTC	263
	Three Files, Three Skills	263
	The Content File	263
	The .css File	264
	The .htc File	264
	Chain Reaction	264
	Steps in the Process	264
	HTC Elements	266
	Element: <COMPONENT>	266
	Element: <PROPERTY>	266
	Element: <METHOD>	267
	Element: <EVENT>	267
	Element: <ATTACH>	268
	HTC-Specific Elements	268
	ondocumentready	268
	oncontentready	268
	Summary	271
Appendix A	**CSS Reference**	**273**
	Color and Background Properties	273
	Color	274
	bgcolor	274

background-image	274
background-repeat	275
background-attachment	275
background-position	275
Fonts and Text Properties	276
font-size	276
font-family	276
font-style	277
font-variant	277
font-weight	277
line-height	278
text-indent	278
text-align	279
text-decoration	279
text-transform	279
letter-spacing	280
word-spacing	280
Position and Visibility Properties	280
position	280
left	281
top	281
display	282
z-index	282
Spacing and Area Properties	282
clear	282
float	283
height	283
width	283
border-color, border-style, border-width	284
border-top-width, border-bottom-width, border-right-width, border-left-width	284
border, border-top, border-bottom, border-right, border-left	285
margin, margin-top, margin-bottom, margin-right, margin-left	285
padding, padding-top, padding-bottom, padding-right, padding-left	286

Appendix B The Companion Website   287

Glossary   289

Index   293

Foreword

Understanding XML

I joined Microsoft in May 1996 with great faith in the Standard Generalized Markup Language (SGML) and a dream that its potential might one day be realized. As soon as I arrived at Microsoft, Jon Bozak of Sun Microsystems (as well as Tim Bray from Textuality, and a lot of other friends from the SGML world) and I began discussing the possibility of simplifying SGML and creating an XML standard. We shared an incredible enthusiasm for markup language and structured information, and we understood what it could mean for the web.

The web as we know it began when documents became widely available to everyone, when access to the Internet became as easy as "reading a page." Documents are the magic that make the web appealing to the world. This "magic" is what specialists call structured information. Since its inception, the most fundamental building block of the web—the HTML document—was actually organized as a set of smaller portions of information assembled in a logical fashion. But that was only the beginning! Since then the web became more and more pervasive, used in many new fields and for many new purposes. We needed more and more ways of slicing and describing smaller portions of information, and for describing data in a more universal way. We needed information to be independent of any platform and adaptable to any language in the world. We needed it to be text based because that was the only way to make it universal and this is why we created XML, the universal language for data. Now, three years later, the achievements of XML are amazing! Hundreds of small innovative startups and every large, established software company have implemented and delivered XML support. The magnitude of support is exhaustive, from word processors to databases to productivity applications to data exchange. Companies and entire consortia are created everyday, and create XML applications and vocabulary in every kind of human knowledge possible (e-commerce, law, medicine, math, sciences, and more). XML has already made a substantial and real impact.

This phenomenon occurred because of standards, which are so important to the web; in fact, this is what the web is all about. You could not view a document in a browser or even connect to the Internet if standards did not exist. The beauty of XML, and something that I personally can attest to because I lived it, is that XML and all the standards that have been built around it have been developed in a truly cooperative spirit, in a process involving many intelligent, passionate individuals and competitive companies which had as their sole driving passion the purpose of making the web a better place for the user. This remarkable and perhaps seemingly idealistic achievement has been a difficult but beautiful process to watch and to live.

With XML's inception in 1996, Microsoft began to develop a huge set of applications, tools, and vocabularies supporting XML that grew from these original efforts of a few dedicated professionals in the W3C. Now, in February 1999, with the release of the first XML-enabled browser—Internet Explorer 5.0—Bill Gates, a well known XML fan, publicly acknowledged that virtually all Microsoft presentations from now on will mention XML in some capacity.

In this book, Teresa Martin gave depth and meaning to something that might otherwise have seemed theoretical (after all, XML is a language for defining languages!). It is an achievement to attain an intimate understanding of a new field; it is even more remarkable to convey an understanding of this field to others. To see our work and progress with XML explained in a way that gives it credence in reality is extraordinary. This book conveys the essence of XML to HTML and web users, showing them how to expand their knowledge and augment their dealings with structured information by using XML.

It is a very good guide for learning XML itself and learning what a DTD is, and the book is full of examples of XML applications. Teresa insightfully captured the intentions of the creators of XML and accurately conveyed the XML philosophies. In particular, she understands and presents the integral nature of the creation of standards on the web, reflecting the internal, intrinsic, overall standards process. This in particular will be very important for the reader and will help him or her to plan ahead, because more new standards will be added to the XML family.

The web is moving now to a more meaningful place with regard to structured information, and XML is effectively preparing a Web Version 2. This book will certainly help many users to participate in this journey.

Enjoy the book!

Jean Paoli
Redmond, May 17, 1999
Product Unit Manager, XML Technologies
Microsoft Corporation
Coeditor of the XML Specification

Acknowledgments

Thank You!

You know who you are. You are the people who helped to improve this book and to keep its author somewhat sane during its creation!

To Bruce Rosenblum—this book owes a great deal to you and your generous reviews and editing. Your input on topics ranging from SGML and XML implementation issues, to DTDs, to confused paragraphs in need of gentle revision, to notes about the class of 2015 (in which we both have a vested interest!) have helped more than you know. Bruce is part of Inera Inc., <http://www.inera.com>, and is an awesome programmer who understands documents inside and out and who can explain it all in understandable terms. A rare combination indeed.

To digital artist extraordinare Lyn Bishop, <http://www.zama.com>—thank you for pulling me out of the Illustrator quagmire! When you need professional art, I strongly recommend turning to the professionals. I wish I had done so earlier and I am grateful that Lyn helped me pick up the pieces.

To Jean Paoli of Microsoft—our multiday phone conversations and your review of structure and XML set me on the best possible path for thinking about the issues surrounding XML.

To Lauren Wood of Softquad Software—the time you spent explaining both the DOM and the reality of creating a specification helped me focus those chapters and your reviews of them kept me clear and concise.

To Tim Bray of Textuality—our email exchanges about XML and its future provided a valuable sanity check. I hope my endless questions about what namespaces really are weren't too frustrating!

To Terri Molini and Jon Bosak at Sun—for adding depth to the history of XML and for their persistence in working the system.

To Mary Fernadez of AT&T Labs' Research Facility—for her generous explanations of query languages and the deconstruction of what a language does.

To Eve Maler of ArborText—for reviewing and clarifying the differences in XLink and XPointer. And to Steve DeRose of Brown University and INSO for adding additional linking insight.

To Simon St. Laurent—for demystifying Xschema and keeping me updated on its process into the W3C submission process.

To Jeffrey Veen of Wired—for sharing with me his reasons for working on W3C projects.

To all of the folks at Wiley who helped take this book from idea through the final printed product you hold in your hand today.

To everyone at Project Cool—Edna Chavira, who follows up on endless details, listens to me babble, and even tangled with Photoshop and a balky printer for this project; Mike Sweeney, who is wonderfully cynical about XML (and all technology for that matter) but who keeps the servers happy and prevents me from doing bull-in-a-china-shop damage to directory structure (well, mostly!); and Glenn Davis who is, well Glenn—annoyingly talented and able to figure out how to make HTML components, JavaScripts, and CSS dance while I'm still slogging through the spec.

And most importantly, thanks to the lovely Miss Allie, who helped make this book possible with random keystrokes, grabbed mice, crumpled paper drafts, and the occasional toddler screech…all of which serve to remind me of the really important things in life.

Teresa A. Martin
Palo Alto, CA
March 1999

Introduction

Round and Round We Go…

Sometimes I think that everything is destined to go full circle. I got into the publishing business in 1979 because I needed to make money. I was a freshman in college, our campus paper needed people to typeset, and I figured type, typeset, what's the difference, right? I could wing my way through it.

In short order, I ended up as a production coordinator, tucking the paper into bed at the printer across the river in the wee hours of the morning one night a week. This was a volunteer position. Somehow the hourly job had become, well, something else. I did, however, sometimes typeset things, enter the command to print, and process the film. Actually, it was RC paper. We stuck thumbtacks in one end and pinned it to the wall to dry.

This touching-of-the-machine came in handy the following summer when I needed a paying summer job. I stretched the truth a little to a local type shop that was advertising for a temporary typesetter. I mean, I *had* produced typeset copy. In the following whirlwind month I proved that I could dance really fast, staying exactly one half-step ahead in learning what I needed to know to do the job. It was the fastest crash course in point size, leading, line length, kerning, and typesetting coding you've ever seen.

The following fall I found myself addicted to those volunteer nights. I would often find myself standing on the BU Bridge (the link between the newspaper's office on Cummington Street, behind the Boston University campus, and the printer's plant across the river in Cambridge) just as the sun rose. I'd gaze down at the slowly brightening Charles River as a lone car rolled up the usually bumper-to-bumper Commonwealth Avenue, and I'd know that our night's work was currently rolling off the press and that maybe in a few hours the driver of that car would be reading a copy of our work with his or her morning coffee. It made the publishing process visceral, human, and very, very real.

I also found myself working at a weekly paper as a part-time typesetter. I didn't quite expect the ancient blind keyboard (made by a company called AKI) and paper tape, but I learned how to splice, how to translate eight rows of dots into a letter, and how to code yet another typesetting system. I also became very good at handling large glass type disks with great care—we were threatened that if the owner of the shop found a scratch, he'd dock our pay. Does anyone still remember those glass disks? They weighed what felt like a ton and went into machines made by a long-defunct company named Photon. Designers did not touch these machines, and type purists sneered that the output wasn't what it used to be.

A few years later, I was still working part-time at this local weekly. I had graduated to setting ads, town warrants, and even boldly specing incoming jobs myself. Then we got this new system, from a company called Compugraphic. The system had the catchy name of Modular Composition System, or MCS for short. Suddenly we could see our code on a screen. And with a special separate preview monitor we could see how the text would look—more or less—when it rolled out of the processor. And, even more incredibly, we could typeset borders and rules! Instead of applying sticky border tape to a block of type, we could paste up a single unit. The typesetters were suddenly designing ads, not just following a designer's marked-up hard copy. We had the power.

I didn't realize it then, but that moment marked the beginning of a convergence of formerly distinct tasks. These tasks continued to meld together until desktop publishing came along. Suddenly everyone was supposed to be able to do everything. It sort of matched the 1980s credo of super-achiever. You can do it all, you can have it all.

A decade later, the World Wide Web made its appearance. The single part of the desktop publishing process that a one-person band couldn't do was print many copies quickly and distribute them. We still needed some sort of press and post-press process. But with the web, that barrier went down, too. In those early, heady days of web publishing it seemed that all the walls were stripped away, the barriers had fallen, anyone and everyone could publish anything.

Publishing, though, is a collaborative process at heart; as the web grows more pervasive as a publishing medium, it seems we are asking it to do more and more. And that's where the long trend to one-person-does-it-all publishing is beginning to turn back on itself.

You see, as we moved to the one-person/one-stop model we were also losing capabilities along the way. Part of what enabled everyone to do it all was good tools; the other part was simplification of the tasks. With the old CG MCS and PowerPage, or the old Q5000 systems, we could do some pretty amazing things. We could create what were essentially programmatic routines that would test for conditions and apply certain styles based on the value in counters and variables. (Of course, no one would even suggest that we were programming—that required special knowledge of computers, and we were just setting type.) We could batch process a 350-page book with varying headers and footers and even different styles, chapter by chapter. We could make UDKs, user-defined keys, that let us perform a string of common functions—text and code—with one keystroke. UDK values could include variables, so we could push a key and automatically enter the first part of a string, type the name of, say, the book in the book list we were building, and push another key and watch the string of commands finish entering automatically.

On the post-press end, our counterparts could selectively bind different sets of pages based on values in a database and deliver quasi-custom packages to different individuals. R.R. Donnelley & Sons invented a process called Selectronics, which could be used, among other things, to deliver targeted advertising. In one well-publicized example, Buick ran several different ads in the same ad slot in a magazine. The ad that appeared in any given issue would be the one that best matched the demographics of the subscriber to whom the issue was going. Was the subscriber in a suburban family zip code? That subscriber's magazine would be bound with the family vehicle ad. For a price, you could even inkjet print the name, address, and telephone number of the nearest dealer in the ad. Selectronics, though, wasn't just for ads. A magazine about parenting could target editorials and ads based on information it had about the age of the reader's child or children. A different cover could be delivered to urban and rural areas or to eastern and western regions.

In those pre-web, pre-desktop publishing days, no one person was expected to know it all and do it all. It just wasn't possible. We demanded a lot from the process, and it took many skill sets to meet those demands.

I can't do it all!

Say this now, aloud, with me:

I can't do it all. I can't do it all.

This is important to remember as we begin, again, to add complexity to the information publishing process. With JavaScript, Dynamic HTML (DHTML), Cascading Style Sheets (CSS), and now Extensible Markup Language (XML) and its stylistic cousin, Extensible Style Language (XLS), we're adding tremendous power and exciting new functionality. And we're creating a process that requires many different skill sets.

There's a lot of hype around XML. Anxious web designers and developers fervently believe they need to know how to "use" XML. XML, however, isn't one set of tags that you memorize, pop into a document, and voila! XML is now in your list of skills.

XML is a way of working with information in a structured form. Yes, there is a technical specification and some syntax that you can memorize, but syntax alone won't let you actually do anything. XML applications work at several different levels, and to take full advantage of what XML offers you'll be working with other people, with complementary skill sets.

Your task will be to understand what XML and a structured document allow you to do to present and display and how to use the tools and your design skills to take full advantage of these capabilities. You'll need to understand the dynamics of a structured document sufficiently so that when a client says, "I want to deliver this information on both a computer and a PDA, and I don't want to create different versions of my material," you can say, "That sounds like a possible XML application." Or when said client wants to bring 300 product spec sheets online and make them easily searchable by part number and product category, you can say "Let's explore the possibility of implementing an XML-based solution for this project." Then you'll pull together a team that includes programmers, database gods and goddesses, designers, and production types. Together this team will explore and implement the solution, each person working on the parts that match his or her skills.

Yes, you will also need to know how to structure tags within a web page and how to be sure your document is "well-formed," but the tags that you use will depend on the larger structure that you and your team are creating.

This isn't as simple as it sounds. You will have to learn new technology—for example, you might want to learn how to program Internet Explorer 5.0 behaviors (now called "HTCs"). HTCs, or HTML components, are a display feature that takes advantage of XML structure. At the very least, you'll want to understand how HTCs work and how you can adapt the styles of behavior libraries so that your page elements will look the way you want them to look.

There is almost-new technology you'll need to know. For example, you'll want to have a basic understanding of CSS (Cascading Style Sheets), a standard that lets you define the display characteristics of elements on a web page. You certainly don't need to be a JavaScript expert, but it helps to have a general sense of what JavaScript is and know that it is one of the tools you can use to control the actions of a web page. (One place to learn the basics of both of these is our very own Project Cool Developer Zone, <http://www.projectcool.com/developer>.

XML from a designer's perspective requires an understanding of both concepts and a set of related technologies. Together, these pieces combine to add some exciting new opportunities to web-based publishing.

About This Book

This book is written for the web designer, web development team leader, or web publisher. You know who you are—you're the one who makes sure the site looks good, functions well, gets updated routinely, has a good user interface, interacts with readers, and displays content appropriately.

You create attractive forms that are easy for people to use and integrate them into the site, but you might have your engineer write the back-end CGI that processes data and work with a database programmer to tie the site into database-driven applications.

You are the visionary who sees and specs the potential of the site, but you're already learning that you can't do it all by yourself (remember to chant after me, "I can't do it all, I can't do it all."). You coordinate with programmers, scripters, and system administrators. You're part of a team that includes people who make art, people who design, people who write, people who program, and people who perform page production tasks—much like the publishing teams of the past.

This book is explicitly not written for the database experts who will be getting down and dirty with XML implementation in the data trenches, although if you are a database type, this book will provide a useful background that positions the potential applications of XML within the web environment. This book isn't targeted at SGML DTD gurus (document type definition experts) either or people who want to debate the minutiae of back-end server applications, although there is something here that everyone in these groups can learn.

What this book does is teach you about the potential of structured documents and the role XML plays in creating those documents. It will de-hype XML, exploring what it is and what it isn't. It will position XML within the alphabet soup of HTML, DHTML, CSS, XSL, DOM, and SGML. It will teach you enough about XML and related standards so that you can talk intelligently about them and understand the issues they raise. It will show you how to create well-formed and valid documents. It will teach you to build a simple DTD. It will teach you how to attach styles to an XML document and display it in a web page. It will teach you how to work with XML and the 5.X browsers to display pages in more powerful ways.

The first half of this book is about structured documents, document object models, metadata, and the big picture behind XML and related proposals. It gives you the fundamentals you need to make good use of the potential of XML.

The second half of the book focuses on working with XML, showing you how to create well-formed and valid documents, how to create elements and attributes in simple DTDs, how to create and use entities, and how to apply style data to an XML document. The final chapter walks through a simple case study of an XML document from a designer's perspective.

The Chapters in This Book

Chapter 1, "The Structured Document," introduces the key concept of structured documents, which is essential to understanding the potential of XML.

Chapter 2, "What Is XML?," presents an overview of XML, talking about what it really is and how it fits into the structured document. It also introduces the concept of metadata, another critical concept behind XML.

Chapter 3, "The Document Object Model," discusses the Document Object Model (DOM) and the role it plays in displaying an XML document on a web page.

Chapter 4, "The Standards Process," explores the process that created XML and is developing other related technologies. Because XML is standards driven, understanding the process helps you better understand XML's larger potential.

Chapter 5, "Alphabet Soup," overviews the many proposals that work with XML and provides additional sources of information on each.

Chapter 6, "XML Document Basics," teaches you XML syntax and how to work with an XML document.

Chapter 7, "Creating Well-Formed and Valid XML Documents," teaches you how to create both well-formed and valid XML documents, introduces you to the internal DTD, and shows you how to parse a document.

Chapter 8, "Other Pieces of an XML Document," explores CDATA sections, entities, namespaces, and other components that may be part of an XML document.

Chapter 9, "Understanding a DTD," shows you how to read and understand an existing DTD.

Chapter 10, "Creating a DTD," walks you through the process of creating your own external DTD, including creating elements, attributes, and entities.

Chapter 11, "Under the Hood: A Simple XML Example," explores the necessary thought processes behind creating a DTD that will work in your environment.

Chapter 12, "Displaying an XML Document," provides you with an overview of CSS and how it applies to XML documents.

Chapter 13, "HTC Behaviors," provides you with an overview of IE5 behaviors, a way of displaying XML with scriptable display characteristics.

Appendix A, "CSS Reference," is a summary of CSS commands.

Appendix B, "The Companion Website," gives you some information about the website that is offered as a companion to this book, which is full of additional references.

The Glossary contains definitions of XML terms, concepts, and proposals.

Summary

XML sounds much more intimidating than it is. The key to working in an XML environment is to remember that you can't do it all. You'll need to match skill sets with different levels of XML implementation.

This book will help you understand the potential of XML, where you fit into it, and how you can get started working with it.

The Structured Document

In an HTML-only web world, the process of creating all documents is pretty much the same: Open the file, put in some HTML code around the content to describe how the page displays in a web browser, and close the file.

We use HTML, for example, to make a headline blue, Helvetica, and centered; to give a table a two-unit border and a pale yellow background; to place a specific image on a page; or to make hypertext links to other sites on the web.

We don't use HTML to identify pieces of a page. We don't specify, for example, that a certain set of words is a book title or that a certain headline is a section chapter head. Instead, we use HTML as a design tool that specifies the way our work will appear in a web browser window.

Understanding how we use HTML and what we use it for is important as we start to explore XML.

HTML Past

HTML wasn't always a designer's tool. In its infant stage, HTML started out with a somewhat different focus than the display creature we've come to know and, well, tolerate, if not love. In its earliest incarnation, HTML tags described the elements of a document by what they did. The tags created a structure, a sort of outline of the pieces of the page.

You didn't use tags to tweak the document's appearance. Or, at least, you weren't supposed to. There were different levels of headlines, there were paragraphs, there were lists. These were the pieces that made up a web page. You identified everything on your page as one of these elements.

With a small handful of tags you could build a very simple page. It was easy to do, and it met the initial purpose of the first web browsers: to provide a visual way to display and link to information around the Internet. It was not about displaying aqua text that matched a corporate identity color. It was about function.

The browsers had a small amount of built-in default intelligence that displayed information in a top-level headline at a larger size than information in a second-level headline. Both were displayed larger than the information in a paragraph. This simple display intelligence helped make the elements easier to separate when displayed in a browser.

This little bit of default display information was enough to hint that the web page had a future beyond gray and black, with blue links. It was enough to whet the creative appetite of us human users—and HTML began to morph from something that described a very basic structure into something that displayed fonts in 18-point Arial type, colored lime green on a background of a photo of Spot the dog and Whiskers the cat standing in front of the new corporate headquarters. The notion of structured documents on the web quickly disappeared under a tidal wave of creative design.

That change opened the door for creative possibility, and it helped make the web feel like a friendly place to millions of everyday users. But when structure disappeared, a certain level of potential also disappeared. Now, with the advent of XML, the notion of a structured document is back.

Documents

Before we get to structure, let me first say a word about documents in general. There, I've said it again: the word *document*. It sounds rather dry and academic. Wouldn't you rather say *the book*, or *the brochure*, or *the web page*? Don't be put off by the term! *Document* is a catch-all term that describes any set of information presented to a reader. A document can be presented in different forms and different media: books, web pages, magazine articles, advertisements—these are all formats for displaying a document.

One of the interesting characteristics of documents is that the same document can take on many different forms. You can create a headline and 18 paragraphs of text and put them on a web page. You can take those same paragraphs and print them on your printer and suddenly you have a flyer. You can bind the headline and paragraphs into a book. You can put the headline and paragraphs into a database. The document stays the same; it just manifests itself in different types of presentations.

One way to think of a document is as a collection of small elements. Ah, there's another word that can feel awkward: *element*. An *element* is simply a single component, a piece, a part. The headline we just talked about is an element. Each of the 18 paragraphs is an element. The headline and 18 paragraphs, taken together, constitute a document.

A document is really quite a lot like a home theater system. You have cable and connection elements, a large-screen TV element, a surround sound element, a DVD player element, and a digital processor element. Together, all these elements form a home theater. You can arrange all the elements one by one in a row, you can stack them, you can place them in a rustic pine armoire or a sleek hidden cabinet. You can make the outward appearance of the system look different, but no matter how you slice it, you have the same set of elements interacting with each other.

Thinking of the document as a collection of elements has a lot of advantages. For starters, when you think of a document this way it suddenly becomes flexible. It isn't something printed on a piece of paper that sits there, unable to change. It isn't a web page, displayed in a certain font, married to the technology in vogue at the time it was built. It isn't a word processing file, forever tied to the program that created it.

By treating a document as a collection of elements, you free it from the constraints of a time, place, and presentation format. A flexible and fluid document can pour itself from printed page to electronic page, adapting itself for the form. It can move from word processing program X to text editor Y without losing its integrity. You no longer need to worry about whether a paragraph is indented or set in 12-point Times Roman. All you need to do is know that the document contains headline and paragraph elements.

Here's another cool thing about documents: The elements from which they are formed aren't a random group of things tossed together willy-nilly. They are a group of elements that have a defined set of rules and relationships to each other. At first this idea might take a little getting used to, but the relationship and rules for interaction are extremely important.

Think about that home theater system again. It works as a system because the audio plug goes into the audio jack, and the video on the TV connects via a certain type of cable to the video on the DVD player. Each element of the system has a set of rules that guides its interactions with the other elements. Some elements won't work unless another element is already in place—you can't make use of video-in unless you have in place a connection to video-out. Some elements aren't allowed to work next to each other—you can't cram a VCR tape into DVD holder.

The rules are part of the elements. When you move an element into a different environment, the rules come with it. You can move your home theater from your living room to your neighbor's basement, but the video-in still needs a signal carried over a cable from the video-out.

And the rules aren't affected by display issues. You can put the VCR on the kitchen counter instead of in the AV cabinet, and you can paint the front panel with pink and purple polka dots, but the VCR still won't play a DVD.

Apply this thinking to a document. If it is made up of elements and if the elements have rules for interaction and a relationship to each other, you can move a headline and 18 paragraphs from my computer to yours, and it will still have a headline and 18 paragraphs. You can print it, you can sing it aloud, you can paste it into a chat room, and the headline will still be a headline and the paragraphs will still be paragraphs. Each element might be visually very different, but the headline still has the same relationship with the paragraphs, no matter where or how it is displayed.

Seeing a web page through this document lens is important because the primary use of XML and its affiliated technologies is to define the document and its elements.

Structure

The word *structure* gets a bad rap. It reminds many of us of dreadful school experiences in which we had to recite the multiplication tables at a certain time of the day and couldn't visit the restroom without raising our hands and getting a pass. We cringe at the thought of using something called *structure* in our creative work of building for the web.

In the document world, though, structure has a more biological meaning. A document's structure is a little like a lizard's skeleton. It defines the physical outline of the beast and describes what elements appear and the order in which they appear. In the lizard's case, there's a main backbone, off of which hangs back legs and front legs. The legs have appendages that end in claws. In the lizard's case, structure is not only a good thing, it is a necessary thing. It defines a lizard by the sum of its parts, not by the color of its tail, the size of its claws, or any other lizard display description.

If you relied on description, you might say that the creature is green and has a long tail. One listener might envision the lizard you are describing.

Another might envision an alligator. Because you're relying on description, you lose the meaning that is imparted with and inherent in a defined structure. The display isn't portable from one person's mind to the next, but the structure is.

Remember that old fable about the blind men and the elephant? Each man is asked to describe the animal. The one who touches the leg describes the beast as a thick tree. The one who touches the tail describes it as a rope. The one who touches the trunk describes it as a snake. Each of these descriptions misses the elephant. If they had been able to rely on structure instead of display, the elephant would have appeared quite clearly to each man, no matter what display lens he had.

In a document, structure plays much the same role. Structure defines the document by describing each of the elements and how they all fit together.

Suppose you're writing a guide that tells people how to take care of their pet lizards. This guide has a number of elements. It has chapters, headlines, subheads, paragraphs, glossary terms, photos of lizards, nutritional values for different foods, guidelines, reference sources, and procedures. These elements combine to make a document titled *The Lizard Guide*. No matter what format the document takes—whether it is printed on an 8x10-inch sheet of glossy paper using 12-point Bembo type or displayed in a web page using the Arial font—it is still *The Lizard Guide*.

The features that define *The Lizard Guide* are not 24-point headlines or italic style or double-spaced paragraphs; many different types of documents can be formatted with 24-point headlines, italic style, and double-spaced paragraphs. *The Lizard Guide* and *The Bible* could both be formatted and presented in the same way. The structure—the elements within each and the way the elements interact with each other—is what sets apart *The Lizard Guide* and *The Bible*.

Structure versus Format

One of most important things to understand about a document is that there is a difference between structure and format.

- Structure is about the content of a document.
- Format is about the way a document looks.

We have spent most of our lives working with documents in which structure and format are intertwined. When you think of telephone directories, odds are that a particular look and color come to mind. Few people think about telephone directories as a combination of phone, name, and address elements. Instead, most of us picture thin newsprint, a thick book, yellow, white, and blue paper, small type, bold words and nonbold words.

The form and format are what let us interact with the document. That's why we remember it. It is the surface level, the most obvious feature of the document. It is about the way the page feels or the sharpness of the image. Format is about having green hypertext links that stand out instead of black links that can't be distinguished from the rest of the text. It is about putting the legal disclaimer in tiny type: "Only one winner per galaxy; prizes can be claimed after the moon turns blue." Formatting conventions are what dictate the use of a script font for a formal invitation, a font that is larger for headlines than for tables, and an indent at the beginning of paragraphs.

Format is incredibly important. It gives us critical clues for using the document. It guides us through a document, implies meaning, adds value to the document, and makes a document work for its audience.

But format is not structure. As we move into a publishing environment that incorporates XML, the two must be separated. And because we have had a lifetime of training in format and thinking in format, the transition to thinking in structure can be somewhat difficult, especially for designers.

Figure 1.1 compares a formatting (style/display) description with a structural description.

The technologies for dealing with structure and format are, of necessity, different. They are also complementary and work with each other. As we move forward into the future of the web, XML is the preferred method of defining a document's structure. CSS (Cascading Style Sheets) and XSL (Extensible Style Language) are or will be the preferred methods of defining a document's format.

And HTML? It started out trying to deal with structure and was hijacked to present format. The little-from-both-camps approach was exactly what we needed to jumpstart the web and bring it to the state it's in today. HTML isn't going away anytime soon, and it will leave a legacy to all the web technologies that follow it. Much as the web publishing world is no longer a one-person-do-it-all world, web publishing technology can no longer be a one-format-do-it-all solution either.

Enter SGML

Both XML and HTML have their roots in SGML, the Standard Generalized Markup Language (also known as ISO 8879, for those of you who like hearing standards-speak).

The Structured Document

Formatting Markup

Times Roman 24 bd — Happily Ever After

Zapf Chancery It 18/24 — Once upon a time ...

Times Roman x36 12/14 —
There was a prince who thought he was a frog. Sad young man. He insisted he be fed bugs and flies and other creepy-crawlers, all of which he licked from the plate, sticking out his toung and making little grunts as he swallowed.

"The prince is mad," the court wispered.

2 em p. indent

But they didn't dare say it aloud for fear the king would hear. The king had only one son, the Frog-Prince.

If he heard the court make fun of his son he'd shout, "Off with their heads," and the unfortunate to whom he pointed wouldn't criticize the Frog Prince again.

The King began to seek a bride for his son. This was no easy task. Who wants to marry a Frog?

Structural Markup

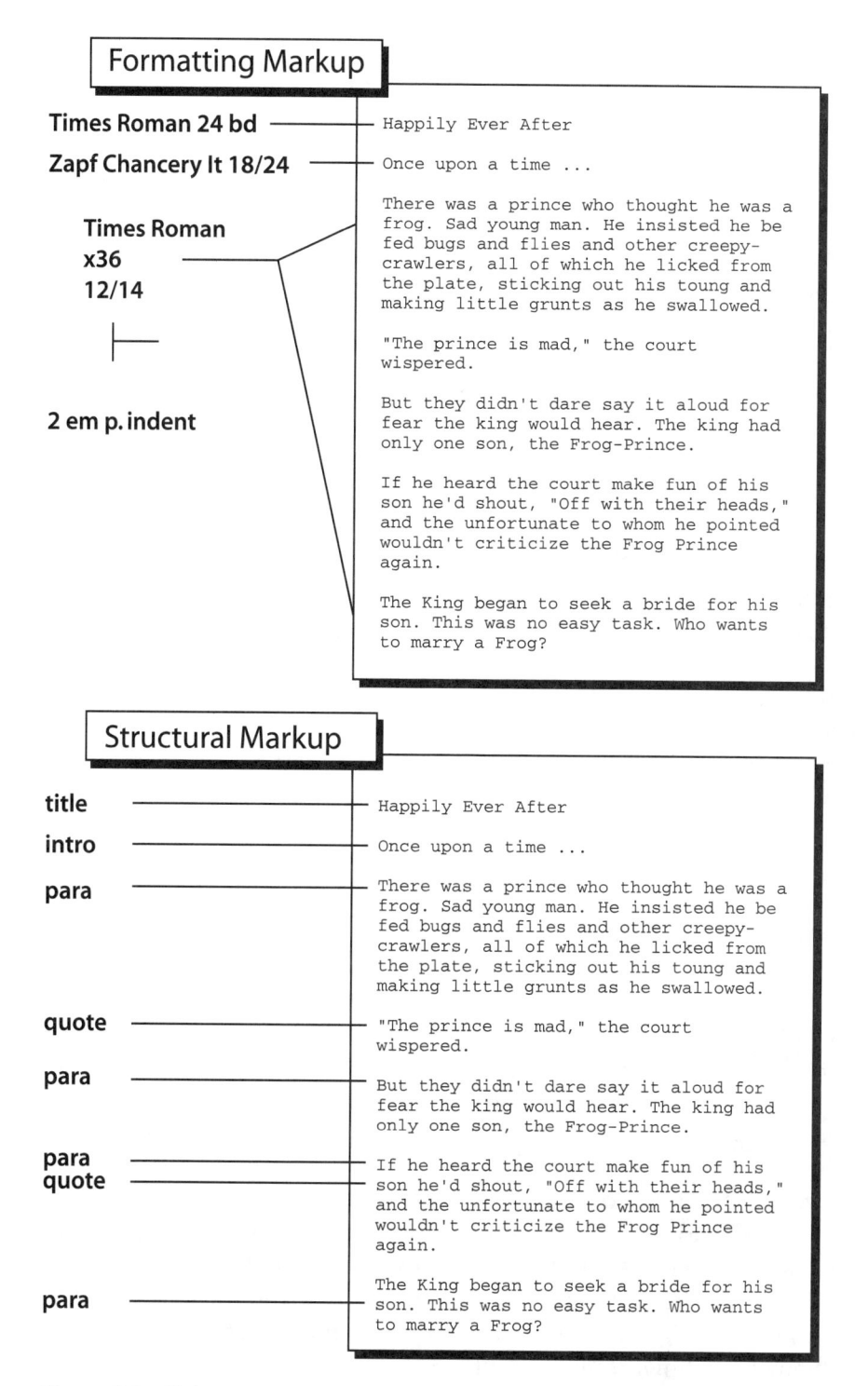

title — Happily Ever After

intro — Once upon a time ...

para — There was a prince who thought he was a frog. Sad young man. He insisted he be fed bugs and flies and other creepy-crawlers, all of which he licked from the plate, sticking out his toung and making little grunts as he swallowed.

quote — "The prince is mad," the court wispered.

para — But they didn't dare say it aloud for fear the king would hear. The king had only one son, the Frog-Prince.

para
quote — If he heard the court make fun of his son he'd shout, "Off with their heads," and the unfortunate to whom he pointed wouldn't criticize the Frog Prince again.

para — The King began to seek a bride for his son. This was no easy task. Who wants to marry a Frog?

Figure 1.1 Style versus structure.

HTML has, of course, veered off into a space of its own, turning from a structuring tool into a web formatting tool. XML, however, has retained the vision of SGML, which is that structure is what makes a document flexible.

SGML came about because people were creating documents that needed to be adapted, reused, and passed along to other people. In the late 1970s and early 1980s this meant, in practice, that the same document was retyped into several different sets of word processors and typesetters along the way. Yes, you could pass along ASCII text, but the raw text was just that, raw. Headlines, paragraphs, subheads, and tables were blurred together in the same text stream. The relationships between elements in an ASCII document were completely lost. The result was that millions of hours and millions of dollars were wasted in duplicating efforts—each ASCII document would have to be reformatted whenever it was transmitted.

Large organizations with heavy document processing needs led the charge to SGML. The U.S. Department of Defense, for example, came up with a plan called CALS (Computer Aided Logistics and Support). Under this plan, all text would be in the form of SGML documents. This meant the text could be easily transferred from one type of system to another without losing its structure. Headlines remained headlines, paragraphs remained elements that appeared after headlines, steps in a process remained steps in a process. In other words, the document retained its structural integrity no matter what type of text processing or publishing system used its content.

What this meant in real production time was that when the people who created the subwheel assemblies for Fighter Jet X completed their documentation, that documentation could be passed along and incorporated as one intact piece into the documentation created by the people who built the full wheel assemblies for the same fighter jet. This combined documentation, in turn, eventually ended up—without repetitive rekeying and potential entry of errors—in the documentation set for the finished jet.

Under this plan, the days of endless retyping and re-creation of the same documents would become a thing of the past. By adding structure, millions of dollars and hours would be saved as documents became truly portable.

The idea of structure could also take us one step further. When SGML reality was tied into the DoD's dream of the "big database in the sky," the documentation, the parts, the related part numbers, and the current inventory data could all be tied together for one-stop, electronic access. Need to replace an interior light in the jet? Log in from your secure laptop, define the problem, learn how, when, and where to acquire the part, find out what other parts might be needed, and get step-by-step directions for fixing the problem. It would offer instant access, provide up-to-date information, and save literally billions of dollars. What's not to like?

Exit SGML

SGML and CALS have been implemented in one form or another, but they've never become truly widespread across the entire publishing industry. They have remained in the purview of the big-budget, big-project, technical documentation segment. It turned out that the answer to the question "What's not to like?" was "the process."

Although the idea of SGML and the structure it brought had applications far beyond the production of technical documentation tomes, the tools and the presentation of the tools by and large remained in and of the community that created these massive documentation products. The tools spoke this group's language and met its needs. They offered a level of complexity that this particular market required. SGML in action always felt like a detailed tech-doc solution, and publishers of other stripes tended to shy away from it. And, on the surface, at least, it certainly didn't seem to offer anything of interest to designers.

In addition, SGML required you to create something called a DTD, a *document type definition*. This is a complex description of the document structure, a very formal sort of rule set that had to follow a very specific and, some say, awkward syntax. The DTD tested each SGML-tagged file to make sure it complied with the defined rules. For large projects with very specific requirements, the DTD played an important error-checking role, making sure that the documents complied with the project's requirements. DTDs were never easy to write. This added step created a technical barrier to using SGML for any but the largest projects, or for projects where SGML was mandated.

In many ways, XML is designed to meet the same set of needs as SGML but to do so in a way that is easy to learn and implement. Those needs are the ones that every content creator shares: to be able to create a document that is easily transportable across media and display formats. In other words, XML is designed to help you create a document that you can write in your word processor, that I can edit in my word processor, and that we can turn into a web page, a printed page, and a PDA brief—all from the very same file.

In a world where people might read the same information online, in print, on a PDA, on a television monitor, and in yet-unknown formats, this offers an immediate benefit, but it does so without some of the extra complexity that turned off potential SGML users. XML lets you use a structured approach with a minimum of overhead and a shortened learning curve.

The Structured Model

To understand what XML can do for you, you need to understand the structured document model. The structured document model has two key principles:

- In the structured model, each part or element of the document has a relationship to the others.
- This meaning is separate from the visual appearance of the element.

This model is the key to understanding how, at its base level, XML works and how much power it can bring to your documents, whether they are newspaper pages, aircraft specifications, or a guide to music CDs.

Each piece of the document is defined by how it fits into the larger document, what role it plays, and how it is related to other pieces. XML doesn't care if a top-level headline is blue and 24-point Helvetica or if it scrolls across the page in a fancy animation. What it cares about is that there is an element called *tophead* and that a tophead is always the first element on a page. XML can also be used to specify that a tophead is always followed by something called *intro*.

In a way, XML is building a sort of navigational guide to the document: We start here, at the tophead. Then, we go to the intro graph. After that we go to a second head and a lot of paragraphs and bulleted lists and quotes.

A structured document doesn't need to be rigid; it just needs to follow a consistent set of rules. Think of the structure brought with XML as being a little like grammar in a human language. To understand what someone is saying, you need to understand that there is a subject and a verb and that they usually follow each other in the expected order. There are many variations on subjects and many variations on verbs, but if you understand the basic structure and the basic rules, then you can translate the language into meaning. And it doesn't matter if that language is spoken, written, presented in person or remotely. It doesn't matter if the words are shouted, whispered, spoken in a spooky tone or a happy banter. If you understand the structure, you can understand the meaning.

The same is true for a document. If you know what to expect from it, you can do powerful things with it.

You might want to consider an XML structured document as being a little like a vector file and an HTML file as being like a bitmapped file. The vector file contains information for creating the illustration it contains, but it doesn't actually draw it out. The way it is finally drawn depends on the device doing the drawing. An oak tree will still come out as an oak tree, even if in one version the lines are thick and in another they are aquamarine. It is a file that contains meaning without display data.

The bitmapped file, in contrast, contains very specific information about how to display the oak tree. The file has no intelligence about what it is drawing—it hasn't a clue that it contains something called an oak tree—but it will know the color, shape, and size of each and every pixel in that tree. The file contains display data without meaning.

Exploring Structure

All documents have a structure, but the depth and complexity of the structure vary, as you can see in Figure 1.2.

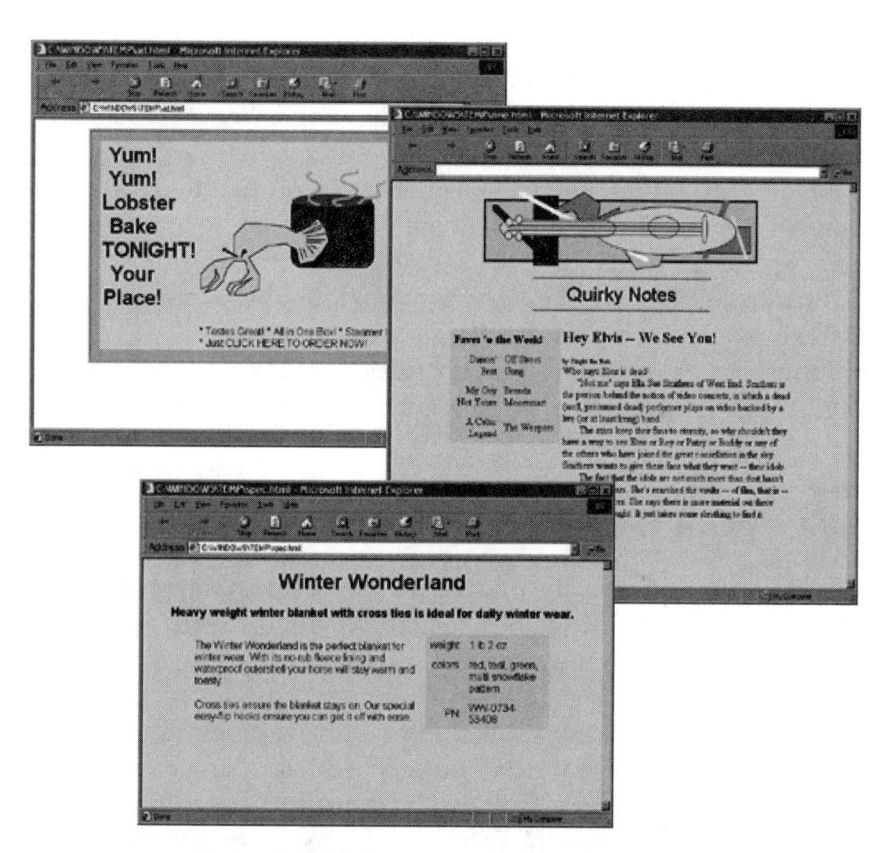

Figure 1.2 There are many different applications of structure.

Some web pages serve as the template for similar types of documents. You may be creating these pages in sets of hundreds. They are likely to follow very specific rules. This type of document clearly and definitely has structure behind it, structure you can count on, structure you'll use over and over again.

Other pages contain more loosely related information. These groups of pages might be similar but not identical. They may live in an archive or be constantly accessible over a long period of time. Their rules may be specific, but perhaps not as detailed as the template-type pages. These documents have a strong structure, but it might not be as readily obvious as in the template-type or rigid document. It might take a little looking under the hood to see what is really happening within this looser document in order to find the structure.

Other of your web creations are destined to live only once, for a specified period of time. They may be single, unique pages that you tweak and tweak until they look exactly the way you want them to appear. They have a structure, but it may not be one that you'll use repeatedly in document after document. This type of document has a structure, too, but it is quite free-form in comparison to the other types of documents. Appearance is of primary importance. The information you have and the way you display it are tightly linked. You probably wouldn't want to have one with the other.

All documents have structure. But the way you handle structure will vary depending on the type of document with which you are working.

Is one type of document better than another? Certainly not. Some types of documents, though, will benefit more obviously or more quickly from the structured approach of XML. If you understand the ideas behind the notion of structure you'll be better able to judge for yourself which of your documents can take the most advantage of XML and exactly how you'll use XML's strengths.

Example: Rigid Structure

The first type of document, the one that serves as a template for other documents, clearly and definitely has structure behind it, structure you can count on, structure you'll use over and over again.

For example, you may be creating 32 different product spec sheets for the beach toys line. Each spec sheet will be pretty much the same as the next, except that one describes a "pack 'n go beach chair" and another describes a "set of sand castle molds." The content changes, but the fundamental structure into which the content is placed does not change. There will always be exactly the same elements in exactly the same order. The elements will contain the same type of content from sheet to sheet. The product color element will always contain color values for the product. The list price element will always contain a dollar value. The description element will always contain a few sentences.

This type of document features the most easily-understood application of a structured document: the repeated, rigid template. In large part, the structure is so obvious in documents like these because the format is rigid and is often designed to highlight the structure.

When you look at this type of application, though, be careful to keep format and structure separate. With this type of document, it's easy to focus on a design template and be distracted from the structure, or to see the format as the structure. The layout of the page isn't what gives this product sheet structure; it is the elements and their relationship to each other.

Let's look at a website that contains the product spec sheets for your company's product line of horse blankets. Odds are that every spec sheet has pretty much the same information:

- Product name
- Description (a brief product description)
- A set of product specifications, such as colors offered and price

Using the idea of a structured document, the spec sheet can be described like this:

- The document is a spec sheet.
- The first element in the document is something called *product name.*
- After product name is something called *intro.*
- After the intro are one or more elements called *paragraph.*
- After each paragraph is either another paragraph *or* something called *specs.*
- After specs is any one of these elements: *height, width, depth, weight, color, part number.*
- Each of these elements has particular attributes, such as number of inches or a color name.

If you step back a second, you'll see that this description has created a document tree or a sort of relational outline. In visual terms it looks something like Figure 1.3.

The structure has created a set of elements that are arranged in a certain order. Each element has a place and a relationship with other elements. Taken together, they form the document you know as a spec sheet.

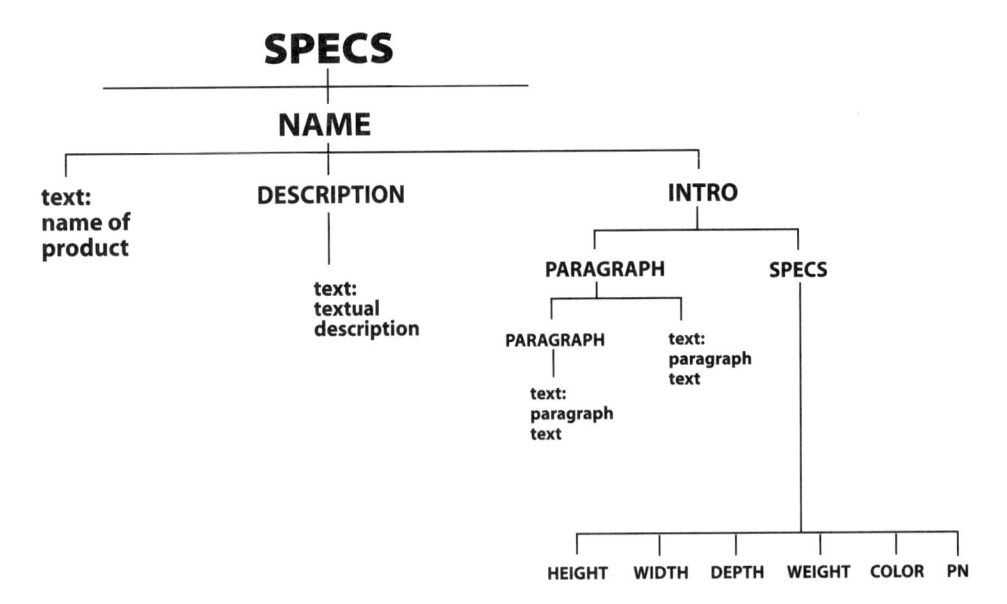

```
                           SPECS
                             |
          ┌──────────────────┼──────────────────┐
                           NAME
                             |
   text:           ┌─────────┼─────────┐
   name of      DESCRIPTION          INTRO
   product          |                  |
                    |            ┌─────┴─────┐
                  text:       PARAGRAPH    SPECS
                  textual        |
                  description    |
                             ┌───┴────┐
                         PARAGRAPH   text:
                             |       paragraph
                           text:     text
                           paragraph
                           text
                                            ┌────┬────┬────┬────┬────┐
                                         HEIGHT WIDTH DEPTH WEIGHT COLOR PN
```

Figure 1.3 Document tree.

You'll notice that no place in this structure do we say that the product name is 18-point Helvetica. That information is not part of the document structure. It is part of the display or formatting information. The same structure can be displayed in many different ways. Figure 1.4 shows the spec sheet structure applied to a line of horse blankets. The documents are displayed as a simple web page and use style data to display the structure in this way.

It can look like a list, a brochure, or an outline. It is completely and totally transferable because it is described as a series of interrelated elements.

Now let's look at something a little less rigid, say, an online 'zine, something like the one in Figure 1.5. The 'zine has lots of different articles. On first glance, the design-heavy presentation doesn't look like it has much of a structure. Let's look again.

What do the articles have in common? Well, it seems that all have a title and a byline. Most use pull quotes, many cite books by name, and others reference popular music. Each was posted on a specific date. All contain a series of paragraphs. Most contain quotations.

On closer inspection, it turns out that each member of this group of documents does indeed share elements with other members. Maybe a structured approach isn't totally out of line.

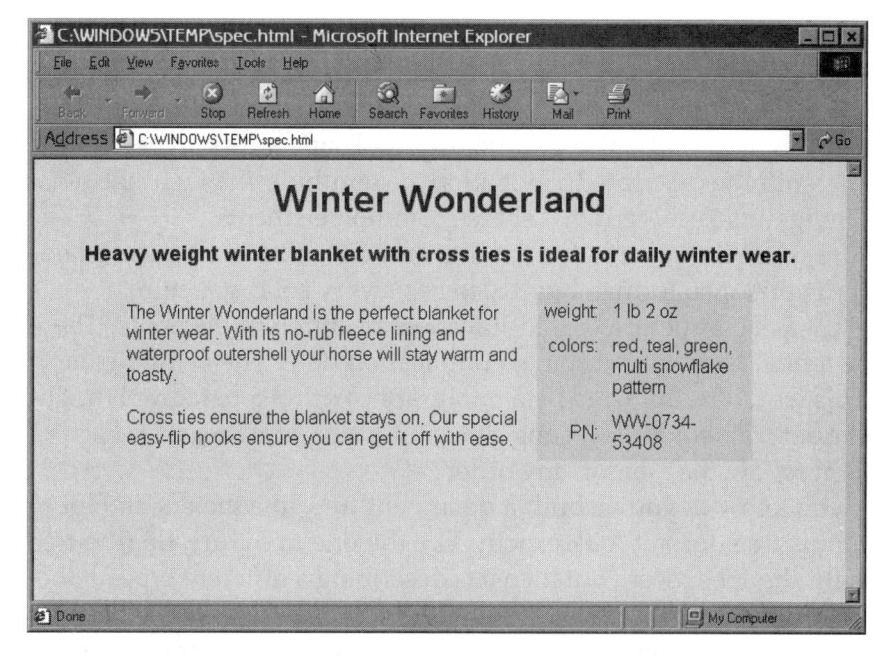

Figure 1.4 Style applied to the same structure. Example: Hidden Structure.

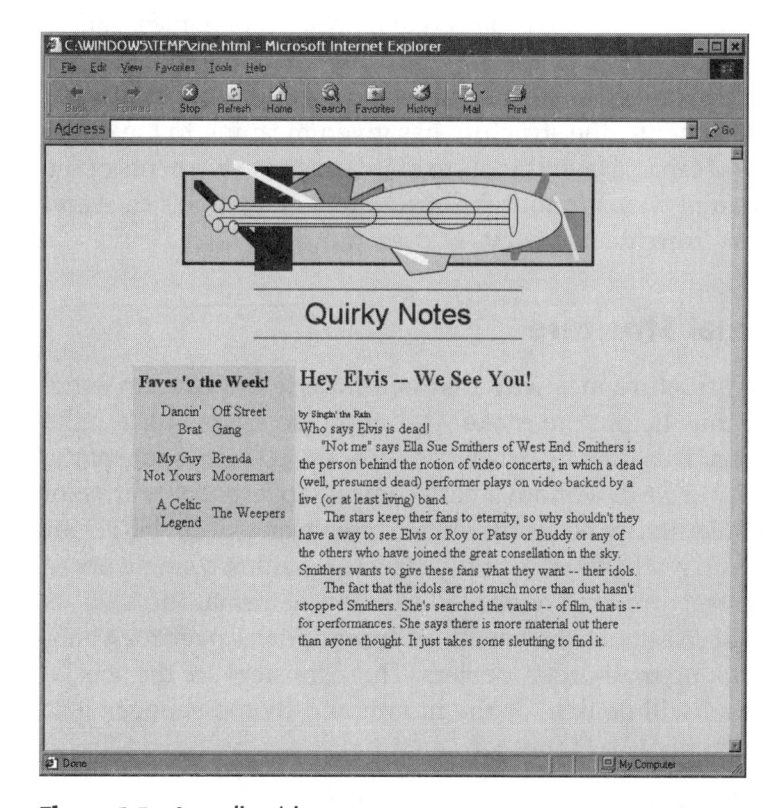

Figure 1.5 An online 'zine.

Remember, structure is about describing what elements are part of a document—not how the elements look. Don't be thrown by the fact that pull quotes use DHTML to have the first word pulsate. That's a display issue. Don't be thrown by funky use of typography. That's a display issue, too. Don't let a spiffy JavaScripted navigation system hide the fact that what you are navigating is content that shares common elements.

Structure is not the same as formatting, and this 'zine is a perfect example. It has a very open format, but it also has a very solid structure.

In this case, the structure would have lots of different elements. There would be a title. Next would come a publication date. Then could come a byline. This would be followed by a paragraph. Within a paragraph might be a pull quote, a book title, a song title, an author, and an artist. Each of these might follow the other in any order.

Before you know it, you've built a document tree, like the one in Figure 1.6. Sure, this tree doesn't look exactly like the one in Figure 1.5 (the tree you built for the spec sheet), but then it is describing a different type of document.

Because you've added structure you can now do some interesting additional applications with the 'zine. For example, suppose you have an article talking about women-led bands. You can display a list of names, bands, and best-known song as a sidebar without creating a separate file. You can do this because you've tagged elements as *song names* and *bands* and *names* within the main document—the structure has given meaning to the document's elements. You can use layout tools to display certain elements of the document in a different way. Without the structure, you couldn't slice and dice the information to create new ways of presenting it.

Example: Internal Structure

XML thinks about structure in a way that is a little less formal in some ways than SGML, thus helping to make XML more accessible for a wide range of applications. This difference is what allows you to use some of the power and flexibility of XML without a very complex external definition of the structure. It would hardly be worthwhile to create an external DTD for a single page ad! With XML, you can apply structure within a single document and use that structure as a connection to external formatting.

Let's say you've been asked to create the underlying sales page for a banner ad that is promoting mail-order lobsters. These lobsters are the special of the month. The ad will be live for the month and then disappear. The page will look something like Figure 1.7.

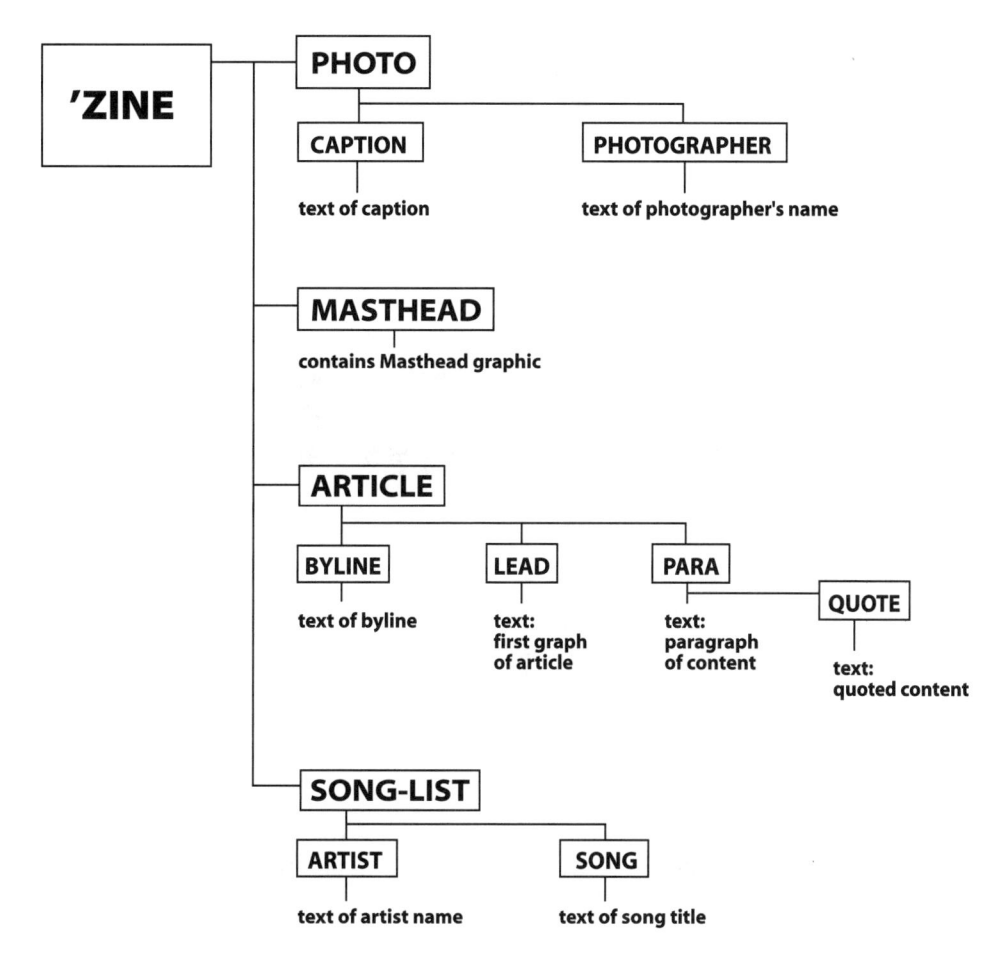

Figure 1.6 Document tree for a 'zine.

If you created a document tree for the ad page, it would look something like Figure 1.8, one clump of elements. You could move the elements around with little loss of meaning, as long as the display and presentation were strong.

Your job is to present these darn crustaceans in a way that makes them so appealing the orders will just pour in and there will be a lobster bake in every online household.

Are presentation and display important in this application? You bet!

You want that headline to be a luscious boiled lobster red. The selling features of the one-pounders should sound like they are dripping with but-

Figure 1.7 Ad page.

ter. And the call to action—to buy, and to buy *now*—must be powerfully presented.

With a document like this you have a choice. You can create it with HTML. There is nothing wrong with that option, and that's the route many people will take.

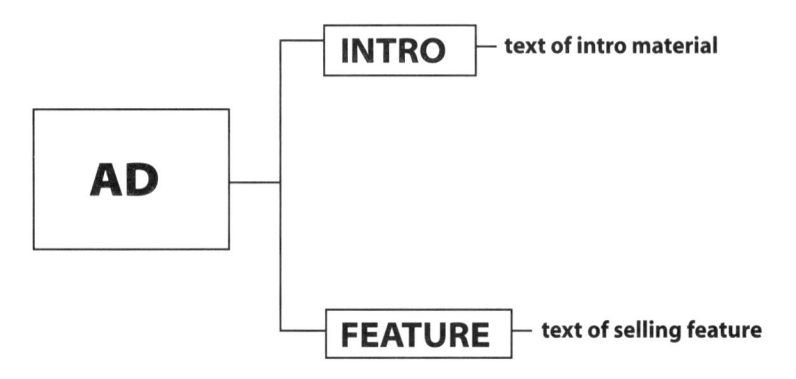

Figure 1.8 Document tree of ad page.

Alternatively, however, you could create a simple structure and use XML to separate content from form. This enables you to make formatting changes quickly and easily, without altering the lobster ad file. It also allows you to send the lobster sale data to other types of devices and use a style application to display the lobster in the best manner for that device.

Right now, to do this, you (and most of your audience) need to be on 5.X browsers, which support both HTML and XML. You'll mark up the file and connect it to a separate set of style information that tells the browser how to display your marked-up pages. (In the near future, as something called Extended Style Language becomes more widely used, you'll be able to translate your XML style decisions into old-fashioned HTML that can be displayed on any browser.)

By adding structure tags, you'll also be adding the framework for creating and adapting other future ads, or for reusing the same ad with a different presentation, or for presenting the ad on a different display device, such as a PDA. HTML works fine, but XML gives you an extra set of options with only a little additional up-front work.

Structure Benefits

The beauty of a structured document, such as the kind you create with XML, is that once you have structure, you have meaning. And once you have meaning, you open up some very interesting possibilities.

You can do useful searches. For example, if you used the HTML *bold* tag to highlight your glossary terms, the best you can do is to search for <b>. Not very useful. Sure, you'd probably find glossary terms (along with lots of other unrelated stuff). If you have structured your document, though, you'll not only find the glossary terms, you'll be able to organize them in alphabetical order or by order of appearance in your file.

Remember that 'zine example? Well, because you've applied structure, you've set up an environment in which you can let a reader search for all references to a Hole song or all mentions of Courtney Love, but not just a raw search. You can do contextual searches, looking for all mentions of Courtney Love in which she (a) is a singer of a song, (b) is the author of a song, or (c) appears in the title of a book.

But that's not all. Because you've applied structure, you can have the results of those searches displayed in a certain way, say, by date with the title and byline followed by the first paragraph in smaller text. XML structure lets you choose what to display; style technologies working side-by-side with XML let you choose how to display it. The combination can be quite powerful.

You can create custom presentations. Asking the browser to display all the bold text is an impossible task; even if you could do it, you'd end up with a mish-mash of random phrases that you happened to format as bold. Creating a page that displays only a list of *part numbers* and *price* elements, however, might serve up just the document you need. And imagine if you could also sort by those elements! The doors of possibility begin to swing open.

Because structure and format are separated, you can display the page in different ways. For example, if you want to test the difference in rates of lobster purchases based on background and headline color, you don't need to create two totally different files if you've taken a structured approach to the document. You can just create two different style applications and apply them based on your test criteria.

You can display the same information on different devices. One form of custom presentation is to display your document in different ways based on the viewing device your reader is using. For example, if the reader is using a web browser, you might want to display a full product spec sheet, complete with illustrations. But if the reader is using a PDA, you might want to display only the *part number*, *product info*, and *price* elements in bold, easier-to-read text. Because the structured document has intelligence, you can display the data in a way that works on the little PDA screen, without creating a separate file.

You can easily add a new type of information to the document. If you have a structure in place, adding new elements becomes fairly easy. For example, you can create a new element called *discount price* that is part of your product spec document, and you have a new, usable component without reworking the entire page. You can add a *record label* element to your 'zine and begin adding the label information right away.

Remember, *structured* doesn't mean suffocated. A structured document is open to possibilities and growth. Giving something structure is a way to add value and meaning. It doesn't trap you into a single approach or a single set of possibilities.

Are you starting to get the feel for this structured approach?

Customized Meaning

The structured environment as created by XML lets you tag elements with names that have meaning to you. For example, if you are publishing screenplays, you could create a tag for *stage-direction* and a tag for *music-cue*. These tags aren't part of any preexisting bundle; they are tags that you create for your specific needs.

This is nice because it not only adds meaning to your documents but also helps the people who are producing your documents. When elements are coded in ways that make sense, the job becomes much easier.

If you're a publisher of legal texts, you can create a set of tags that identify elements that are specific to your application and your document's structure. You might have *case numbers*, *dates*, *defendants*, *litigators*, and so on. You can ask all your authors and production staff to use these element tags. Suddenly you've added meaning in a, well, meaningful way.

By working as part of a group, you can take tags beyond your own local use, too. For example, back in SGML days, the Association of American Publishers created a set of SGML tags that it believed would greatly simplify the production process of books. In the XML arena, discussions are underway in a variety of discipline areas to create sets of tags for, say, e-commerce, which could be used by everyone running an e-commerce site, or math, which could be used by everyone working with equations.

There is a flip side to customizable tags, though. Some people find it easier to have a fixed list from which to work because the alternative is so open-ended that they feel overwhelmed. If you're one of these people, either find an association tag set that works for you or assign yourself the task of creating a small manageable set of tags and start working with those. You can always go back and add new tags later.

By consistently implementing tags that make sense for your application, you'll also end up with a set of documents that can be displayed, searched, and presented in various ways in different media.

Getting to Structure

The following section describes some general steps for creating a structured document.

Step 1: Planning and Analysis

First, and perhaps most important, is taking the time to analyze your document set. If you have a series of related documents take a look at them as a group and see what they have in common. Look for the different elements that make up the documents and identify them.

The elements that make up your document set will be unique to your needs. Do you have book titles? Do you have scientific species names? Do you have employee first and last names? Do you have chapter titles? Do you have product list price? Ask yourself "What are the different pieces of the document that I might want to identify and work with, or to identify and store additional information about?"

For example, you might decide to make *quotation* one of your elements. You think you might want to display quotes in a special way. You might want your readers to be able to search for quotes. And you might want to store information about who said the quote and when and where they said it.

Be careful not to confuse style with format. For example, a bulleted list is a way of displaying information—it is a format decision, not an element. Look at the type of information being displayed in the bulleted list. Is it a set of city names? Is it troubleshooting questions? Is it color options?

This exercise will also help you think about the internal dynamics of your documents. Do you see a pattern in which every second-level headline is followed by an illustration? Are book titles, authors, and publishers often discussed in the same paragraph? The more you understand about your documents, the better you'll be at presenting them to your readers.

As you go through this process ask yourself these questions:

- What bits and pieces can you identify that all or many of the documents share?

- Which of these are elements that you might want to search on or sort or display in combination with other elements? For example, will your readers be searching for someone by last name, or will they want to see a directory that lists first name, last name, and phone extension?

- In what order do these elements appear, and why do they appear in that order? Is it a design decision, or is there a structural reason that one element must always be with another? For example, in your set of marketing materials for your company's line of beach toys, is it essential that part number and price always follow one after the other and that both must be part of every product?

- What do you want to name each element? Think of options that are both clear and easy to remember and type. For example, maybe you've decided that one of your elements is *scientific name of each lizard*. That's descriptive, but do you want to be typing that tag over and over again? Maybe you want to call it *sname* to make production easier. But will people remember *sname* easily? Hmmm, maybe you want to consider calling it *sci-name*. The names you select don't really matter, but your selections can make your production process easier.

- Do these elements have certain value attributes? For example, is there an element called *edition* that can have a *booktype* value of hardback, paperback, or clothbound? Does the quotation element have a *source* attribute that identifies who said it? Does your *vendor* element have a *vendor ID* attribute attached to it? Attributes aren't things that necessarily display on a page—they are bits of data that you might want to store with the element. You can use this data later to, say, sort quotes by the name of the person who said them or to sort products by the vendor ID of that product's vendor.

In many cases, analyzing your documents is more than a one-day project, so be forewarned that you'll probably need to set aside a block of time for review, discussion, and general mapping. Understanding what is going on in your documents, and your site, lets you apply structure in a way that makes sense and maximizes its benefits.

Up-front planning really does make a difference. In fact, if you try to apply structure without going through this planning and analysis step, you're setting yourself up to fail. Someone who has been working with structured documents for years told me that one can't underestimate the importance of planning.

"Not doing the up-front planning is a recipe for guaranteed disaster!" he counsels.

Take his word for it—take the time to understand your documents *before* you go into production with them.

Step 2: DTD Writing

If you are working with complex data or a great many large documents, if you have very detailed and specific project requirements for your content, or if you are working on a database-focused project, you may want to write an external definition of the document structure. This is called the Document Type Definition, or DTD.

One of the nice things about XML is that you don't need to have a DTD if you don't want to. You need a DTD only if you want to ensure that the elements in your document conform to a certain set of rules, the rules that are contained in the DTD.

DTDs serve as document structure rulebooks that will validate the tags in each document to ensure that they are entered correctly and in the expected manner. This is the most difficult step of the process, and if you're a designer you'll likely be working with a programmer to create the actual structure definition. (Some tools, such as Microstart Near and Far Designer, display the DTD visually and can help you create the DTD yourself without outside programming assistance.) The structure definition codifies what you sketched out as you analyzed your documents.

Step 3: Marking up Your Documents

The third step is defining the tags and inserting them within your documents. There are some specific syntax rules to follow when entering the tags, but the process is no more difficult than entering HTML tags (except that you won't have a finite, stock list of tags to memorize and pick from). The tags you use are the ones you create and define.

Some people prefer to separate this step as part of a production process; others expect their authors to insert tags as they create the material. Again, look at your own material and pick a process that matches your needs and the needs of your organization.

If people don't follow through with marking up the documents correctly, all the structure in the world won't do you the least bit of good. Take some time to find a process that will really work; whatever you do, don't force an inappropriate process down everyone's throats just to put structure into your documents or to be able to crow that you're using XML. In some cases, this may mean you need to reexamine your production process or add new tools. For example, you might find that one of the emerging XML editors makes it easier for your staff to insert tags. Or you might separate the tasks of writing and document production, so that each team can focus on one area and be more productive. If that's what it takes, do it. Nothing is more frustrating than getting an idea up to the point of final implementation only to have it fall flat because it clashes with the reality of the everyday workflow. After all, for many applications, that was the fate of SGML.

An important thing to remember with structure is that you need to be consistent if it is going to provide real benefits. If you're identifying an element called *species* you need to be sure that your process makes it easy for every reference to a species by name to be tagged.

This is the part of the process where all the good intentions can disappear in a byte of ether. You can plan for structure, you can design for structure, you can see the potential of applications using structure, but if your documents don't become structured through the correct addition of XML tags, all your great plans and potential will end up by the side of the I-way.

For example, if you have people writing original material, you might want to consider separating element tagging from the primary writing chore. If you try to merge disparate tasks it is highly likely that the quality of the writing will deteriorate, the writing will suddenly become a much longer process, or tags will be missing.

If you already have HTML coders working on the production of your site, XML will be a natural addition to their jobs. Tools are beginning to emerge that simplify the process of tagging XML; in fact, some of these tools are joint HTML/XML production tools. Companies like SoftQuad Software, ArborText, and others are exploring ways of making it possible to create HTML and XML from the same editor.

If you are making heavy use of elements—certain types of applications, such as aerospace technical documentation or directory publishing, might find they're tagging virtually every word—it's well worth your while to investigate the available tools and give some thought to ways to make your tagging process both effective and efficient.

Tying Structure to Display

Now you've got a document structure. You've tagged documents. That's all very nice, but left to themselves, the tags don't do anything. They're just markers. For designers, the big question is "How do I make all these structure tags display the way I want them to?"

That is indeed the big question and the question that, at this writing, contains the largest number of holes.

Many of these holes are in the form of browser support for standards. To get the maximum display benefit from XML, the browsers need to be fully compliant with XML and related standards, the DOM, CSS1 and CSS2, and XSL specifications.

This is easier said than done. As of this writing, the forthcoming 5.X browsers from both Netscape's Navigator and Microsoft's Internet Explorer (IE) offer a mixed bag of support. Both will be able to identify an XML document as such. That's a good first start.

If you are using a DTD, the browser will recognize your pointer to that rulebook. That's a good start, too.

Microsoft's IE is offering a category of interesting display applications called *behaviors*. (These have been submitted to the W3C under the name HTC and could end up becoming, in part or in whole, a recommended standard.) These behaviors tie together XML, CSS, the DOM, and scripting to create some exciting possibilities. Later in this book we've devoted a chapter to behaviors.

What is likely to be the most common method of applying style to structure is, in the near future at least, Cascading Style Sheets (CSS). You'll set up external style sheets that define, using CSS syntax, the display information that will be tied to each XML element.

If it seems that a lot of pieces are involved, you're right; there are. And the specifications, tools, and support for the specifications are quite varied. Later on in the book we'll go into more detail on a few specific methods for creating and displaying XML data. For now, it's just important to remember that there is a display step and that you'll be using a specific style-focused technology to define that step.

Holes and all, though, the style side of the equations meshes very nicely with the underlying concept of the structured document approach. Each component of a document is identified by its role in the document, totally devoid of formatting information. From that base, the structure can be tied into style through a variety of approaches. The approaches and the actual visual format can change at will without affecting the content. The document becomes truly flexible and truly transportable across time and viewing devices.

Summary

As you can see, structure is simply the set of rules by which the document is organized. Structure describes the elements—the building blocks—of the document. Structure isn't some rigid set of restraints that constrain creativity. It is just a way of making sense of the document and adding meaning to its parts.

With structure comes the potential to search the document in a more powerful manner, to use different pieces of the document for different purposes, and to display the document in many different ways.

Structure is not the same as format. The two are quite separate. Structure defines what makes up a document, while format describes very specific display information. Structure moves with a document, while formatting is typically best applied in the context of the viewing environment.

Structure can add a great deal of power to your documents. It can make the documents truly come alive and respond to the reader's needs. A certain amount of up-front work is involved in creating structured documents, but that work pays off many times over in more flexible, adaptable, and reusable documents.

CHAPTER 2

What Is XML?

XML stands for EXtensible Markup Language. It's a way to structure documents and give meaning to different elements on a page.

XML is being used in documents in many different forms. Although this book focuses on web applications, people are starting to use XML as a way to mark up everything from databases to Office 2000 files.

By itself, XML does absolutely nothing. Insert some XML tags into your page and . . . they'll just sit there. But, combined with style data, scripting data, and a browser that handles all of the above you can create some powerful new ways to present information.

In this chapter we'll explore what XML is, where it came from, and what it can do for you.

Data about Data

At its most basic level, XML is a *metadata language*. Metadata is data about data. That might sound a little circular at first, but let's step back and take a look at the idea of data about data.

Data are the basic building blocks of publishing. They are the words and other content that you combine to create a web page, a printed book, or automotive classified ads. Data doesn't necessarily mean "database." Data can be a memo, a note, or a word processing file.

Data are what you see, touch, manipulate, display, and work with in various ways. You might store data in a database, in an ASCII text file, or in a spreadsheet.

Data can be easy to take for granted—they're always there, and you just sort of use them as you need them. You never give much thought to their background, their features, or what factors shape and define them.

Sometimes those things can be very important and can make your data more powerful. That's where XML comes in.

XML enables you to add information about your data. You can describe where you found the data; you can quantify, qualify, further identify, and define data. With XML you no longer have to take data at face value—you can add all sorts of information about them, information that can help you process and interpret the data and make your presentation and understanding better and stronger.

Most people who have built a web page have worked with metadata, but they might not realize it. Remember adding a keyword metatag, something like <meta name="keyword" content="dogs, obedience, CD, sit, heel, stay">, so that the search spiders would index your site better? That tag is a very simple form of metadata. It describes the data in your site by listing keywords that people might use when searching for it. It is data about data.

XML uses the same idea but takes it much further. Applications of XML are enabling e-commerce by storing data about digital signature data. XML is making digital forms a reality by adding data about form data. With XML, people are able to build multimedia applications by adding data about each multimedia element and how it works with other multimedia elements.

As a web designer, you'll mostly encounter XML in documents and in databases, but the uses for it extend far beyond what anyone imagined when the standard was first created. It seems that data about data is a much-needed concept.

EXtensible

The first word in XML is *EXtensible*. This is a very important word, one that gives XML so much strength.

Extensible means that there is not one single set of XML tags that everyone uses. What a difference from HTML! In HTML, there is a core set of tags. If you want to create a list, you can go to a reference guide and see what the list tag is and how to use it. If you want to identify a second level of heading, you can go to the HTML spec and learn about the <h2> tag. With HTML there is a defined world and all your tagging works within that world.

XML is different. You are not limited to one set of tags. You can create what you need for your own applications. This is both very exciting and very scary.

It is exciting because you are not limited to the tags that someone else thinks you should use. You can create any tag that you want, any tag that makes sense to you. If your pages include lots of quotes, you can have a tag named <quote>. If your site includes glossary terms, you can create a tag called <glossary>. The EX of XML means that you can extend tag definitions so that you can adapt the tags for your needs, marking up your documents in ways that make sense for your data.

It is scary because it means you can't just go to a book or a reference list online and look up what tag to use. The tag you use is the one you or your organization agrees on. Having no limits at all can be quite disconcerting and simply throws many people into a state of inertia. XML need not be overwhelming, though. If you break it into tasks and pieces you'll find that you can begin to use it without feeling as if you've undertaken an endless task.

The best way to do this is to begin working with XML by working with your documents. Get to know them and their characteristics. Before you sit down to code your first character with XML, you need to spend some up-front time looking at your different documents, analyzing what's in them, and matching this analysis to a list of sensible tags. You'll create a list of tags that you will use across your site. You'll need to communicate this list, and when and how to use each tag, with everyone who is also working on your site.

Extensibility can deliver power, but with power comes an extra level of complexity and planning. The idea of working as part of a team becomes important—you can't just go off on your own and randomly make up tags. (Well, you could, but that would defeat the purpose of XML.) To tap into its power, you'll not only want to develop tag sets that make sense for you, but you'll also need to be sure they are applied consistently across all your documents.

Extensibility means you get more options, but it also means you'll need to do up-front planning, make some decisions, and document those decisions. If you are part of a larger group or an industry-wide project, you'll need to contact your counterparts and learn what tags they are proposing and consider sharing the same tag names.

This is quite unlike the HTML world because HTML is not extensible. HTML contains a standard set of tags. You use these tags (and only these tags) to mark up an HTML file. What you can and can't do is very clear. If you want a tag that indicates something other than the predefined set, you're out of luck.

This factor makes HTML easy to learn. You can quickly memorize some of the most common tags and put them to use right away. It's a simple matter to remember that <H1> is a top-level heading and <p> is a paragraph. Anyone can learn to build a page in less than an hour—and millions of people have. That's a wonderful thing! HTML's relative simplicity is one of its great strengths and a key factor in its success.

This, however, is also one of the factors that eventually limits HTML. For some percentage of the people creating web pages, an <H1> is just perfect. They won't ever want another type of headline. They are building basic, personal pages and sites, creating an important voice on the web. HTML is enough for them, at least for now. Eventually they may begin using XML, but not until the tools are consumer-strength.

But the remaining people? Well, we're the ones who say "But, this isn't just an H1—this is really a chapter heading. The thing after the chapter heading is an H1. Why can't I call this a chapter heading? And then display just my chapter headings when the page first loads?" XML lets us make that chapter heading we've been longing for. And, by combining XML with style and scripting technologies that work with it, we can make the chapter heading perform and interact in the way we specify.

XML lets us display subsets of the page in any order we want. It lets us create custom search options for a site. It lets us build pages on the fly, pages that match our reader's specific needs.

Even more importantly, XML separates structure from format. Your suite of HTML tools increasingly describes how an element on the page looks. You can make it bold. You can center it. You can hide or display it. But you can't define it by what it is.

Because XML describes elements by what they are rather than how they look, XML's extensibility quickly becomes even more exciting. You can create tags that identify book authors, product color, or court case citations. This list really is endless—it is limited only by your needs and your imagination. You aren't stuck with using bold over and over again, sometimes to identify glossary terms, sometimes to identify keystroke names, sometimes to identify song titles.

Imagine creating a document that contains descriptions of the boots your shop sells. You could create a <boot> tag that lets you define each boot. Within the tag, you could set attributes for type of leather, style of toe, colors, and manufacturer. Try that in HTML! Without extensibility, the <boot> tag is impossible.

By the way, you'll notice that the <boot> tag contains metadata, too—that is, data about the boot. The actual data might be the phrase "Justin's Original Cowboy Boot." The metadata is all the behind-the-scenes information that describes what "Justin's Original" is all about. It is a boot. It is made of cowhide. It is black. It has a round toe. It was made by Justin.

The extensibility of XML actually lets you add intelligence to your document. An XML document can contain all the information it needs to introduce itself to you and present all its pieces in order.

Wait a second! Don't rush right out and start making up tags. For XML to be truly useful, you'll need to have consistency in your tags. You'll need to decide what elements are part of your page and what you want to call them. Then, you'll need to be sure you consistently and accurately use the same tag for the same type of element. Creating your own tag set isn't very useful if you apply your tags all higgly-piggly, so that nothing can make sense of them.

This might sound like stating the obvious, but in the excitement of being able to create a <crazy> tag to identify the oddball characters in your company directory, it is very easy to forget that there's more to using XML than making your very own tag names.

You don't need to create a huge tag set, either. You might be able to describe your documents with four or five simple tags. XML isn't about complexity. It is about creating the number of tags that you need—no more, no less.

Markup

The second word in XML is *markup*. Markup means that XML is a way of identifying different portions of your file. You aren't programming those sections to act in a certain way or display in a certain color—you are merely identifying them.

This is an important distinction. By itself, markup doesn't do anything. Markup codes are containers for storing information about elements within the document. This information can later be used in many different ways.

Markup of some sort—be it XML, HTML, or proprietary word processing markup—is essential for documents to make sense. Without markup, your document is one big glob of text that runs to infinity in a long single line, with each character following the other and all characters treated exactly the same. Without markup, people can't read your document. They can't see paragraph breaks. Even other computers can't do much with the data because it's just one big clump, all alike.

Markup defines the document. It turns 10,000 characters into pieces of meaning. These pieces of meaning are what let you use and interpret the document. That is, after all, the bottom line—to make information more useful to us.

Remember when you first learned HTML? The line break (<br>) and paragraph (<p>) tags were among the first tags you learned. You used them to turn the one large glob of text into separate lines or groups of lines. Markup, like the line break and paragraph tags, adds meaning to ASCII text and lets you display it, read it, print it, and understand it.

But wait a second, you say. HTML stands for Hypertext Markup Language. HTML *is* a markup language, right? Why does HTML do something and XML doesn't? Why does typing an HTML level-three heading tag (<H3>) have an immediate impact on the text you see in the web browser?

This is true. HTML, like XML, is a markup language. And, yes, you do see immediate results by adding an HTML tag to your file. The difference between HTML markup and XML markup is twofold. First, HTML has a known universe of tags. Second, the web browser has built-in processing instructions for what do to with the HTML tags. One of the web browser's primary functions is to display HTML in a particular manner.

And not all HTML tags are processed by the web browser. In fact, you might think of XML markup as being a little like metatags. Metatags are the way you add information such as keywords and textual descriptions to your web page. The metatags you add aren't understood by the web browser. They aren't part of the web browser's processing instructions, but they are markup tags known to search spiders. The metatags sit there in your file until some program that recognizes them—like a search spider—comes along and makes use of their information.

For example, suppose you added these metatags to your web page:

```
<meta name="description" content="Catfish are nature's vacuum cleaners.
This page talks about the role catfish play in keeping a healthy ecology
in ponds in the Southeastern United States.">
<meta name="keywords" content="catfish, ecology, southeastern US, pond,
bottom-feeders, scavengers, ecosystem">
```

When you pulled the page up in your web browser, it might resemble the page in Figure 2.1. Look closely and you'll see there is no sign of either metatag. The tags and their contents don't display. They don't format. For

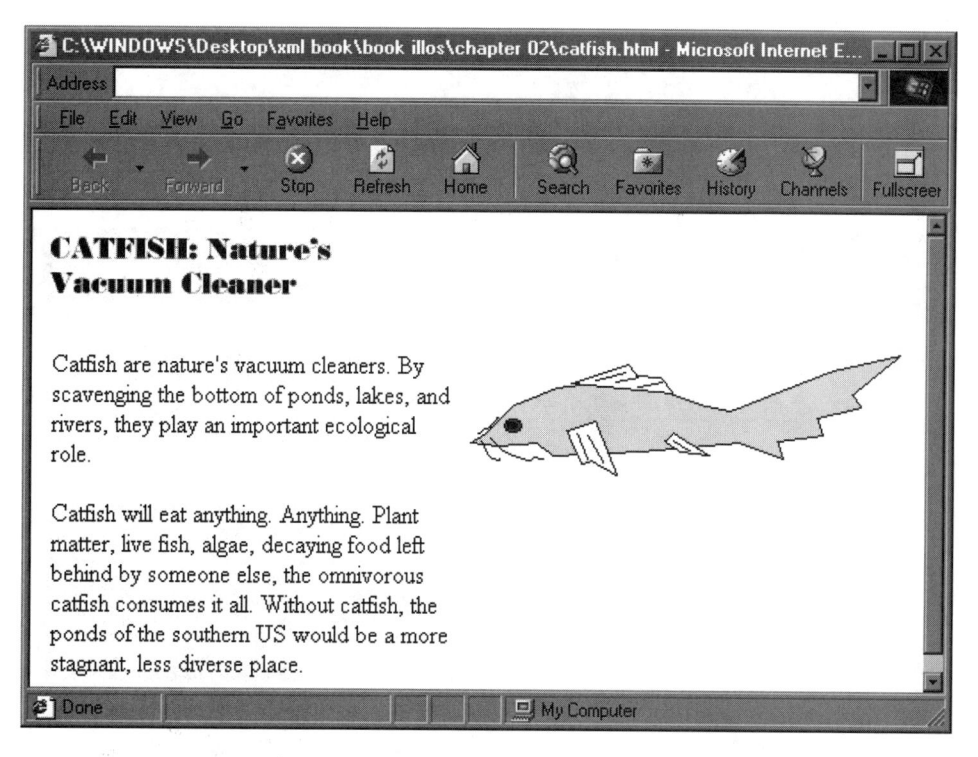

Figure 2.1 Description and keyword metatags don't appear in the browser window.

all intents and purposes, they don't do anything. They just sit there holding information.

Put this page through a search program that has been set up to understand and make use of a metatag named description and a metatag named keyword, and suddenly the tags will show their usefulness. Figure 2.2 shows how the Alta Vista search engine displays the catfish page in a search page result. You'll see that the description, as defined in the metatag, is displayed as the text that describes the page. The keywords influenced the order in which the files were ranked. Suddenly the meaning contained and defined by these two markup tags is put to use. The tags show their value when they are used in conjunction with a program that understands this particular form of markup.

In these types of environments, people often configure their web servers to perform actions based on the information contained in certain metatags. For example, if you have worked in an intranet environment you have probably also used metatags to store information such as the date the file was created or the name of the person responsible for updating it.

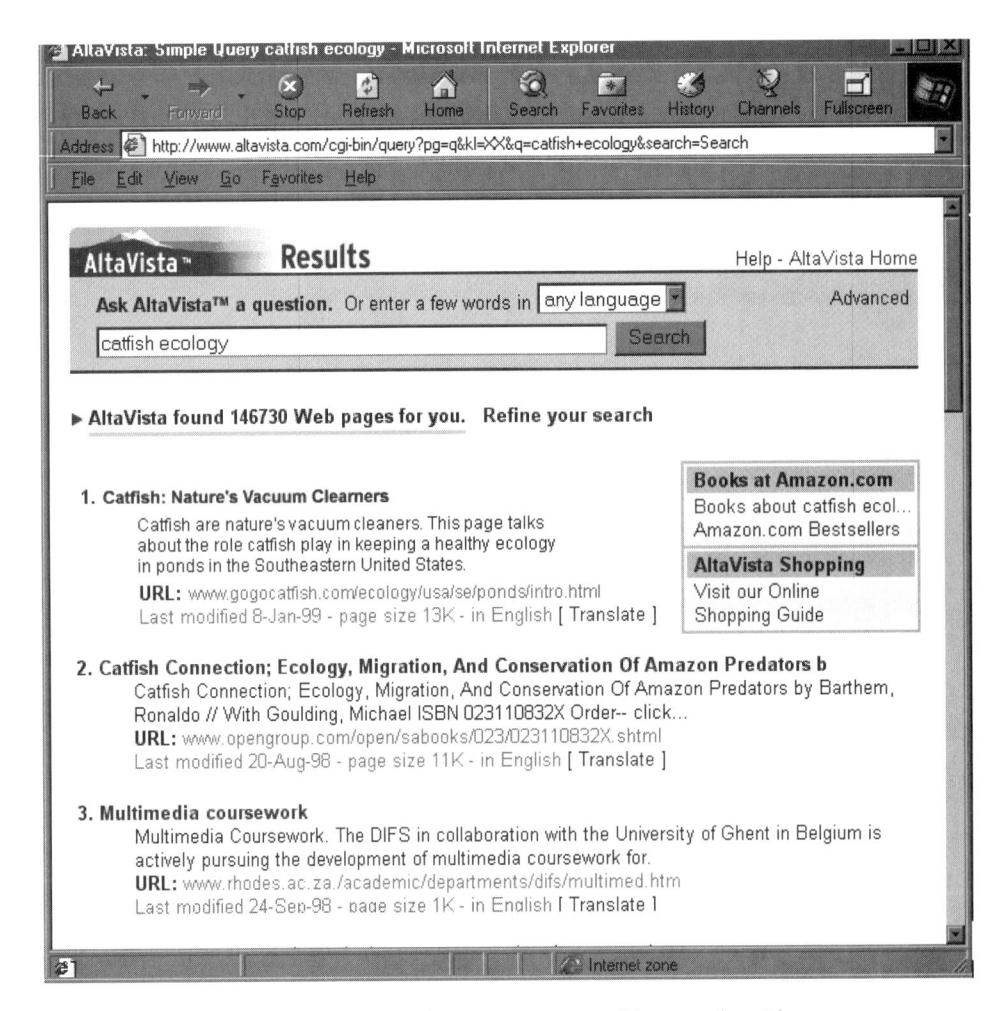

Figure 2.2 Description and keyword metatags are read by search spiders.

Using metatags makes it possible to run a monthly report identifying all files that are more than 30 days old, for example, or all files that were created by the marketing department. The server software uses the metatag markup, much as the search engines did, because it has been configured to understand the meaning added by the tags and to process this information in some way. The web browsers, though, will ignore the markup and display the pages as if the tags weren't even there.

Extend this idea of markup as a means of containing information about an element on a page and you'll start to get a sense of what XML is all about.

Remember that concept of data about data? Well, we're coming back to it again. Markup is data about a document's data.

You could identify the creation date using a metatag. You can do the same thing with XML, but you can take it even further. You could create an <about> tag. The <about> tag might have the attribute's creation date, creator, last edited date, editor, and expiration. This metatag makes is easy to display a list of documents created by marketing that have not been updated in the past six months.

XML markup adds meaning to elements within your document. When you are working with XML, at some point in your process a piece of software will understand the meaning of the XML tag and perform some action based on it. For example, you might not display the <about> tag, but you might use the data in it when you are doing a query.

Once a document is marked up, you can do a number of things with it.

For example, you may be using CSS or XSL, which are style languages that can interpret XML tags. You can match up style information with XML tags to make your document display in a way that is appropriate for either a PDA or a web browser, based on user variables. You don't actually need to create and deliver separate files—by using XML, you can create a new document on the fly.

Or, you might be using an XML query language to search through XML marked-up documents. The query language understands what the markup tags mean and will deliver results appropriately.

Scripting is another way to make use of XML. You can have a script perform actions based on the XML markup in a document, translating certain XML tags into HTML for display or displaying only certain XML elements.

Again, the caveat is that in order to be truly useful, markup tags need to be consistent in their structure and use. Randomly marking up one word in a document with the tag <mine> won't do a bit of good, unless you want to expend the energy to create a support structure for the single use of that tag in one lone document.

Language

The third word in XML is *language*.

The word *language* has taken on some unintended meanings. When many people hear the word *language* in a computer context, they immediately add the word *programming* in front of it: programming language.

Not all languages are used for programming. Programming is a way of describing a set of actions. XML is not a programming language. It doesn't make action happen. Instead, it is a markup language, just as HTML is a markup language. It places an emphasis on identification and information. XML code is used to define and describe a document.

The real meaning of language is much like the meaning we imply with human languages: a way of communicating using a set of rules and syntax.

Based on that description, XML is very much a language. You learn to use it by learning its basic structure and syntax and following those rules when you create XML-tagged documents. Yes, XML is extensible, but that doesn't mean it is random—it is a thought-out and defined language.

Nouns and Adjectives

XML's language rules are much like the rules that govern other languages. Parts of speech combine together in specified ways. For example, elements are a bit like nouns, and attributes are a bit like adjectives.

Elements are a component of your document, such as <paragraph> or <quotation> or <species>. They are *things*.

Attributes are values that describe the element, such as "color" or "speaker name." They are *describers*.

One way to think about the difference between elements and attributes is to try using the words "is a" and "has a." An element is a type of thing. Elements always work with "is a." The headline is a way to get you to read the story. A boot is something the store is selling. The quote is something a person said.

On the other hand, an attribute is a "has a" belonging to something else. The boot has a name. The boot has a color. The boot has a manufacturer. If you aren't sure if you are looking at an element or an attribute, ask yourself this: Is it one of these or does something have one of these?

For example, you might want to identify all the quotations in your documents. To do this, you would create a quotation element. Every time an XML-compliant browser encounters the tag <quotation> it will treat the contents of the quotation—the words between the start and end quotation tags—appropriately. Your code might resemble Figure 2.3.

```
<QUOTATION>Fourscore and seven years ago, our fathers brought forth on
this continent a new nation, conceived in liberty and dedicated to the
proposition that all men are created equal.</QUOTATION>
```

Figure 2.3 The text of the quote is the contents of the quotation element.

The quotation tag might mean the browser will display the quotation in a certain way based on style information. It might mean your reader can ask to see only the quotations in the document.

You can do more with XML than just identify the element as a quotation. You can provide additional information about that particular quotation.

Every quotation has a speaker—the name of the person who said the quote. And it has a date—the date the quote was made. And it might have a source—the context from which the quote came, such as a public speech or a private interview. You can add this information to the quotation by adding attributes to the element. The attributes contain additional information about a specific use of the element. The resulting code might resemble Figure 2.4.

Now, inside this one tag, you've identified a set of words within the document to be an element called a quotation, and you've identified that the particular use of the element has a speaker value of "Abraham Lincoln," a date attribute value of "1863," and a source attribute value of "Address at Gettysburg."

This adds another layer of possibilities. You might choose to display all quotes from Abraham Lincoln in green. Or, you might want to search for all quotations made by Lincoln in Gettysburg. Or, you might want to display all quotations from the entire document, ordered by date. Once you have identified elements and attributes of those elements, the possibilities expand.

You'll learn more details about elements and attributes later on in this book. For now, just remember that they are two of the basic components of XML, just as they are of HTML. Elements are the nouns, and attributes are the noun's adjectives.

Syntax

XML has clear structure and syntax rules also. You saw some of these in the examples above. They probably looked very familiar if you are accustomed to HTML.

```
<QUOTATION speaker="Abraham Lincoln" DATE="1863" SOURCE="Address at
Gettysburg">Fourscore and seven years ago, our fathers brought forth on
this continent a new nation, conceived in liberty and dedicated to the
proposition that all men are created equal.</QUOTATION>
```

Figure 2.4 Attributes further describe the element.

XML Tags Start with < and End with >

XML tags start with an open delimiter, like this:

```
<
```

And they close with a closed delimiter, like this:

```
>
```

The material in between is the XML tag and its attribute and attribute values, just as in HTML.

For example, this is the HTML image tag. Its attributes are src, width, and height. Its attribute values are "sitting-dog.gif," "50," and "100."

```
<img src="sitting-dog.gif" width=50 height=100>
```

As another example, here's an XML tag called dog. Its attributes are breed and sex. Its attribute values are "husky" and "F."

```
<dog breed="husky" sex="F">Snowy Peak </dog>
```

XML Is Case Sensitive

Unlike HTML, however, XML is case sensitive. Under XML, <QUOTE> is a different tag from <quote>. In contrast, HTML pays no attention to capitalization.

XML Empty Tags Must End

In XML, all tags are called either container tags or empty tags. Container tags are ones that surround some content in your document. There is an open tag, the content, and a closing tag:

```
<QUOTE>
"And then, just when we were ready to eat, the dogs ran by and grabbed
the thick juicy steak from the grill. But we had the last laugh -- it
was a tofu steak."
</QUOTE>
```

Empty tags are ones that do not encircle content in your document. They either insert data into your page or are containers for information. In HTML, the image tag (<img>) and line break tag (<br>) are examples of empty tags.

The difference between using a tag like this in HTML and in XML is that in HTML you insert the tag and that's it. In XML the empty tag must end. You can end it by adding an ending tag, like this:

```
<IMG src="happydogs.jpg" width=100 height=150 alt="dogs eating
steak"/></img>
```

You can also combine the beginning and ending tags together and create one tag that ends with a slash just before the ending delimiter, like this:

```
<IMG src="happydogs.jpg" width=100 height=150 alt="dogs eating steak"/>
```

You'll see that it looks like an HTML image tag except that it ends with a slash. Here's how an HTML line break tag looks in an XML-compliant document:

```
<br/>
```

The start and ending tags are combined into one.

XML Attributes Are Surrounded By Quotes

In XML, all attribute values are enclosed in quotation marks; in HTML, some attributes are and some attributes aren't. In XML the syntax rule is very simple: Quote all attribute values, like this—the speaker and the date are attribute values and each is enclosed in quotation marks:

```
<QUOTE speaker="Marty Davis" DATE="4/01/99" SOURCE="interview by aemd">
And then, just when we were ready to eat, the dogs ran by and grabbed
the thick juicy steak from the grill. But we had the last laugh -- it
was a tofu steak.</QUOTE>
```

XML versus HTML

By now you've probably figured out that XML and HTML are in some way related. They look similar. They feel a lot alike. Some of the examples you've seen even use HTML tags.

You're right. XML and HTML are siblings that share a common parent. That parent is SGML, the Standard Generalized Markup Language.

SGML was a product of the 1980s. It is an international standard that was created to solve the problems of data interchange. By describing a document by its structure (headlines, paragraphs, captions) rather than its format (24 point, Helvetica, italic) SGML made it possible to move a document across different types of computer systems without losing its meaning.

With SGML, instead of reverting to a long string of ASCII text, the document kept its structural markup information, allowing it to be adapted, reused, and passed along to other people. The way to specify bold might be different on every computer and word processing system, but in every system you could apply a bold style to "head level 1" structural elements.

Large organizations with heavy document processing needs led the charge to SGML. By implementing SGML, many organizations saved millions of dollars in document processing. But there was also a cost.

SGML was very flexible and powerful, but it was also very complex. It was so complex, in fact, that only the largest companies or companies working within an industry that required it had the resources to set up and implement SGML. It never caught on in the general marketplace, although it continues to play a role in government, aerospace, and other specialized publishing sectors.

SGML used something called a Document Type Definition (DTD) to define the structure of a group of documents. All installation guides, for example, might share a DTD. Or all U.S. Air Force aircraft documents might share a DTD. What we know as HTML is, in actuality, a DTD as well.

That's right, the HTML that we've all mastered is really a flavor of SGML. Originally the connection was much more obvious. Remember those first tags (<H1>, <P>, <LI>)? They were more structural than format-focused. The browsers used a standard DTD and a standard style interpretation to display HTML. As soon as people saw the possibilities of the web, HTML became more and more of a formatting tool and less of a structuring tool. As it did, it moved further and further from its SGML roots and took on a life of its own.

HTML worked because it was simple. It couldn't do everything for everyone, the way SGML claimed to—but it could be learned by anyone and everyone very quickly. Its results were obvious. HTML provided immediate feedback that made people say, "Hey! Cool! I can do that too." The rest, as they say, is history . . . and millions of HTML pages.

There was a lesson here: Even good things can sink under their own weight. SGML made sense, but it was just too complex and demanding for nontechnical users—and for the vast majority of people who are publishing information. HTML, on the other hand, was accessible, understandable, and downright friendly in comparison to SGML.

XML was a response to both the success of HTML and the continuing needs that SGML was designed to fill. It was designed to be accessible and easy to implement, but it would retain the focus on structure and extensibility of SGML.

Thus was the genesis of XML. It would retain the structure-centric approach of SGML, providing all the possibilities that structure brings. And it would also share the simplicity and ease of implementation of HTML, so that it could be quickly, easily, and widely adapted.

That's why you see HTML tags (following XML syntax guidelines, of course!) used within XML documents. The two are variations of the same original parent. You don't have to throw out everything you know about HTML in order to work with XML. In fact, HTML helps you work with XML.

A Brief History of XML

Much of the drive to create XML came from people who were working in the SGML community, managing and producing SGML documents or building SGML tools. They saw the success of HTML and realized that the time was right for the development of a simplified SGML—and not only was it right, it was increasingly necessary.

One of these people was Jean Paoli, who was then working with an SGML tool company in Europe. Today he is Product Unit Manager, Windows DNA XML Technologies with Microsoft.

> I spent 10 years working with SGML, and in one year Tim Berners-Lee introduces 10 tags and everyone uses them. We had to ask, where did we fail with SGML?
>
> In 1995 I started to be invited to speak to a lot of web conferences. At the time I had multiple papers where I talked about how we needed an API for HTML. I would tell people at these conferences that it is important to identify the information as information—not only as display. And that it is important to have an API which permits you to manipulate the information. It is very important to push people to understand that there is a life for information after the presentation part. It was wonderful to see all this excitement around tags, but we can't forget that there is data and logic also.

An API is an application-programming interface. It is the definition that lets you access one part of your page. The idea that Jean Paoli talks about became something called the Document Object Model, or the DOM. It works hand-in-hand with XML and is covered in detail in Chapter 3, "The Document Object Model."

In May 1996, Jean Paoli joined Microsoft and began working with IE 4.0 and dynamic HTML. "I saw all these cool things on the presentation side but realized that what we needed was something that dealt with content as more than just display," he said. "We connected with Jon Bosak (from Sun) and in June 1996 created the XML Working Group."

The XML Working Group is part of the World Wide Web Consortium, the W3C. This is the standards body that sets guidelines for the web.

We finished the specification in December 1997. It was really fun because we had the best people, a lot of people who were visionaries, people who had created great SGML tools, great technical people . . . We really wanted to do the best we could to simplify SGML. We didn't want XML to be too complicated to implement . . . We thought very hard about the 80-20 solution in which you identify the 80 percent of the features that are most used and the 20 percent which are nice but increase the difficulty so much that in a web environment no one would be willing to implement it.

Jon Bosak has been one of the driving forces behind the creation of XML from the very beginning. Today he is the Online Information Technology Architect at Sun Microsystems; prior to that he worked for Novell.

XML arose from the recognition that key components of the original web infrastructure—HTML tagging, simple hypertext linking, and hardcoded presentation—would not scale up to meet the future needs of the web. This awareness started with people like me who were involved in industrial-strength electronic publishing before the web came into existence.

I learned the shape of the future by supervising the transition of Novell's technical documentation from print to online delivery. This transition, which took from 1990 through 1994 to implement and perfect, was based on SGML. The decision to use SGML paid off in 1995 when I was able single-handedly to put 150,000 pages of Novell technical manuals on the web. This is the kind of thing that an SGML-based system will let you do. A more advanced, heavily customized version of the same system, built on technology from Inso Corporation, is used today for Solaris documentation under the name AnswerBook2. You can see it running at <http://docs.sun.com>.

Like many of my colleagues in industry, I had learned the hard way that nothing substantially less powerful than SGML was going to work over the long run. So from the very earliest days of the World Wide Web Consortium, there was a small group of us who kept saying, 'You have to put SGML on the web. HTML just won't work for the kinds of things we've been doing in industry.'

Now, the people in charge of the W3C were far from ignorant about SGML. Dan Connolly, in particular, saw very early the need to standardize HTML itself as a proper SGML language, and by the beginning of 1996, he had created a placeholder for some future SGML work within the W3C. But W3C didn't have the resources to pursue this direction, and outside of the few of us who had already been through the development of large-scale electronic publishing systems, no one else really understood the problem.

I had been pestering W3C about SGML and about DSSSL, the SGML style sheet language, right from the beginning, while I was still working at Novell, and I kept this up after I went to work for Sun. Finally, in early May of 1996, Dan challenged me to put Sun's money where my mouth was—to organize and lead a W3C working group to put SGML on the web. This was an unprecedented offer because up until then, all W3C working groups had been organized and run by W3C staff. Dan's willingness to go beyond established practice was the first key development in the process that led to XML.

This happened just as I was beginning a three-week series of web, SGML, and ISO conferences in Europe. When I got back, I was able to tell Dan that some of the world's leading SGML experts had signed on for the new working group and that I had secured funding from my management at Sun to carry out the work. This was the second critical turn in the path to XML. Many people know that XML grew out of the expertise of the SGML community, but few people realize even today that the whole two-year effort to develop XML was organized, led, and underwritten by Sun.

It was obvious from the beginning of what was originally called the Web SGML Activity (the name XML was suggested by our technical lead, SGML/DSSSL guru James Clark, several months later) that it would need the support of at least one of the two major vendors of web browsers.

In June of 1996 I succeeded in persuading Jean Paoli of Microsoft to join the working group. This turned out to be especially important because in addition to his SGML expertise, Jean was able to convince Microsoft to publicly adopt the technology much earlier than any of us had expected.

The basic design of XML was accomplished in 11 weeks of feverish activity under the guidance of editors Tim Bray and C. M. Sperberg-McQueen. The work started in the last few days of August 1996, and ended with the release of the first XML draft at the SGML '96 conference in November. While it took another year to finish working out all the details, virtually every basic feature of XML as we know it today was specified in that first published draft. This remarkable achievement is a tribute to the team spirit and world-class expertise of the original design group. I am proud to have had the honor of leading this group and proud of my management at Sun for having had the vision to support the effort.

The group wasn't looking at web-only solutions, either. One of the reasons XML is so needed is that information is increasingly fluid. A document is seldom created for just one format. The document might be a web page. A subset of it might be a printed page. A version of it might be delivered via some push technology. And the whole thing might have started in a database, with different portions being used in many different documents.

Tim Bray, a member of the original XML Working Group and co-editor of the XML specification, talked about this part of the project. "We tried to make XML a general-purpose tool, and evidence shows that we succeeded," he said.

> The only common thread I see between all the current XML projects/implementations/consortia/protocols is that they are behind-the-scenes computer-to-computer stuff. Any time you want to build an app that has a network dimension—and what app doesn't these days?—you are going to have to exchange information. In a very high proportion of cases, XML is a good syntax to use for structuring this information.
>
> I think everyone on the (W3C XML) committee would agree that whatever our original orientation was, we're flabbergasted by some of the things people are doing with XML.

HTML might have been the building block of the web, but XML could end up being the building block of data interchange for the next generation of information publishing.

But What Does XML Actually Do?

So now you understand that XML is extensible and that you can create your own tags. You know that it is a markup language that identifies elements within your document. And you know that it is language that plays by a specified set of rules. You even know about its relationship with HTML. But that still leaves one question: What exactly do you do with XML?

First and most important, you need to know that XML by itself doesn't actually *do* anything. It just sort of sits there in your file, harmlessly. Despite the hype flying around XML, it in and of itself is just some defined tags sitting among your ASCII text.

Remember, XML is a way to mark up your content. Unless you tie that markup information into something else, like style information or a search tool, it provides no benefit other than a full-employment act for XML markup jobs.

As with many technologies, you hear people say that they want to learn to use XML. There is the implication that you can go to a book, memorize the information, and start making things happen by typing in a few XML codes. It doesn't work that way.

You can learn XML's basic syntax, but that alone doesn't do you much good. To make use of a markup language, especially one that is extensible, you need to understand your documents, define your markup tags, mark up the actual documents, and then process those documents in some way that makes use of the markup information.

This is the number one misconception about XML—that it is a set of tags you memorize and start adding to your files. That might describe HTML, but it does not begin to define XML.

What XML does is provide your documents with a structure that is transportable across any type of computer platform or processing program.

XML identifies your information as information rather than as a set of display tags. This means that each and every bit of identified information can be selected by itself, acted on, combined with other information, displayed in a certain way, delivered to certain people . . . the list is endless.

This is the single most important thing to understand about XML: By identifying content pieces as individual bits of information, the document can be reshaped and reassembled in many different ways, yet retain its underlying structure.

It can be a difficult concept to grasp. What XML does, at its very core, isn't something you can hold in your hand. It isn't something you demo in three easy steps on a website. It can't be shrink-wrapped. It isn't an action or an activity. It isn't a process. It is a very basic way of describing information, a sort of DNA that turns a quote and a title and a caption into something called a document.

XML is the very anatomy of information. It is a way of describing and defining the components. And by describing the components, it builds the whole.

Summary

XML is a markup language. It identifies elements in your document and lets you record data about those elements.

With XML, you separate format from structure. This makes your document interoperable—a chapter title remains a chapter title no matter to which system you transfer the data. And content tagging adds meaning. You can search for "book-title" rather than "everything in italic."

By itself, XML does nothing but sit there identifying data, yet when combined with style elements, it gives you enormous power over how to display your pages.

CHAPTER 3

The Document Object Model

"The Document Object Model provides a standard set of objects for representing the HTML and XML documents, a standard model of how those objects can be combined, and a standard interface for accessing and manipulating them."

—DOCUMENT OBJECT MODEL LEVEL 1 SPECIFICATION, W3C

The Document Object Model, or the DOM (rhymes with Mom), is the key to being able to display both XML and HTML documents dynamically. Without a DOM, your scripts and applets can't "talk" to your XML and HTML documents on a piece-by-piece basis, telling them, for example, to move the sun graphic across the sky, show only elements with an attribute of Cleveland, or hide a section of the page until a reader clicks on the *tell me more* button.

The DOM specification is the standard that defines a specific document object model—in this case, the DOM that will be used with web pages. The term *document object model* is a broad phrase that encompasses many different types of specific DOMs.

49

You can find the full DOM specification on the web at <http://www.w3.org/REC-DOM-Level-1/>.

"What the DOM does is give you a standardized, interoperable way of doing mouseovers, changing text, and doing other interesting things dynamically," explained Lauren Wood, Chair of the DOM Working Group of the W3C. "The DOM is way of viewing the document as a set of little pieces, as objects, that you can manipulate and change independently each other."

Document Object Model

The general phrase *document object model* means that you treat the document as a collection of individual objects, instead of as one single solid unit.

The objects are arranged according to the document model and, taken together, form the document as a whole. You might think of the DOM as being a bit like a blueprint for the displayed document, a blueprint that explains how the pieces fit together to form a whole unified building.

Under the DOM model, you can address any component on the page and change it in some way without bothering the rest of the document. For example, you can change the color of a link without downloading a whole new page. You just tell the link object to display in lime green instead of goldenrod whenever someone puts the cursor on top of the link.

By using a document object model, you can easily change just parts of your page, instead of sending a request back to the server for a full page reload.

The Pizza Analogy

You might think of the displayed XML or HTML page as being a bit like a pizza. A pizza? Bear with me for a moment and you'll see.

In the non-DOM-accessible world, you can pick up the pizza, you can take a bite of the slice, you can savor the whole melange as it melts in your mouth. When you look at the pizza carefully you can see that it contains sausage and mushrooms and mozzarella cheese. The pizza has baked together and become one single unit: Crust plus cheese plus sauce plus sausage plus mushroom have merged to become *The Pizza*.

The integrated pizza is a great thing . . . except when the pizza arrives at your door and you realize you don't really like sausage. The only way to change that pizza to the way you want it is to order a whole new, sausage-free pie. Back goes the delivery van, the request goes to the kitchen, the new pizza comes out of the oven, and a very long 40 minutes later you see your new sausage-less pizza on your doorstep.

Now, if that pizza had an accessible document model underlying it, things would change. You won't be drooling from hunger for 40 extra minutes. Under a document object model approach, you still have a pizza, but all the elements that make up the pizza can be picked up and moved around individually. If you don't want the sausage, no need to send the whole pizza packing. If you want olives instead of mushrooms, no problem either. You just make the change on the fly. You tell the sausage element to disappear and the mushroom element to become an olive.

By changing the underlying philosophy of the pizza—of the web page—you suddenly open up whole new possibilities for customer-specified combinations, created on demand, without kitchen—or server—overhead.

Objects

DOM's middle name is *object*. Objects are any individual piece of a program or document. (If you liked the pizza analogy, think of mushrooms as being one object and cheese shreds as being another object.)

In an XML document, each element is an object—it has a name, and it has attributes that describe it. You can address or "talk to" each element individually. For example, you can use a style sheet to tell all *booktitle* element objects to display in bold italic. Or you can display all *booktitle* element objects in order based on their *date published* attribute.

In a displayed web page, each component of the page is an object. Each has a name and attributes and certain ways of acting. You can tell all the images to display at 100×100 pixels, for example.

If you know the objects and what they can do, you can create a page that acts exactly as you want it to act.

Object orientation is not a new concept; it has been around academic computer science circles since the 1960s, but only in the past few years has it gained commercial ground. The time seems to be right for the object approach. As people have begun to understand it, it has increasingly been seen as the path to the future of programming—and more.

As a result, the notion of objects has become quite popular in both software and documents. Both the programming language Java and the scripting language JavaScript have an object-oriented philosophy at their core. The adoption of the standard DOM enables web pages to share that object approach, too.

With an object approach, you create components that have characteristics; the components interact with other components based on these characteristics.

Proponents of this approach say it is more flexible and powerful than a traditional linear approach to programming or data. An object-oriented approach creates a development environment in which it is faster to create code and easier to debug code. Under an object model it is easy to add new modules. You simply create the module and teach it to follow the rules for interacting with the existing modules. Plug in the new piece and you're up and running.

Each object is a little like a template. You can use an instance of the same object over and over again. For example, you might have multiple instances of the paragraph element in a document (or multiple instances of a mushroom slice on a pizza!).

You might think of an object approach as being a little like a collection of Lego blocks: Different pieces do different things, but you can combine and recombine them into many different finished projects.

API

The DOM specification describes the Application Programming Interface—the API—for HTML and XML documents. An API is the set of rules that describes how you can access and manipulate an object.

It isn't enough to know what the objects are; you also need to know how to talk to them. The API says that you talk to the objects using, for example, a certain naming convention and certain programming models.

When you are building with Legos (or Duplos or Primos, depending on your age!), one of the first things you do is learn how to handle them. You pick them up in a certain way. You connect them with a certain motion. You snap them apart with another motion. You give them names so you can identify them—this is the two-pointer, this is the four-square, this is the Duplo-Lego connector. Some of the blocks require a certain touch—the four-square needs a special sort of wrist flip to separate it from another block; the two-pointer slips into place with a gentle tap. This set of rules for handling the blocks is their API.

If someone had never seen a Lego before, you could tell him or her your rules for handling them and from those rules the newcomer could also pick up the blocks and assemble and disassemble them. This set of rules is the block set's API. Once you know the API, you can access, manipulate, and work with all the individual objects.

The Lego blocks don't care whether you use bare fingers or woolen-gloved fingers to snap them together and apart. They care only that the motion matches the motion described in their "API." You could even have a robot arm building a block tower. The type of arm—or language—doesn't matter as long as it addresses the blocks following the API guides.

The same is true for the web page. You can access a document's DOM through many different languages as long as you follow the API. The DOM doesn't care if you adore Java or are a JavaScript guru, as long as you follow the rules.

For example, you could write a Java applet that displays all elements with an attribute value of *Cleveland*. You'll end up with a page that displays the weather, the current time, and the wind speed in Cleveland. You could also end up with a page that displays weather, time, and wind speed in Cleveland by writing a JavaScript script to perform the action of displaying only elements with an attribute value of *Cleveland*. Because there is a standard DOM, you know how to address the objects, regardless of the specific language you choose as your means of directing the action.

DOM and DHTML

You may have encountered the term *DOM* in a few other places on the web.

One of these is Dynamic HTML, or DHTML. Microsoft's DHTML was part of IE 4.0 browsers. It allowed you to change elements of the web page on the fly.

Another was Netscape Navigator 4.0's "layers," which let you work with different elements as if they were on overlay transparency paper.

Both MS-DHTML and layers were ways to expose the individual elements of the page to the designer, so that the page could display in different ways dynamically.

For example, at Project Cool we used MS-DHTML to animate our planet Saturn, making it travel across the page. We used Microsoft's version of the

DOM to address the image object that contained the planet Saturn image. We told it to display the image at a certain XY location on the page, and then, after a certain number of seconds, to display it at another XY location. By stringing together a number of these commands addressing that particular instance of the image object, we were able to make Saturn "move." We also did a variation on this using Netscape Navigator 4.0's implementation of the DOM, so the effect would be cross-platform compatible.

This effect works as shown in Figures 3.1 through 3.3.

Another handy DHTML feature is using the hide and show attributes of an element to hide the element under certain circumstances and show it under others. One great use of this is for an expanding outline. In Figures 3.4 and 3.5, you can see how we used it in our CSS Reference section. Both

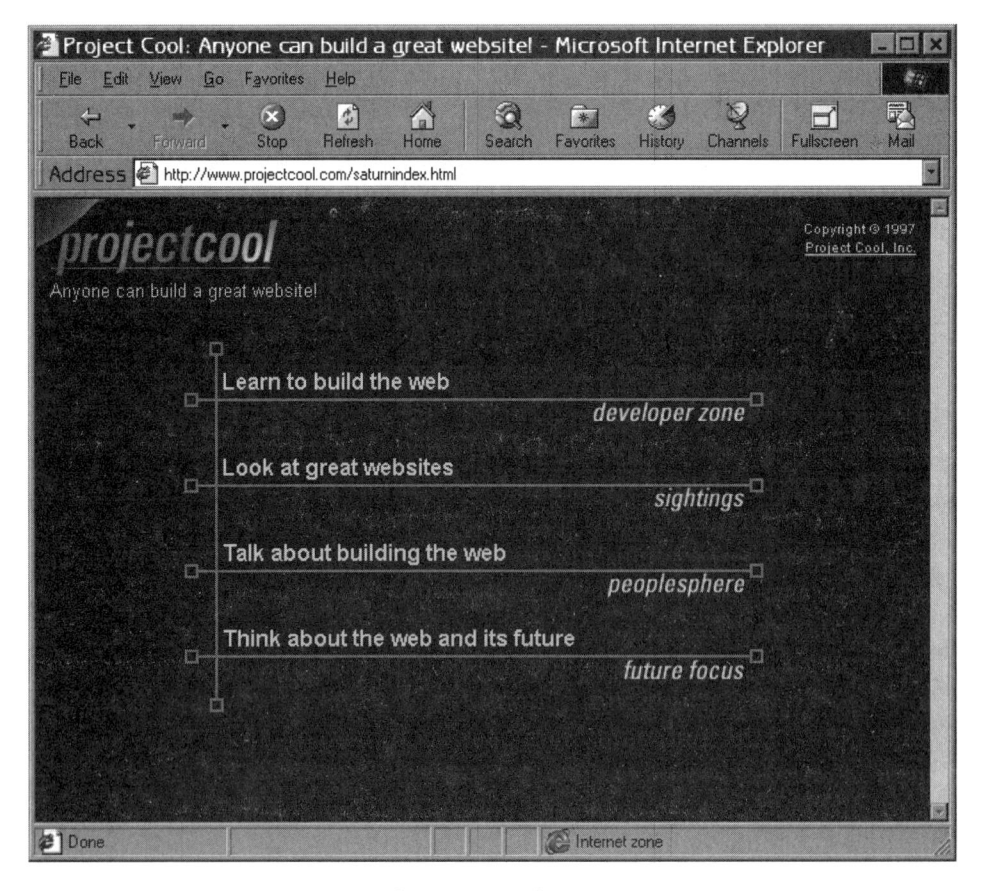

Figure 3.1 Saturn creeps in from the corner of the page.

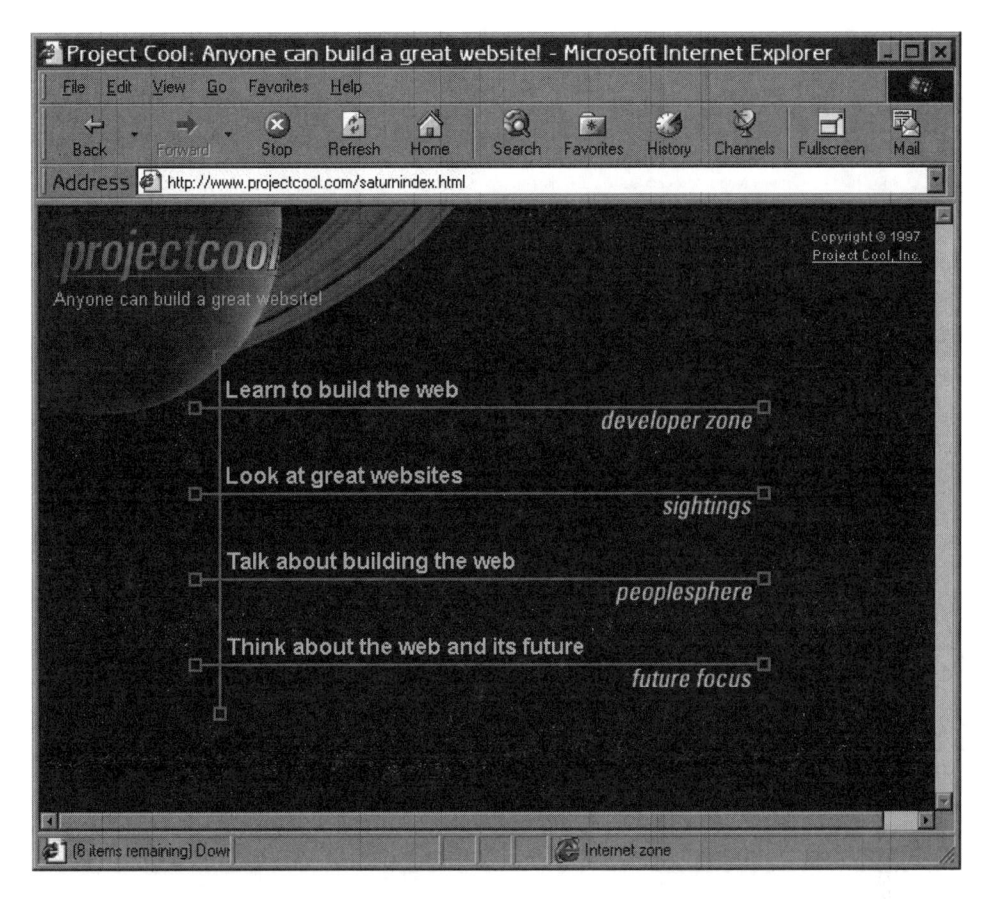

Figure 3.2 Changing the XY location of the object via the DOM makes Saturn appear to move.

the "flying Saturn" and the expanding outline are linked and live at the companion website to this book, <http://www.projectcool.com/guide/xml>.

Figure 3.4 is the way the page looks when it first loads. Only certain elements display. When the reader clicks on one of the topics—on Innovators, for example—the hidden elements appear, as you see in Figure 3.5. This is all done by using the DOM to address specific objects in the page.

The current W3C Recommendation for the DOM is somewhat like the DOM that Microsoft implemented in IE 4.0, but it is not exactly the same. It has been updated to take XML documents into account, for example.

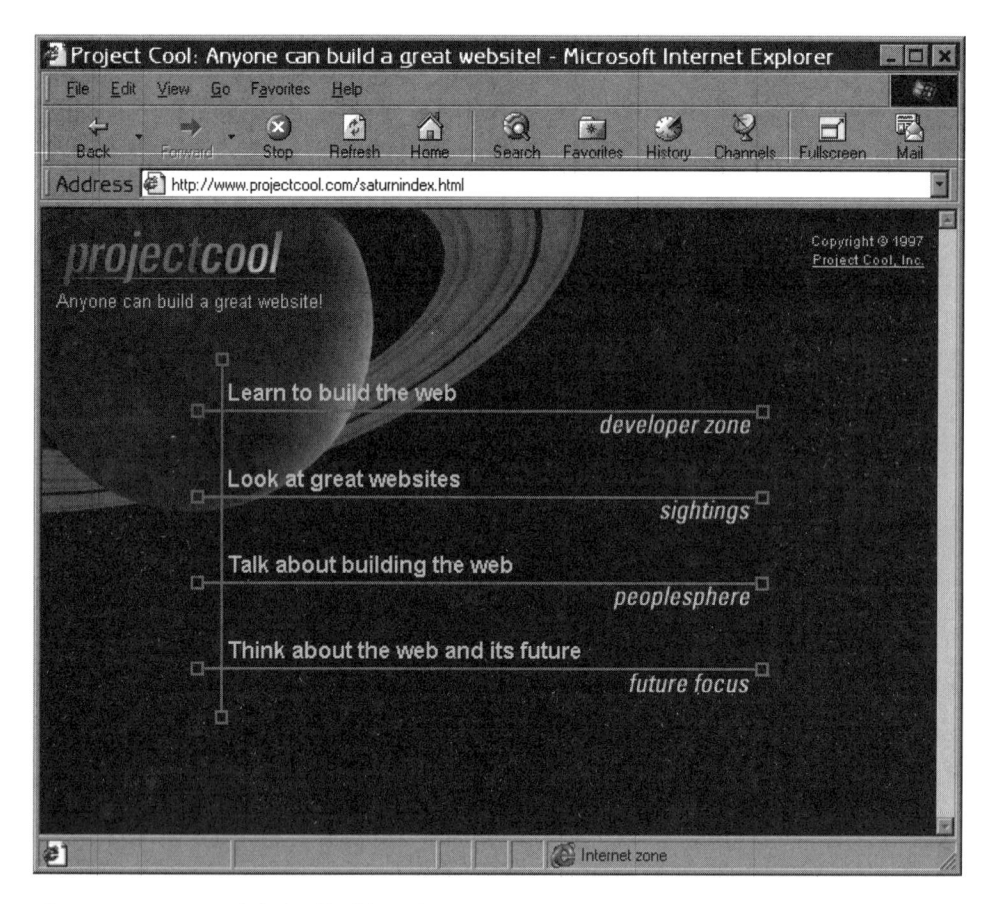

Figure 3.3 Saturn is in its final location.

And parts of the API have changed to reflect the needs of a broader audience.

DOM and JavaScript

You may have encountered the idea of a DOM, as well as the concept of an object, in JavaScript as well.

Like the DOM, JavaScript was created to work with web pages. It calls elements of the browser—the window, the status bar, and so on—by name and performs actions on or with them.

JavaScript has objects. Each object has attributes that describe it. JavaScript objects also have methods, verbs that let you perform action. JavaScript does more than describe—it makes things happen.

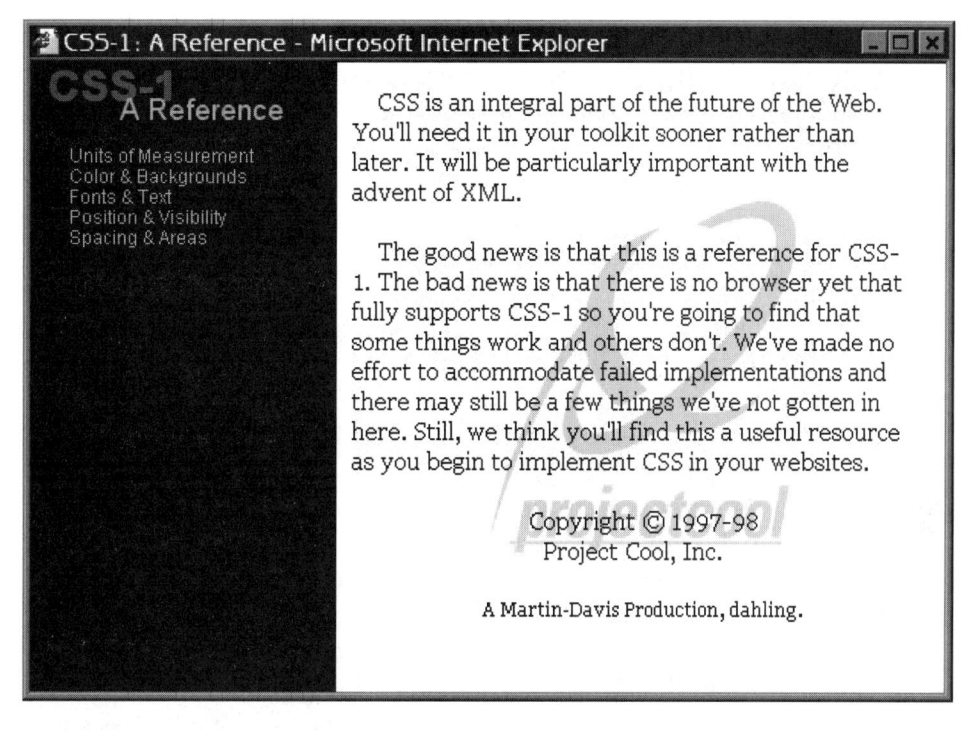

Figure 3.4 Outline before.

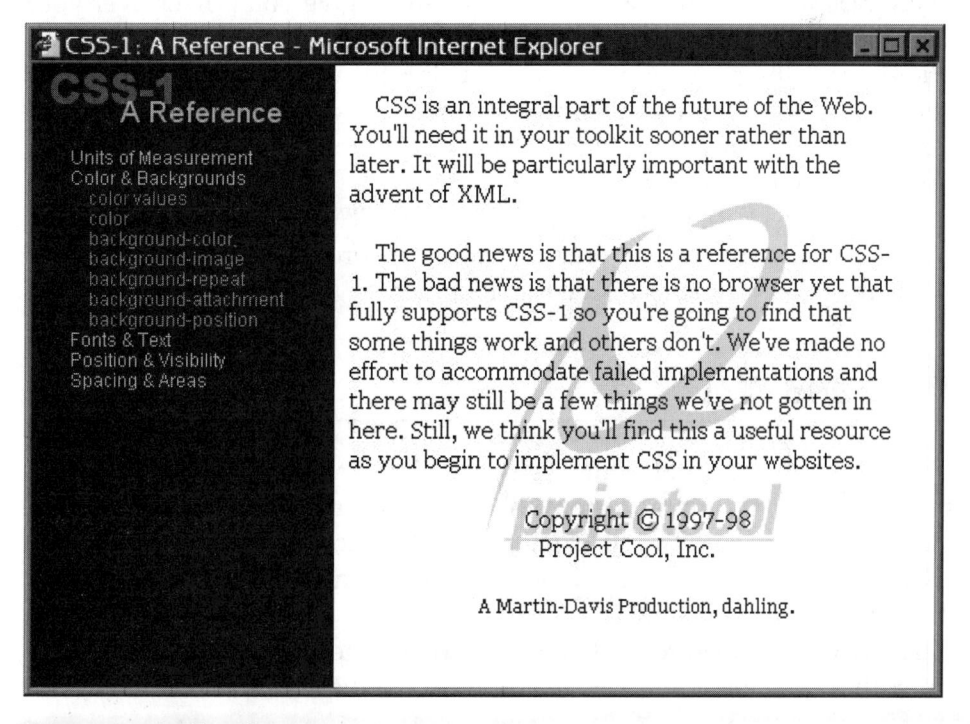

Figure 3.5 Outline after.

For example, the browser window is one of the JavaScript objects. You can use JavaScript to tell the window object to perform an action; for example, to open a new window with a height attribute of 200 and a width attribute of 400.

JavaScript also understands actions that a reader does. These actions are called events and include things such as clicking on a link and closing a window. You can make actions happen based on the appearance of one of these events.

For example, you can open a new window when the reader clicks on a certain spot in the page, or you can display an alert box when the reader enters a certain value in a form.

JavaScript objects are pieces of the browser, not specific pieces of the document. With JavaScript you can open a new window and make it a specific size. You can also display an alert box with a specific message. With JavaScript alone, though, you cannot hide a paragraph or turn a headline green. JavaScript has no built-in knowledge about *your* data and *your* documents.

JavaScript—without the DOM beside it—cannot access elements within a document. Without the DOM to describe the image object or the <booktitle> object, JavaScript doesn't even know that images or book titles exist, let alone know how to access and manipulate them.

JavaScript—combined with the DOM—does give you power over your document. Combining the two technologies, you can make that Saturn glide across the page. You can make a link turn pink when your reader runs the mouse over it. JavaScript is one way of accessing the DOM and its objects; it lets you tell the document objects what to do and how to act under what circumstances.

Because the DOM gives you an API to the HTML/XML document, you can use JavaScript (or any other scripting or programming language) to perform actions on items inside the document.

DOM and XML

If the idea of objects and elements is new to you, you might be asking how the DOM and XML interrelate. When you read the introduction to XML, you read about objects and elements, too. In some ways, XML and the DOM sound as if they do the same thing—defining a document as the sum of its parts.

The two are indeed related, but they are not the same. XML is a *metalanguage* that describes data. The DOM doesn't know data from diamonds.

What the DOM does is describe how XML documents can be represented as objects. These objects can, in turn, be accessed by a programming or scripting language.

JavaScript doesn't understand XML. You can't tell a script to interact with the <booktitle> tag. There are no programmatic guidelines around XML and its elements. To interact with <booktitle> you need a go-between that turns <booktitle> into an object with an API. That go-between is the DOM. The relationship resembles Figure 3.6.

Here's a sample application of how the DOM and XML interact (thanks to Lauren Wood for this example).

Suppose you are running an online bookstore and you have thousands of titles. If your customer searches for Jane Austen's *Emma* using some sort of search tool in the page, he or she might get back a list of 50 different results. Some are the book itself, in various editions, while some are literary critiques of the book. This search is better than nothing, but if you have marked up the data using XML you have the potential to make this search much more useful.

Under XML, you could have added tags that identify the author, the author of the introductory notes, the publication date, the type of edition, whether it is a hardback or paperback copy, the price, the delivery time;

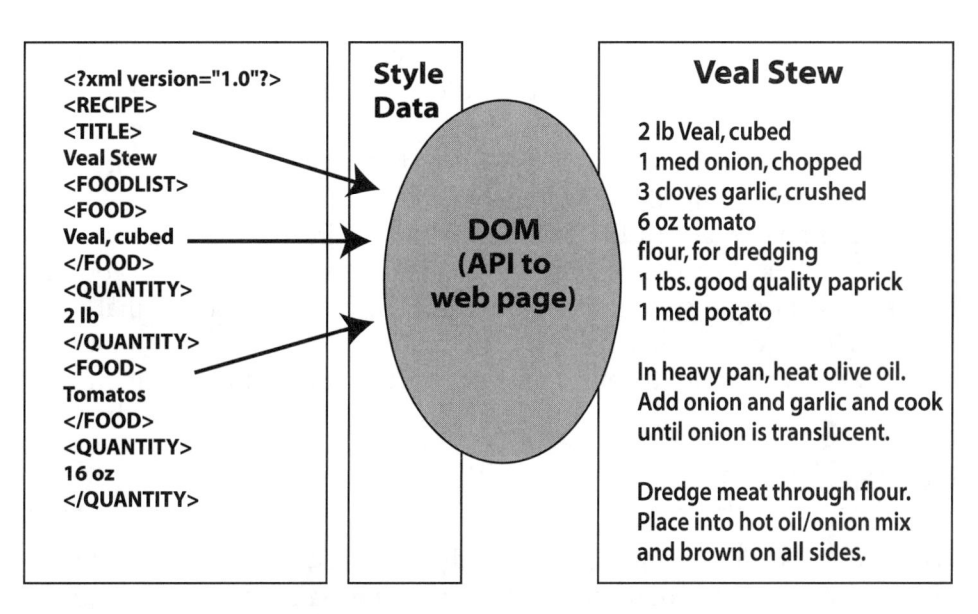

Figure 3.6 The relationship between the DOM and XML.

you could add all sorts of information about each different book. Once you have the information, you can write a script that lets you sort these entries according to any criteria—show the hardcover books first, show the most recent release first, and so on.

It is XML that lets you add the data, but it is the DOM that lets the script manipulate and display the data on command. XML provides the means of marking up the information, but alone it is not enough. You also need a way to work with that data, a piece at a time. And that's what the DOM provides.

DOM and CSS

You're hearing a lot of talk about "display" in this chapter, and you might be asking yourself, "Hey, isn't display what CSS is all about? How do the DOM and CSS work together?"

You're completely correct. As you remember, one of the important things that XML does is to separate structure from format. CSS (and, in the future, a style language called XSL as well) is where you specify the appearance of your XML elements.

CSS, however, doesn't address the specific elements in any sort of programmatic way. It doesn't give action commands. What it does is offer a sort of element-name-to-format-description translation table. It matches element information with style information.

CSS says, for example, that each <booktitle> tag means "bold italic sans serif" display attributes. Or that <quotation> has display attributes of "14-point Futura Bold, green."

The web browser matches the style information with the element name and displays the element appropriately.

By being able to access the DOM, you can do interesting and dynamic things with style. Because you can access the <quotation> element, you can also access its style information. This lets you write a script that, say, increases the size of the text inside the quotation and displays the quotation's *speaker*, *source*, and *date* attributes when a reader clicks on the quotation.

Interaction

When you talk about displaying a page dynamically, you're looking at four pieces of technology coordinating and working hand-in-hand with each other.

Remember that quotation example you just read about? The desired effect looks like that shown in Figures 3.7 and 3.8. The quote displays in one way until a reader clicks on it. Then, the quote displays in a different style and some of its attribute values are displayed.

Here's how it all works:

XML is the technology that identifies the element as a quotation and stores the *speaker*, *source*, and *date* of the quote.

The *script* is the technology that does the talking and sends the "change your display attributes when someone clicks" message to the quotation.

CSS is the technology that stores information about different display attribute values for the quotation and delivers this information to the browser when the script asks for it.

The *DOM* is the technology that lets you find and talk to the quotation and deliver the script's message.

If any of the pieces are missing, you can't create a dynamically-changing document.

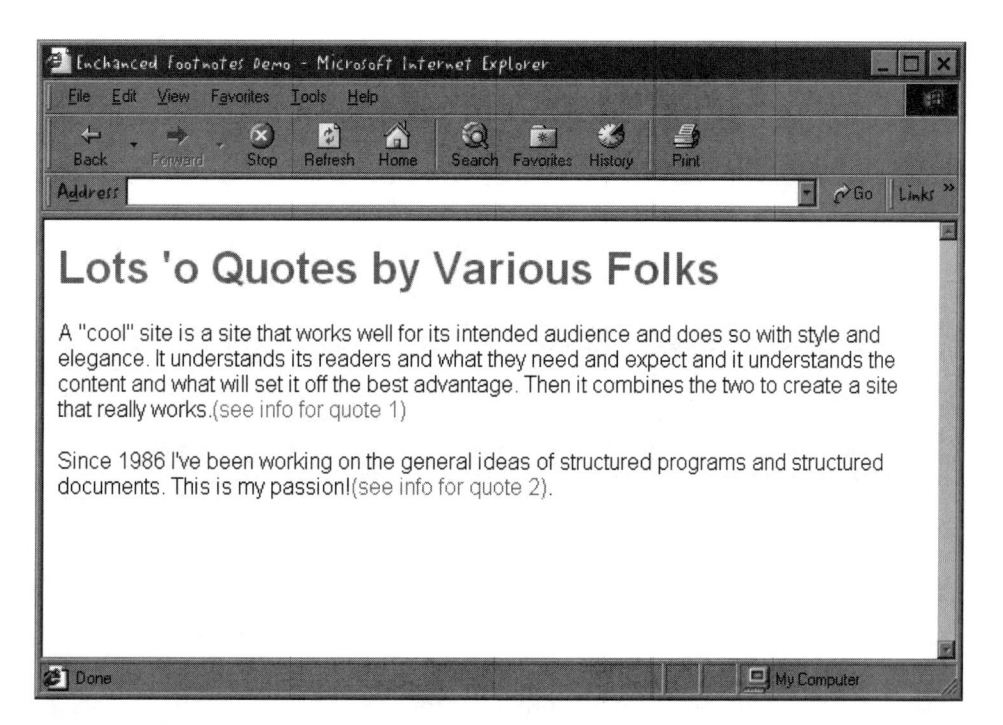

Figure 3.7 The quote in its unclicked state.

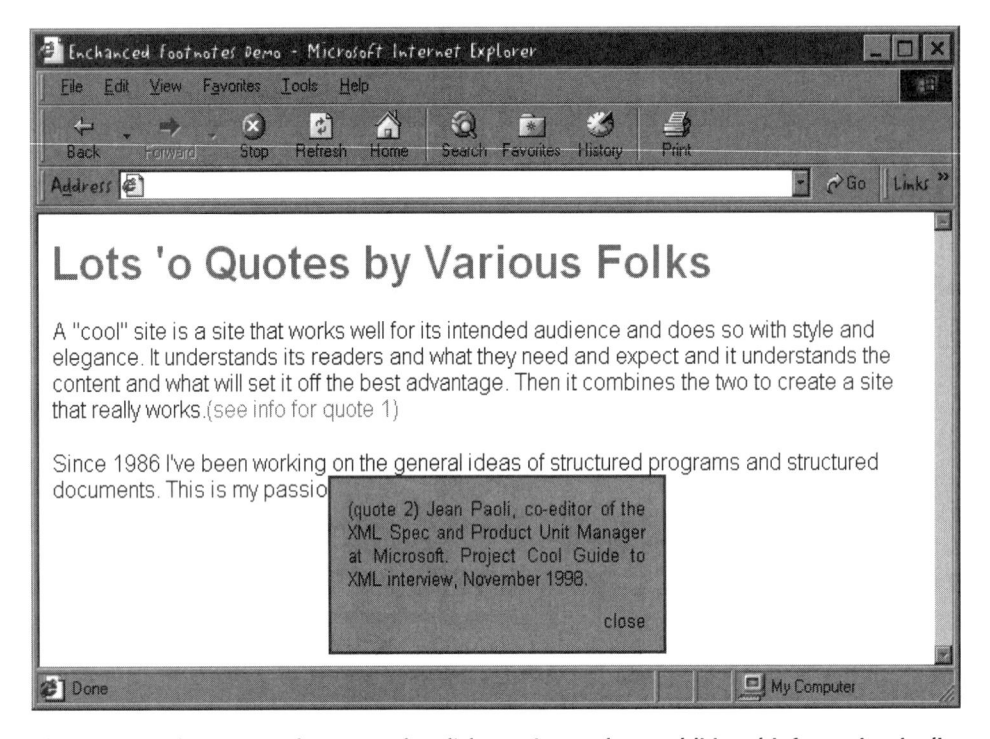

Figure 3.8 The quote when a reader clicks on it. See how additional information is displayed.

This also shows why standards are so important. Imagine the variations and the potential for very bad results for the poor reader if each of the four pieces is implemented differently in different browsers!

The DOM Specification

If you are going to do anything with a web page besides display it in one way in a browser window, you need to be able to do three things:

- You need to know what objects make up the document.
- You need to understand how those objects act.
- You need to know the rules for interacting with the objects.

The DOM specification does all three things.

First, it defines a standard set of objects for displaying XML and HTML pages. Second, it defines a model of how these objects work together. Third, it defines a standard interface for accessing these objects.

By combining these three features, the DOM achieves its stated goal of "defining a programmatic interface for XML and HTML." That is, the DOM opens up the HTML and XML document for manipulation, it exposes the individual parts, and it tells you how to talk to each of them directly.

The DOM specification is specific to HTML and XML documents. It is not a multipurpose, use-anywhere-and-for-every-reason spec. It is designed to allow people to access individual components of the web page and perform actions on those individual pieces.

Even with this specific scope, it covers a lot of territory, and so the DOM spec is divided into multiple parts. When you read about support of the DOM standard you'll often hear that the vendor is supporting something called the *DOM Core*. The DOM Core is, as its name suggests, the base level of specification.

The Core spec outlines the basic interfaces. These interfaces apply to both HTML and XML documents and are the basic interfaces that everyone has to implement, whether they do XML or HTML implementations of the DOM. The interfaces include those for elements, comments, and text.

The Core spec also includes a number of extended interfaces. These extended interfaces apply to items that are used in XML but are seldom used in HTML. These include CDATA sections and processing instructions. XML implementations of the DOM must implement both the fundamental and the extended Core interfaces.

The HTML interfaces were placed in a separate chapter of the spec, and they are implemented by HTML DOM implementations. HTML implementations also have to implement the fundamental Core interfaces.

An implementation of the DOM can, of course, implement all three sets of interfaces (fundamental Core, extended Core, and HTML) if it chooses, but most implement the sets of interfaces appropriate to their market. If a vendor isn't dealing with HTML, it wouldn't necessarily need to implement the DOM HTML—it could implement the Core and Extended interfaces and be completely standard compliant for the XML DOM.

The DOM became a W3C recommendation in October 1998. This means that as of that date, the DOM working group decided that the specification was ready for prime time and the W3C membership agreed. Various ideas had been tested, and different approaches had been tried; the October 1998 version reflects all this testing and trial.

A Brief History of the DOM

Very early on some people said that the HTML document needed an API. These aggressive developers saw that there was more to the browser window than a static page and suggested that the only way to make the web truly dynamic was to open up the page to programming commands. And the solution shouldn't belong to just one vendor—it should be an open standard that everyone could use and that would work on all browsers.

Every software tool that manipulates data uses a DOM of some sort. Usually it is a proprietary DOM that works only with that software, and it might be an internal part of the tool. If you want to expose the DOM to the user and let the user manipulate the information directly, then it makes sense to have a standardized interface. That is part of the reasoning behind the DOM standard.

If you have done any work with DHTML, you can understand why addressing individual elements is cool—and why a standard DOM is important. For example, remember that moving Saturn example earlier in this chapter? Or the table of contents that hid or displayed based on what the reader did? These were both great effects that didn't add any server overhead. One made the page more visually interesting; the other made the content easier to navigate.

Creating these pages was very exciting and started to show us some of the potential of working with individual objects on a page. We started thinking of other possibilities and how we could implement them—then reality hit. That's because implementing them meant creating multiple versions or having versions that worked on only one browser.

Because there was no standard DOM, we had to create the "flying Saturn" page several times so that it would work in the different browsers. And we couldn't make the hide-and-show outline work at all under Netscape Navigator. It is usable under NN, but it doesn't do the dynamic display. The work-around was to have the whole list show all the time.

And that Saturn page—yow! It was created once for IE 4.0 using MS-DHMTL and a second time for NN 4.0's layers. Then, it was created a third time in a static form for browsers that didn't allow you to access the DOM—in practice, all 3.X and earlier browsers. This is not a process any designer or developer wants to do very often. Standard procedure without a standard DOM is a huge, time-consuming, cost-inflating pain. For dynamic pages to be practical, there needs to be a standard DOM.

The DOM specification we have today originated as a description of how to make JavaScript scripts and Java programs be portable among all web browsers. It builds on the work done for DHTML, but it takes into account other needs and handles some things a bit differently.

SoftQuad's Lauren Wood, chair of the W3C Working Group for the DOM, tells how the DOM standard came to be:

> I was on the HTML Editorial Review Board at the time that Microsoft submitted their proposal for dynamic HTML and Netscape submitted their proposal for JavaScript Style Sheets. It was obvious that these two proposals were for things that the world needed, and needed to have standardized. It was also obvious that there was too much work to do for one ERB, so the decision was made to split the HTML ERB up into three Working Groups, one for the HTML language itself, one for the CSS style sheet language, and one for the Document Object Model.
>
> SoftQuad was one of the companies that thought the DOM work was extremely important, and for reasons slightly different to those of several other companies. We wanted a standardized interface that could be used for editors as well as browsers, and that wouldn't be limited to HTML. Since SoftQuad has a lot of experience in SGML, we could see that XML would be very important (though we didn't foresee just how fast XML would grow!). So I talked it over with my management, and we decided that I should offer to chair the Working Group, to help make the DOM happen. The Director of W3C agreed that I could chair the Working Group and so from then on a lot of my time was spent on the DOM. I called people at various companies to see if they were interested in joining the DOM WG, and fortunately most were. Many of these companies had experience in the SGML world, so they could see the importance of XML as well as HTML.
>
> We held our first meeting in March 1997, and it was a lot of fun. Since then the Working Group has grown, we've put out our first Recommendation (for Level 1), and now we have the satisfaction of seeing so many people implementing the DOM Level 1 specification. The WG has a number of very bright, experienced, talented people on it. There is no company in the world that could afford to put this much talent on solving this problem, and I think it's a good sign for this industry that companies are prepared to send such good people to meetings to solve problems in a standardized way.
>
> A special mention has to go to the editors, who have spent evenings and weekends polishing prose, checking the accuracy of the descrip-

tions, and updating the specifications every time things changed (which was often!).

It's been sometimes frustrating, trying to come up with a solution to technical problems that works in different languages, on different platforms, and for different types of software, but it's been a collaborative effort. There's a sense of almost magic when the solution to a knotty problem starts to appear and everyone catches hold of it and builds it up further. It's these moments, as well as the times when people send us e-mail (or talk to us at conferences) saying they find the DOM useful, that makes all the work worthwhile.

Using the DOM

If you are a typical web designer, you'll probably access the DOM, without necessarily realizing that is what you are doing. You'll most likely be using a tool to create some effect on your web page, or you'll be using a predefined script to perform some action.

As a designer, the most important thing to know about the DOM is that it is what enables you to work selectively with specific pieces of your document.

The tools for creating dynamic websites need to comply with the DOM, but much of that action will be invisible to you. You want tools that support the standard as well as tools that make it easier for you to control the action of your websites.

Having browsers that comply with the DOM is equally important. If the browser doesn't support the DOM, the effects that you create just flat out won't work. Your code will be sending calls to an API that doesn't exist. Your script will be talking to elements that don't understand what it is saying.

Asking for compliance from your software vendors is important. Understanding that you can access and manipulate individual sections of your web page is important. Knowing the minutia of the DOM spec might be interesting if you're an API junkie who loves the esoterica of code, but for most people that level of learning isn't necessary to create web pages that use the DOM's strength.

Don't be intimidated by this alphabet soup. The DOM might sound a little complicated at first, but it is really just a way of reaching out and touching the mushrooms, cheese, and sausage on your website pizza.

Summary

The DOM is the web designer's friend. With the DOM, scripting, and CSS, you can turn your XML and HTML files into reader-responsive displays without requiring server overhead.

By addressing and manipulating individual elements of the web page through the DOM, you have the power to change elements on the fly. When you combine this power with the metadata power of XML, you can bring a new level of customization and interaction to your websites.

CHAPTER 4

The Standards Process

XML lets you do some pretty exciting things with documents and the web, but that is just the tip of the XML mountain. XML has incredible potential for changing the way data moves around computer networks, the way we work with data, and the way data is interpreted by computers.

XML is leading the development of an entire set of related standards that will make data transportable and interoperable. With XML and XML applications, data will be free from the constraints of proprietary systems. This is very powerful stuff.

Standards, though, work only if they are agreed upon and actually implemented. That's why standards bodies are important. If you're exploring XML solutions, it helps to understand how an idea becomes a standard and how you and/or your company can affect this process.

Understanding the standards process also takes some of the frustration out of what sometimes feels like shifting standards—you can make implementation decisions more intelligently if you know where any given proposed standard is in the process and how likely it is to change.

Lauren Wood, chair of the DOM Working Group, explains the role of standards nicely:

> The basic idea behind the standards process is that you have a lot of people saying 'I just want [the browsers] to be interoperable.' Getting

to that point is part of the standards process—but not only for Microsoft and Netscape products. Every time you use an authoring tool you want to make sure that the code it generates can be read by one of the big browsers, so you want these tools to be interoperable too.

What you want is for all of these people to sit down in a room and talk about how they are going to interoperate. And then, lo and behold, what you get out of the end of this process is what is commonly called a standard. A standard isn't a big thing given from on high—it is something from the people who are working in the industry.

The W3C provides a forum, a name, a mechanism by which people can get together and say 'we need to interoperate' in this area.

Standards Fill a Need

Many people find that the standards organizations are convenient scapegoats for explaining why a standard doesn't work. We've heard people make public statements that standards bodies are unnecessary and that the market will just make the best decisions. We've heard that standards are too removed from the "real world" to be workable. We've heard that standards are just about politics.

We disagree.

The current round of standards, especially those that revolve around XML, are a huge effort, undertaken by a group of people who are volunteers. In some cases, their companies help underwrite the time they spend on standards development; in others, it is work done on their own time. The one thing the folks involved in the standards effort share is a desire for the web to work, and to work well.

Those who pooh-pooh standards are right—the marketplace could decide, but then we'd have something new to complain about. Either we would end up with splintered implementation that leaves us pulling our hair out (picture the variation among browsers for HTML display and then multiply that by a factor of 20 or so), or we'd have one dominant company impose its will on everyone else. In either case, we'd all feel frustrated or angry, and the resulting de facto standard might not be a very good one.

In the past, the cry that standards were too academic had some truth behind it, but in the XML space there has been an effort to throw the standards-in-progress into the web market, to let people try them and test them in real applications. Yes, the proposals change, but that's part of the development process. You and I use them, we complain about them, the specs get tweaked. After a few cycles of this, a firm document emerges and becomes a blessed standard. Then the work begins on version 2. The process more closely mirrors real-life software development than ever before.

As for politics, well, we believe politics are inescapable. They are part of human nature. The standards process, though, appeals to the mutual good. Because people from different companies and different perspectives are part of the process, the force of pure partisanship is blunted. And the vast majority of the individuals involved in developing the standards do care about making a solution that works—not solely about being mouthpieces for their respective companies.

It is easy to believe that "Microsoft always gets its way" or "Sun thinks it can do whatever it wants" or "Netscape has to win," but the reality is that all these companies will do best if the market has a workable standard that everyone can build to and develop for. That's where standards come in: They offer a shared vision and set a base for comparison.

The pressure by grassroots groups like the Web Standards Organization (<http://www.webstandards.org>) on the browser vendors to support Cascading Style Sheets—CSS1 and CSS2 standards—is a good example of the interaction between standards, users, and vendors. CSS1 and CSS2 were developed and approved by the standards body W3C. These specifications provide a baseline to which users should be able to develop web pages. Vendors see the same specifications that users do. When support wasn't fully forthcoming, users banded together to pressure for support. Vendors have responded, and slowly we're moving toward a state where we can develop one page and know that it will display across all browser and platform combinations.

The support isn't complete yet, and not everyone is happy with every aspect of the standard. Having that standard as a stake in the ground gives us a place for which we can aim. We have a set of common specifications around which we can develop and that we can legitimately request vendors to support.

Without the standards, vendors would be throwing out their own ideas, developers would be requesting features, and the poor end user would have no idea what websites might work or break on any given computer and browser. In short, we'd have a mess—and we certainly wouldn't have a mass medium.

If you still aren't convinced that standards are important for the large-scale use of a technology, then picture how the world would work in these situations:

Without FCC-mandated bandwidth for broadcast. Turn on your TV or radio and you'd receive stations cutting each other in and out. Or one single station could dominate the airwaves. Or you'd have no consistent ability to find and receive the station you want to find. How fast would this medium have grown in an environment of cacophony?

Without film speed standards. Put a roll of film into your camera and, well, now guess how much light that film requires for a good exposure. Calculate the speed of action this film can record. Study reams of data to learn how to make a properly exposed picture with this particular model of camera because you would have to consider both camera-to-camera and film-to-film variations. Would there be a consumer market for snapshots without film standards?

Without one set of mailing codes. Imagine if each large mailer used its own codes to speed up delivery of snail mail. Aunt Esther's address would be 02215 if the package was sent via one system, HB542 if sent by another, ne65-12-45 if sent by another. How often would you be sending anything to anyone if you needed to look up postal codes from several different vendors to find the right one?

Standards Come from People

It is important to remember that behind all this work are individual people. Yes, each person has his or her own agenda; don't we all? This variety of viewpoints and backgrounds is important in creating a well-rounded standard, one that works for most web applications. XML will be something we can use only if it works for a large body of applications and is developed via healthy debate and discussion.

By and large, the people involved in the XML and related standards are not academics; they are people who are working with information processing and distribution in real companies, on real projects. They are people like Lauren Wood, who chaired the DOM specification and works for SGML vendor SoftQuad Software. They are people like Jean Paoli, who was a coeditor of the XML spec and developed SGML solutions in Europe before joining Microsoft as its Product Unit Manager, Windows DNA XML Technologies. We'd like to introduce you to a cross section of some of the people who are making XML real.

Lauren Wood

Lauren Wood is smart. Five minutes into a conversation and you know you're dealing with someone very intelligent; you aren't surprised to learn that she holds a Ph.D. in theoretical nuclear physics. She went to Germany to do some postdoctoral work, discovered there were few jobs, took a detour through programming, and eventually ended up in Vancouver working for SGML editing tools (and now HTML and XML tools) vendor SoftQuad Software. She had done some SGML standards work and thought the DOM was an important issue; she volunteered to chair the group.

> Sometimes it's really good, sometimes it's a pain with a certain amount of bureaucracy, t's crossed, i's dotted, everyone notified, liaison, scheduling of meetings and conferences. But I enjoy it. There are some really bright people on the working group—they're not shy about stating their opinions but are also willing to provide their versions of solutions. It is sometimes almost magical to sit back as chair and watch things develop, to see ideas bouncing around . . . all of a sudden after an hour of this the group ends up someplace different than where it started and everyone looks at each other and says 'that's it!'

Jean Paoli

Jean Paoli was one of the coeditors of the XML specification. He is currently Product Unit Manager, Windows DNA XML Technologies at Microsoft, but before that he worked for 11 years in SGML startups in Europe. When he says he is passionate about document structure, he really means it.

Paoli began his academic career with a focus on structured programming and spent the last year of his education studying at the Institut National de Recherche en Infomatique et en Automatique (INRIA), working on technology dealing with structured authoring of programming. He met Vincent Quint (who is now W3C's deputy director for Europe), who got him interested in applying the idea of structured programming to documents.

> I'm an old SGML-er. . . . Since 1986 I've been working on the general ideas of structured programs and structured documents. This is my passion!
>
> [The XML spec process] was really fun because we had this kind of dream. We had the best people, a lot of people who were dreamers who had created good SGML tools. And on top of that I was at Microsoft and part of the Internet Explorer team [so I could have an impact there as well]. We really wanted to make XML the best we could; we wanted to simplify the process. We wanted to have millions of people using tagged languages.

> [Standards] work is done by e-mail, which is very efficient but takes a lot of time. We had 10–12 people who were very involved. We were from companies with similar interests, and lots of these people were working for companies that are competitors. We were doing it very quickly because the web doesn't wait.

Tim Bray

Tim Bray is one of the names you'll often hear associated with XML. He is a founding member (as invited expert) of the W3C XML Working Group; he is also coeditor, XML 1.0 and XML namespaces. In the rest of his life, he runs a web publishing technology consultancy, Textuality, based in Vancouver, Canada.

Bray worked for Digital Equipment Corporation and GTE before joining the New Oxford English Dictionary Project in 1987. He cofounded Open Text in 1989 and built the Open Text Index, the first-generation web search engine, in 1995.

> In 1996, about the time I left Open Text, Jon Bosak invited me to join his SGML-on-the-Web committee that eventually became XML. I was a pretty obvious candidate since I was a veteran of the SGML wars and had also had success building big Web applications. I figured that since I was just starting my consultancy, I'd have some spare time on my hands, so I signed up. I had no idea that it (XML) would get as big as it has!

Mary Fernandez

Mary Fernadez is a senior technical staff member at AT&T Labs' research facility. For the past three years she's been working on developing query languages, the way you ask computers for information. She co-authored the W3C submission, XML-QL: A Query Language for XML. A submission is a proposed solution offered to the W3C by one or more of its members.

Fernandez's work (along with that of co-authors Alin Deutsch, University of Pennsylvania; Daniela Florescu, INRIA; Alon Levy, University of Washington; and Dan Suciu, AT&T Labs) is an example of how a diverse group of people have had an impact on XML, even without participating in a working group. Her experience also illustrates the way submissions can serve as levers for kick-starting conversations and research.

The goal of the XML-QL paper was to initiate discussion on what we perceived as several important characteristics of *a* query language for XML.

It was not our intention to propose XML-QL as a standard or even as the basis for a standard. After submitting the paper to the W3C, Dan and I proposed to the W3C that they hold a workshop on XML query languages, which took place in early December [1998] and was managed by Massimo Marchiori. The goal of the workshop was to bring together different groups of people, in particular, database researchers from academia and industrial research, information-retrieval experts, and technical leaders from industry, who we thought could contribute different perspectives to the technical discussion of query languages for XML. The workshop was a great success and was the launching pad for creation of a working group on an XML query language.

Jeffrey Veen

Jeffrey Veen currently sits on the W3C's CSS Editorial Review Board and has sat on the HTML group as an invited expert on electronic publishing. You might also know him as the Executive Interface Director of Wired Digital or the author of *HotWired Style: Principles for Building Smart Web Sites*. He's also on the steering committee of the Web Standards Project (<http://www.webstandards.org>). As you might guess, standards are important to him.

I began following W3C standards years ago as a foundation on which to base our own internal standards at Wired Digital. Early in the history of the Web, browsers were developing at an insane rate, and the number of innovations was mind numbing. There were new releases nearly every month, each filled with an array of features being slapped together with what seemed like very little thought. But the more I looked at what the W3C was doing, the more I started to fundamentally understand the meaning of markup languages, electronic text, and what would eventually be a totally new type of publishing.

Strangely, however, the browsers seemed to be diverging from this path. As the working groups published specifications on things like cascading style sheets, which abstracted presentation from structure, the browser vendors were filling their software with <FONT> tags, plugins, and other 'sexy' technologies.

That's when I got involved—when it became obvious that the real-world, shipping software was going in the wrong direction, and content providers were the ones who could stand up and say so.

It is easy to vilify standards when you think of them as the work of a generic standards organization. The organizations, however, are just umbrellas for the work of many individuals. The standards process may be flawed, but it is also fully human, reflecting both the good and the bad of any human process.

The W3C

The World Wide Web Consortium, the W3C (<http://www.w3c.org>) is the leading standards organization for web-related standards, including XML.

The W3C's genesis lies at CERN (the European Laboratory for Particle Physics) in Geneva, Switzerland. As most of the web knows, CERN was where Tim Berners-Lee worked and where, in 1989, he started a project to improve collaboration between CERN researchers. Several years later, that project became the World Wide Web.

As the web grew, it became clear that CERN couldn't coordinate the development efforts. In October 1994 the W3C was founded at MIT in collaboration with CERN and with seed funding from the U.S. Department of Defense's Advanced Research Project Agency (DARPA) and the European Commission.

Today, the W3C has more than 250 corporate and academic members and is hosted by MIT in the United States, by Frances' National Institute for Research in Computer Science and Control (INRIA), and by Japan's Keio University. Its goal is the provide "a vendor-neutral forum for its members to address web-related issues ... the Consortium aims to produce free, interoperable specifications and sample code."

To reach that goal, the W3C has four *domains*, or larger areas of study, research, and development.

XML is part of the Architecture Domain, which is leading the efforts to maintain the seamless integration of the "global information space," more commonly known as the World Wide Web. The standards for Hypertext Transfer Protocol (HTTP) are also part of this domain.

Other domains include User Interface (HTML, the DOM), Technology and Society (privacy, e-commerce, security), and Web Accessibility.

The W3C Process (or How an Idea Becomes a Standard)

Most ideas follow a fairly clear path along the standards road: They begin as a submission, become published notes, and then move into a working group, which creates a working draft. After feedback and commentary, the working draft becomes a proposed recommendation, then eventually a W3C recommendation.

It is important to remember that the W3C doesn't issue "standards." It issues recommendations. If enough people adopt them, these recommendations become de facto standards. This is somewhat different from the way organizations such as the International Standards Organization (ISO) work, but it is an approach that has been serving the web-related technologies well.

When you read about XML (which was accepted as a recommendation in February 1998) and its related standards-in-progress, it is helpful to know the current stage of the would-be standard. The earlier in the process, the more likely it is to change, disappear altogether, or be open to input. The further along, the more likely it is to be accepted as it is described and "safer" to consider implementing.

When you hear all the terms—XML, XSL, Xlink, XQL, and so on—being tossed about, you might be tempted to throw up your hands and conclude that you're better off sticking with good old HTML. Look closely, though, and you'll see that many of these acronyms describe either submissions or notes, which means they are simply ideas under development; in the end they may or may not be accepted as standards.

A number of people will shape the idea as it moves through the process. Here are some of those groups.

The Director

The director is the person to whom all submissions are presented. When the director formally accepts a submission for consideration, the backers of an idea can say, "Idea ZYX is a W3C submission."

The Working Group (WG)

Working groups are set up to look at certain areas and turn different ideas into a proposed recommendation. Much of the nitty-gritty documentation work, specification writing, politicking, and consensus building happen within a working group.

The Members

All members of the W3C can comment on a proposal and weigh in on whether it should become a recommendation. All members may also submit an idea for consideration. In essence, the process both starts and ends with the W3C members.

Submissions to Notes

Here's how the process works:

Your company sees a problem in the web information space and formulates a possible solution. You talk to others in the web community, and together you create a submission to the W3C. The submission is a formal package that has been given to the W3C for consideration. The submission process allows members to propose technology or other ideas. Only when the W3C director accepts the submission for consideration can the proposed solution be called "a W3C submission."

You'll hear a lot from vendors about how this or that technology is a W3C submission. All this means is that this particular vendor thinks a particular technology is a good idea and that it would like to see the idea discussed and possibly become the standard around which all rally. Or, it considers a topic area to be important and has proposed a possible solution; making the submission is a way to introduce the topic to the W3C agenda. In any case, the vendor or member group has formally packaged its ideas and submitted them to the W3C for consideration. Being submitted does not make an idea a standard—no matter what any vendor tells you.

After acceptance of a submission, the W3C repackages and publishes documents that are part of the submission package. These documents are called W3C notes. They do not represent any commentary or input from the W3C, and they are not endorsed by the W3C. They are simply published as a matter of record.

Again, no matter what any sales person might tell you, notes are really no further along the process to becoming a standard than a submission is; they are simply the W3C's presentation of the idea that has been submitted and an acknowledgment of the submission.

Sometimes submissions are rejected. The W3C rejects ideas that it considers outside its scope, ideas that run counter to the W3C mission, and ideas that just don't hold up under scrutiny.

Working Groups and Working Drafts

If the director thinks the proposal merits further discussion, he or she accepts it and then either sends it to a related working group or calls for the creation of a new working group to address the topic. Working groups usually contain about a dozen people. The dynamics of each group are different, but in general the group has a chair or cochairs who coordinate the discussion and one or more editors who turn the discussion into a written specification. Some groups meet in person routinely, some seldom meet in person, and all carry on a voluminous e-mail exchange.

Working groups are held to schedules, and they must report results. An idea can't just go into a WG and disappear. Submissions are examined and dropped or, more likely, merged with other ideas and turned into a working draft. The working drafts might build on one or more submissions, exploring how Idea A from Vendor X and Idea B from Member Y can best be used to solve the problem at hand.

The working draft is a work in progress and represents a commitment by the W3C to pursue work in this particular area. A working draft does not, however, mean that this particular configuration of ideas will become a recommendation. If you hear that a piece of technology is a working draft, you can feel comfortable that there will be some sort of standard on this topic eventually, but you shouldn't assume that the end result will exactly match what you read in the working draft.

It is within the working group that issues are debated (sometimes hotly), different approaches examined, and solutions tested. Working groups are also subject to the realities of the market. Vendors have shipping schedules for products, and the vendor members in the working group have the delicate task of balancing proposal schedules with their own product schedules. It's an ongoing question of "Is this the best solution?" set against "When can we support this solution?" The combination helps test ideas in a real development environment and keeps ideas grounded, making them usable instead of merely nice academic exercises.

As DOM Chair Lauren Wood explains:

We have a lot of discussion, which is why standards take a while . . .

It's real people sitting on these working groups. You have to . . . get them talking about things, figuring out where they are coming from, and building consensus. It isn't writing the spec that takes the time—it is building consensus. In the DOM group, for example, we have people who are writing HTML, working with XML, building server-side applications, writing tools, etc. They all have different things they care about. So you take all these different viewpoints, and it can take a while to get this consensus built.

Proposed Recommendations to W3C Recommendations

Once the working group has finalized its working draft, it submits it to the W3C director. The director, in turn, sends it on to the advisory committee for review. At this point the working draft becomes a proposed recommendation. Members of the W3C are invited to review and comment on the proposed recommendation.

When you hear that something is a proposed recommendation, it is just one step away from becoming a recommendation. It means that the working group has agreed on the approach and that it is in its final review stages.

The proposed recommendation has a fixed review period. At the end of that time, the director can do one of four things with a proposed recommendation:

- If it is perfect, he or she can give it the green light and issue it as a full-fledged recommendation.

- If it needs only minor changes, he or she can issue it as a recommendation with the indicated changes.

- If it needs reworking, it is sent back to the working group with a list of "to-do" items, and the process repeats itself.

- If it is unacceptable, he or she can abandon the proposed recommendation and remove it from the agenda, effectively killing it.

When you hear that a technology has become a recommendation of the W3C, it means that it represents a consensus of the membership and that the WC3 considers it fully ready for use.

Standards Support

Once a specification, like XML, becomes a recommendation, it has all the marks of a standard except the most important one: widespread use. A recommendation becomes a "standard" only if people use it.

XML took off quickly because it provided a solution to the problems of data exchange and of separating content from format. It is safe to say that XML is already being implemented widely enough that it will become a standard.

As XML reaches critical mass, more vendors are pressed to offer support for it and tools for working with it are beginning to emerge. We are in the early stages of this as of this writing.

What Say Do I Have?

Now that you understand the evolution of a submission to a recommendation; you might be asking, "So, what does this have to do with me?"

The answer is, "A lot!" Standards become standards only if people implement them and find them of use. As a designer/developer you can make the standards yours by exploring ways to use them, implementing them as they make sense for you, and demanding that vendors support them.

You can push for the support of standards through grassroots organizations like the Web Standards Project. Founded in 1998, this group has pressed browser vendors to offer full CSS support, and it has been active in DOM issues and XML implementation. Its website address is <http://www.webstandards.org>.

If you're interested in the hands-on make-a-standard process, there are three ways you can become a member of the W3C.

First, if you work for a large company, you may already be a member. Full members are charged $50,000/year, with a three-year commitment. If you think your company might be a member, go to <http://cgi.w3.org/MemberAccess/>. Part of the form that appears is a list of all members. If your company is on the list, you can use the form to apply for a password, which lets you see the members-only discussions, newsletters, and other information.

If you are part of a small company or a nonprofit group, your company can join as an affiliate member. Affiliates are charged $5000/year, with a three-year commitment.

There is no provision for individuals to join at an individual rate, but if you are an expert in an area, you could be invited to join as an invited expert.

Even if you aren't a member you can have input into the process by participating in some of the public discussion lists on emerging topics. The W3C runs an extensive set of standards lists; you can see what's available at <http://www.w3.org/Mail/Lists.html>.

The bottom line for standards is this: Use them, test them, and be vocal about them. Get involved, and make the standards yours—because if you don't use them, they aren't standards; they're just some good ideas that someone once proposed.

Summary

It's awfully easy to poke fun at the standards process—sometimes it can feel slow and a little academic. But it plays a crucial role in the development of the web as a medium. To work and truly be a part of our daily world, the web needs to be a form that many people can create for and use, and can do so without an impossible learning curve. Without standards groups—and the smart, dedicated people who volunteer their time and expertise—we'd end up with a system that serves only a few.

We would have a hodgepodge of technology pieces, all proprietary, all competing for our use, many doing the same end application. Content for browser A wouldn't work correctly on browser B, and browser B's developers wouldn't even bother to make their work viewable by users who happen to have Browser A. This isn't the recipe for a mass medium; it's a recipe for technology tinkering.

Or, we would end up with a monolithic, one-company-imposed solution that we could take or leave. Our online experience would be defined by one single "we know best" corporation or media conglomerate. The best technology wouldn't win—the biggest marketing budget would.

Where would this leave the web? I suspect it would be a footnote tucked in with video-text and other good ideas that just didn't work. Support your standards—and get involved. Because you really can make a difference.

CHAPTER 5

Alphabet Soup

XML does not stand on its own. It provides a standard syntax for marking up data (including documents), for providing data about the document's elements, and for adding structure to the document. Once the data is marked up with XML, you'll need to use other standards to display it, manipulate it, and work with it.

As of this writing, we are fairly early in the standards process. XML itself is stable, but XML is just the start. It is one key piece of a larger issue—finding the solution to the question "How can data be made interoperable, so that different platforms, programs, and applications can interpret the same data for their respective applications?" The documents and web applications that web designers develop are an important piece of this mix, but they are not the only piece.

XML is becoming the basis for applications as diverse as database structure, digital forms processing, and multimedia integration. Some of the terms explained in this chapter may not be items you work with directly, but you are likely to hear and see these acronyms used in the trade press and in conversations about XML.

People and companies are creating ideas for the way we should be working with XML documents. These ideas are being proposed, tested, and revised. Tracking these proposals and the changes within them is a full-time job. This chapter outlines some of the leading proposals and explains what each would do.

In addition, Tables 5.1 through 5.8 summarize the current state of the various proposals and list URLs where more information about each can be found. These tables are also part of this book's supporting website at <http://www.projectcool.com/guide/xml/>. From this location you can see updated information and click through to the specs and other data.

Remember, XML and its various applications are still under development. New solutions could be proposed tomorrow, and some of the solutions outlined in this chapter could well be altered, dropped, or replaced with newer ones. Despite its ongoing evolution, XML is clearly here to stay and its applications are already "ready for prime time" and in use in the real world.

Extensions

You'll notice a common theme in many of these acronyms—the syllable "ex."

It all started with XML. The X comes from the sound at the beginning of "extensible" (not from the second letter, as is commonly thought; members of the XML working group are quick to point this out!). Most of these ideas in some way extend the underlying philosophy behind XML, creating applications or presenting ideas that work side by side with XML, to make it more useful and more powerful.

The ideas behind these acronyms provide ways for displaying XML documents, for validating XML documents, for querying XML documents, and for accessing individual elements within an XML document.

On the surface, the result seems to be a tangle of terms, a veritable alphabet soup with a lot of "x"s floating around in it. Don't let these terms leave you confused or frighten you away from XML. You won't be using all of them directly; we explain them here to give you some background so that when you hear the phrases being used you have some idea whether they apply directly to your work.

A Word about Status

Much of the development work for XML and related technology is happening under the W3C umbrella, which you read about in the previous chapter.

There are a couple of important things to remember about the W3C. First, it doesn't create international standards. It generates recommendations for standards—which may or may not be adopted by the community at large and by the formal international standards bodies, such as the International Standards Organization (ISO).

Second, as the idea moves along the W3C process, it tends to evolve as it is tested, beat upon, and explored by people with a variety of backgrounds and needs. Everything is subject to change until the idea is officially declared a recommendation.

As a brief review, here are the steps an idea moves through within the W3C:

1. Submission
2. Published note
3. Working draft
4. Proposed recommendation
5. Recommendation

Guide to the Proposals

Tables 5.1 through 5.8 summarize some of the XML-related proposals under discussion and provide links for additional information. The status noted for these proposals is valid as of the time of this writing, but it may have changed by the time you read this. The companion website to this book, <http://www.projectcool.com/guide/xml>, contains an online, up-to-date reference to these terms and their specifications and other reference material.

Each of these proposals is discussed, in order, in this chapter.

Markup

Markup is the process of adding meaning to raw text. Markup codes are containers for storing information about elements within the document. This information can later be used in many different ways.

Markup of some sort—be it XML, HTML, or proprietary word processing markup—is essential for documents to make sense. Without markup, your document is one big glob of text that runs to infinity in a long single line, with each character following the other and all characters treated

Table 5.1 XML-Related Idea Summary: Markup-Related Topics

NAME	DESCRIPTION	STATUS	OTHER RESOURCES
Standard Generalized Markup Language (SGML)	An international standard that was created to solve the problems of data interchange.	ISO 8879 ISO standard, 1986.	Robin Cover's SGML Overview: <http://www.oasis-open.org/cover/general.html> Lou Burnard's What is SGML page: <http://sable.ox.ac.uk/ota/teiedw25/> OASIS, The Organization for the Advancement of Structured Information Standards (was sgml-open, renamed in early 1998): <http://www.oasis-open.org/>
HyperText Markup Language (HTML)	Basic building block of the web, turns ASCII text into a displayable page in a web browser, is an application of SGML.	HTML 4.0, W3C Recommendation, April 1998	W3C HTML Home page: <http://w3c.org/MarkUp/> GettingStarted.net HTML tutorials: <http://www.gettingstarted.net/>
Extensible Markup Language (XML)	A tagged language that separates form from structure and enables the addition of metadata to information, is based on SGML.	XML 1.0, W3C Recommendation, February 10, 1998	XML W3C Recommendation: <http://www.w3.org/TR/REC-xml> Project Cool's XML Zone: <http://www.projectcool.com/developer/xmlz/> Tim Bray's annotated XML spec: <http://www.xml.com/axml/axml.html> Robin Cover's XML Overview at OASIS: <http://www.oasis-open.org/cover/xmlIntro.html> XML.com: <http://www.xml.com/> OASIS, The Organization for the Advancement of Structured Information Standards (was sgml-open, renamed in early 1998 and expanded to XML also): <http://www.oasis-open.org/> W3C XML Activity Page: <http://www.w3.org/XML/Activity>

Table 5.2 XML-Related Idea Summary: Style-Related Topics

NAME	DESCRIPTION	STATUS	OTHER RESOURCES
Cascading Style Sheets (CSS)	A way of assigning various kinds of display values to web page elements, works with both HTML and XML.	CSS1, W3C Recommendation, December 1996. CSS2, W3C Recommendation, May 1998.	W3C Web Style Sheets page: <http://w3c.org/Style/> Project Cool CSS Reference: <http://www.projectcool.com/developer/cssref/index.html>
Extensible Style Language (XSL)	Contextual style language, works with XML.	W3C Working Draft, December 1998.	W3C latest working draft: <http://www.w3.org/TR/WD-xsl> W3C Note about using XML and CSS together: <http://w3c.org/TR/NOTE-XSL-and-CSS> W3C XSL page: <http://www.w3.org/Style/XSL/>
Document Style Semantics and Specification Language (DSSSL)	SGML's style language.	ISO 10179, ISO Standard, April 1996.	James Clark's DSSSL page: <http://www.jclark.com/dsssl/>
HTML Components (HTC), aka "behaviors"	Part of IE 5.0, a means of using a component approach to setting style through scripting, uses CSS functions.	W3C submission, October 1998 (by Microsoft).	HTML Components Submission: <http://w3c.org/TR/NOTE-HTMLComponents> Project Cool Behavior Library: <http://www.projectcool.com/developer/behaviors/index.html>
Dynamic HTML (DHTML)	Controlling style through CSS, scripting, and the DOM.	A catch-all phrase for dynamically changing HTML; not a written specification.	Project Cool's DHTML Zone: <http://www.projectcool.com/developer/dynamic/> Macromedia's DHTML Zone: <http://www.dhtmlzone.com/index.html> Inside DHTML: <http://www.insidedhtml.com/>

Table 5.3 XML-Related Idea Summary: Structure Rules-Related Topics

NAME	DESCRIPTION	STATUS	OTHER RESOURCES
Document Type Definition (DTD)	A way of defining the elements that make up a document. Required for SGML, optional for XML.	Not a formal standard, just a means of defining elements.	Schema.Net: <http://www.schema.net/> Project Cool's DTD page: <http://www.projectcool.com/developer/xmlz/xmlbasics/dtd.html>
Document Definition Markup Language (DDML), formerly known as XSchema	A schema language for XML documents; a means for XML developers to describe their XML document rules using XML syntax.	Submitted to the W3C and published as a note, January 1999. Developed by the XML-Dev Mailing list group.	W3C Note: <http://www.w3.org/TR/NOTE-ddml> DDML Site: <http://purl.oclc.org/NET/ddml> Simon St. Laurent's personal page:<http://www.simonstl.com/> XML-Dev Mailing List Archives (summer 1998): <http://www.lists.ic.ac.uk/hypermail/xml-dev/>
XML Data	A proposal for using XML syntax to create both DTDs and definition of data in an XML document.	Submitted to the W3C, December 1997, now superseded by DCD (see next).	XML Data Note: <http://www.w3.org/TR/1998/NOTE-XML-data/>
Document Content Description (DCD)	A proposal for using XML syntax to create a DTD.	Submitted to the W3C by Microsoft and IBM, August 1998.	DCD Submission to W3C: <http://w3c.org/Submission/1998/11/> DCD Note: <http://w3c.org/TR/NOTE-dcd> Schema.net: <http://www.schema.net>

exactly the same. Without markup people can't read your document. They can't see paragraph breaks. Even other computers can't do much with the data because it is just one big clump.

There are many different types of markup languages, including SGML, HTML, and XML. These three markup languages are all related to each other.

Table 5.4 XML-Related Idea Summary: Processing-Related Topics

NAME	DESCRIPTION	STATUS	OTHER RESOURCES
Document Object Model (DOM)	A standardized interoperable way of manipulating individual pieces of the document.	W3C Recommendation, October 1998.	W3C DOM Page: <http://w3c.org/DOM/> DOM Recommendation: <http://www.w3.org/TR/REC-DOM-Level-1/> DOM FAQ: <http://w3c.org/DOM/faq.html>
XML Namespace (XML NS)	A collection of XML names, identified by a Uniform Resource Identifier (URI).	W3C Recommendation, January 1999.	W3C Recommendation: <http://www.w3.org/TR/REC-xml-names/>

Table 5.5 XML-Related Idea Summary: Linking-Related Topics

NAME	DESCRIPTION	STATUS	OTHER RESOURCES
XPointer	A way of describing how to get to linked content.	Working Draft.	Working Draft at the W3C: <http://w3c.org/TR/WD-xptr> Steve DeRose's (one of the Xpointer editors) links to Xpointer implementation: <http://www.stg.brown.edu/~sjd/XML-Linking/xptr-implementations.html>
XLink	A language for describing a relationship between data.	Working Draft, March 1998.	Working Draft at the W3C: <http://www.w3.org/TR/WD-xlink>

SGML

Standard Generalized Markup Language, or SGML, is an international standard that was created to solve the problems of data interchange. By describing a document by its structure—headlines, paragraphs, captions—rather than its format—24 point, Helvetica, italic—SGML made it possible to move a document across different types of computer systems without losing its meaning.

Table 5.6 XML-Related Idea Summary: Query-Related Topics

NAME	DESCRIPTION	STATUS	OTHER RESOURCES
XML-QL	A proposal for querying XML data.	Submitted to the W3C, August 1998.	W3C XML-QL Note, August 1998: <http://www.w3.org/TR/NOTE-xml-ql/> Position papers on a variety of query topics from the W3C Query Languages Workshop, December 1998: <http://w3c.org/TandS/QL/QL98/pp.html>
XQL	A proposal for querying XML data.	Proposal by Microsoft et al. September 1998.	XQL Proposal: <http://www.w3.org/TandS/QL/QL98/pp/xql.html> Proposal for Querying and Transforming XML: <http://www.w3.org/TandS/QL/QL98/pp/query-transform.html>

Table 5.7 XML-Related Idea Summary: Metadata-Related Topics

NAME	DESCRIPTION	STATUS	OTHER RESOURCES
RDF	Resource Description Framework.	W3C, Proposed Recommendation, January 1999.	W3C, Proposed Recommendation: <http://www.w3.org/1999/.status/PR-rdf-syntax-19990105/status>/ W3C Metadata Activity page: <http://www.w3.org/Metadata/Activity> Dublin Core Metadata Initiative: <http://purl.oclc.org/dc/>

SGML is an international standard, adopted in 1986. It has been used in a number of large and/or specialized publishing applications for the past dozen or more years.

SGML does not have a fixed set of markup tags. You define your tags—and your document elements, attributes, and document rules—to suit your application.

Table 5.8 XML-Related Idea Summary: XML Application-Related Topics

NAME	DESCRIPTION	STATUS	OTHER RESOURCES
General	General information about XML applications.	N/A	XML.COM: <http://www.xml.com/xml/pub/Guide/XML_Implementations>
Extensible Forms Description Language (XFDL)	A way to digitally represent complex forms, including digital signatures.	W3C note, September 1998.	W3C Note: <http://w3c.org/TR/NOTE-XFDL>
Synchronized Multimedia Integration Language (SMIL)	A way to integrate multimedia objects into a web page.	W3C Recommendation, June 1998.	W3C Recommendation: <http://www.w3.org/TR/REC-smil/>
Ad Markup	A way to submit advertising digitally, developed by the Newspaper Association of America (NAA).	Under development by the NAA.	Ad Markup: <http://www.zedak.com/admarkup/default.htm>
Information Content and Exchange Protocol (ICE)	A way to reuse information across different websites, designed for syndication of content.	W3C Note, October 1998.	W3C Note: <http://www.w3.org/TR/NOTE-ice>
Mathematical Markup Language (Math ML)	A way of describing mathematical notation by both structure and content.	W3C Recommendation, April 1998.	W3C Math page: <http://www.w3c.org/Math/> W3C Recommendation: <http://www.w3.org/TR/REC-MathML/>

SGML is quite complex. Its complexity is part of both its strength and its weakness. The challenges in developing SGML documents discouraged its widespread use.

SGML is the parent of both XML and HTML, and its ideas of structured documents form the underpinnings of XML's philosophy.

HTML

Hypertext Markup Language, or HTML, is the basic building block of the web. It turns ASCII text into a displayable web page.

HTML is an application of SGML, although most people who code in HTML probably don't realize it. HTML applies tags to a document. The web browser converts those tags to a default display within the browser window. Although HTML was originally structural in nature, in practical use it has become a combination markup and formatting language.

HTML has a set of defined tags because someone sat down and created the definition. By creating an understandable set of elements and attributes and enabling browsers to use this set without any additional effort on the part of the content creator, HTML made SGML-style markup accessible.

XML

Extensible Markup Language, or XML, is the topic of this book—and much, much more. It is the language, recommended by the W3C, that enables you to create a structured document that you can use across many different types of publishing applications, ranging from the web to databases.

XML separates format from content. And it lets you add data about your content, giving your documents extra layers of meaning. An XML tagged document can be combined with style standards to display and process in many different ways in many different environments.

XML is rooted in SGML, but is far easier to implement. It combines the simplicity of the HTML application with the power of SGML to create a solution that is practical in the real world for a wide range of applications. It is the best of both worlds.

Style

A number of standards and standards-in-progress deal with the issues of formatting and display style.

Without some sort of style standard, XML is hamstrung from the designer's perspective. Remember, one of the most important concepts behind XML is the separation of content from style. XML lets you focus on adding meaning to the data without getting trapped by design and display constraints. There will come a time when you want to—and need to—display your XML data. That's where the style standards come into play.

The style and formatting standards let you turn tagged data into beautiful web pages that will work across all browsers and platforms. Of all the items discussed in this chapter, it is likely that you'll work most often with the style standards, especially CSS and XSL.

Through the style component, you control the look and feel of the page. Some of the proposed style standards even let you make the style contextual—that is, you can apply one look under a certain set of circumstances and another if other variables apply.

For example, by applying styles, you can make your document display the way you want it to on many different platforms. You can have one set of styles that display in XML-compliant browsers, a set of styles that turns XML into HTML for older, non-XML browsers, and a set of styles that displays a subset of data on the version of the document designed for a Palm Pilot. Your underlying document with its XML structure stays the same; only the overlying styles differ to create custom results.

CSS1 and CSS2

Cascading style sheets, known as CSS1 and CSS2, work with both HTML and XML files. They are a way of assigning various kinds of display values—including font, color, and screen placement—to document elements.

CSS1 became a standard in December 1996, yet the major browsers still do not offer full support of its features. CSS2 became a standard on May 12, 1998. CSS2 is a superset of CSS1 with CSS positioning incorporated as well as support for different media types and many more enhancements. CSS positioning allows you to explicitly position document elements, either absolutely on the display page or relatively to each other, using X,Y coordinates.

CSS authorities speculate that it could be years before CSS2 is fully implemented due to its complexity. For comparison, the CSS1 spec is about 50 pages long, but the CSS2 spec weighs in at about 300 pages.

More and more designers are working with CSS, however, and there is a strong push from the user community as well. We hope to see near-complete support of CSS1, at the very least, in the 5.X generation of browsers. At the same time we expect to see at least partial support for CSS2.

In the CSS view, *style* means just about everything that defines how your web pages look. This includes fonts, spacing, color, indents, line height, hide/display, and many other attributes.

Using CSS you can control the look of your page from one central location. You can make style changes once and have them affect a whole suite of pages. You can make changes to a set of styles and apply the slightly changed set to other web pages, without re-creating all your style-building work over and over again. You can create variations on the look of elements and call those variations in your web pages. Once you've worked with CSS, you'll wonder how you ever got along without it.

The term *cascading* means that the styles you create and apply to a page operate at three levels, with each level cascading into the next.

At the top-level is the external style sheet file. This is a file of ASCII text with a .css extension. In the text, you define the style—the look and feel—for each element in your web page. If you don't define a style, the page uses the default styles, exactly what has happened in the past.

You can create a style for the element, but that's not all! You can create variations of the style, called classes, and use them within your page.

Figure 5.1 shows a page created using style sheets. You can see a live version of this page at this book's companion website, <http://www.projectcool.com/guide/xml>. We used CSS and element classes to display the page.

You can see that there are paragraphs of sans serif text and paragraphs that show HTML code in a monospaced (and purple) font.

Both the copy and the code are paragraphs, but we used style sheets to create two separate classes.

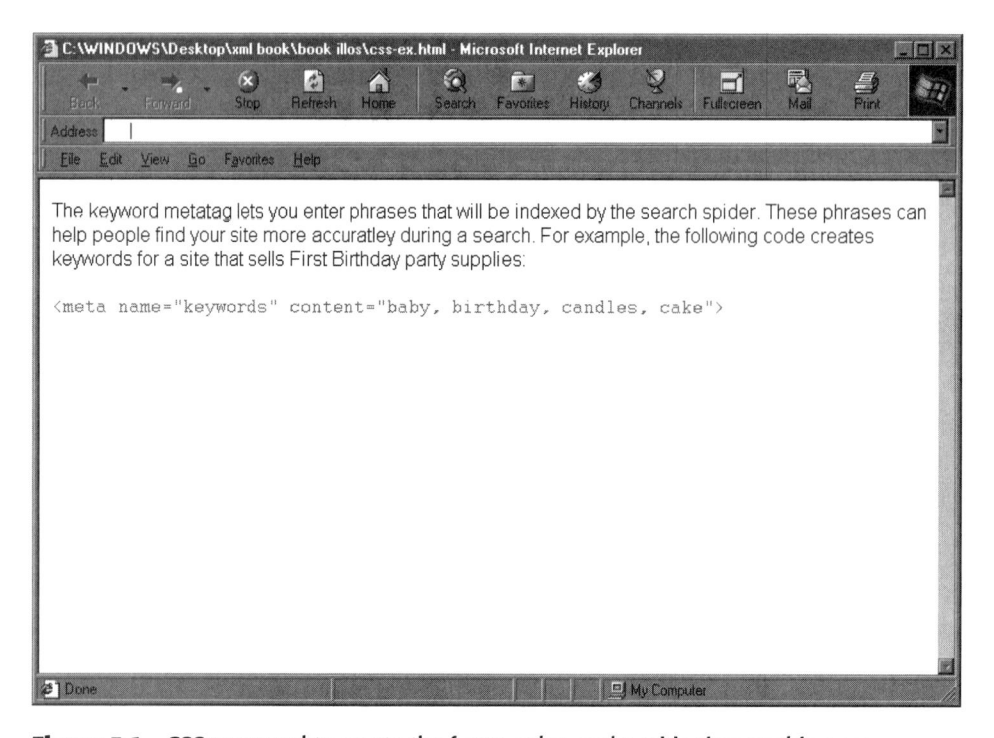

Figure 5.1 CSS was used to create the fonts, color, and positioning on this page.

One class is called *copy* and is used for the body copy.

The other class is called *code* and is used for the code examples.

In the style sheet, we defined the copy class of paragraph to use the sans serif font. In the same style sheet, we defined the code class of paragraph to display in a purple, monospaced font.

The code that does this is quite simple. It sets some baseline values for the paragraph element and also creates two different classes of paragraph elements—p.copy and p.code. Each has its own additional display attributes:

```
P {font-size: 12pt;
    Line-height: 14pt;}
P.copy {font-family: "Arial, Geneva, Helvetica",sans serif;}
P.code {font-family: "Courier", monospace;
color: #9966cc;}
```

When we created the page, we just called the style, like this:

```
<p class="copy">The keyword metatag lets you enter phrases that will be
indexed by the search spider. These phrases can help people find your
site more accurately during a search. For example, the following code
creates keywords for a site that sells First Birthday party supplies:
</p>
<p class="code">&lt;meta name="keywords" content="baby, birthday,
candles, cake&gt;
</p>
```

At a more local level, you can also assign styles within the individual HTML or XML document; those styles will apply just to that document and will override any styles from the linked external style sheet.

At the most local level, you can assign style information for an individual element, overriding both the in-file and external file style information.

Now imagine CSS tied into XML—not only can you define the elements that make up your documents, but you can define exactly how they look using a method that is easy to update and change and that is completely transportable.

XSL

Extensible Style Language, or XSL, isn't actually a style sheet itself—it is a language for expressing style sheets. It consists of two parts: a language for transforming XML and a language for specifying formatting information.

Transformation is an important element of XSL. For example, with XSL, you can turn XML data into HTML documents for delivery to older browsers that don't support XML.

The formatting vocabulary of XSL builds on CSS to create a sort of style sheet with contextual programming.

XSL and CSS are complementary technologies. Table 5.9 shows the differences.

It is quite possible that you will use CSS and XSL in tandem, depending on what you are doing with your data.

The first version of XSL was submitted to the W3C in April 1998. The most recent working draft is dated December 1998. You can see a copy of it at <http://w3c.org/TR/WD-xsl>. XSL is backed by a number of major web players, including Microsoft, and it may well have already become a W3C recommendation by the time you read this.

CSS maps styles directly to HTML and XML elements. XSL takes this mapping process one step further. It lets you specify objects and then map elements in a document to those objects. The objects, in turn, provide formatting and style information to the elements. The benefit of this approach is that you can use XSL to view XML documents in a browser and to transform XML documents to HTML documents or other XML documents.

For example, if you have an XML document that you want readers using 4.X browsers to read, you'll need to do a style transformation that turns your XML tags into some sort of HTML that the 4.X browser understands.

XSL differs from CSS in that XSL is contextual. That is, you can program the way it displays data based on certain variables that you specify.

For example, with XSL you could set a style for displaying elements in a web browser and a style for displaying elements on a PDA. The style would test to see what sort of display device is requesting the style data and deliver the appropriate version of the XML document. There's no need to create separate documents or multiple style sheets. All the style data is stored in one convenient location.

Table 5.9 Differences between CSS and XSL

ACTION	SUPPORTED BY CSS	SUPPORTED BY XSL
Works with HTML	Yes	No
Works with XML	Yes	Yes
Transforms objects	No	Yes

DSSSL

Document Style Semantics and Specification Language, or DSSSL, is SGML's style language. It became an ISO (International Standards Organization) standard in April 1996.

DSSSL plays much the same role in SGML that CSS plays for HTML and XSL will for XML: It is a syntax for describing formatting attributes.

It is unlikely that you'll need to know much about DSSSL, but you may hear the term tossed about. Jade, another term you might hear in passing during XML/SGML discussions, is an implementation of DSSSL.

HTC

HTML Components, or HTC, is not technically related to XML, but the stylistic control it brings can be used with XML. HTC started out as something called "behaviors." It was created by Microsoft, implemented in IE 5.0, and then submitted to the W3C in October 1998. Netscape has a similar submission, called "action sheets."

HTCs provide a way to create components that script a style. They can be used to create effects, like a shaking browser window, or for functional tasks, such as automatically generating pull quote or footnote pop-up boxes. With HTC, you create an action and tie that action to an object in the web page. And, because they are components, they can be reused in many different pages and maintained from a single location.

In our Future Focus section (<http://www.projectcool.com/focus/>) we created an HTC called *pullquote*. We enter the XML tag <FF:PULLQUOTE> around the text we want to display in separate pull quote display style on the page. Every time the browser encounters the <FF:PULLQUOTE> tag it is directed to a script and performs an action—in this case, it creates an 18-point Helvetica block that opens and closes with quotation marks and contains the contents of the <FF:PULLQUOTE> tag, that is, the text between the <FF:PULLQUOTE> and </FF:PULLQUOTE> tags, as show in Figure 5.2.

DHTML

Dynamic HTML, or DHTML, is a blanket term rather than a standard. Both Microsoft and Netscape used the phrase to describe the ability to access and manipulate individual elements in a web page. DHTML describes the process of using scripting to apply CSS display values by accessing the

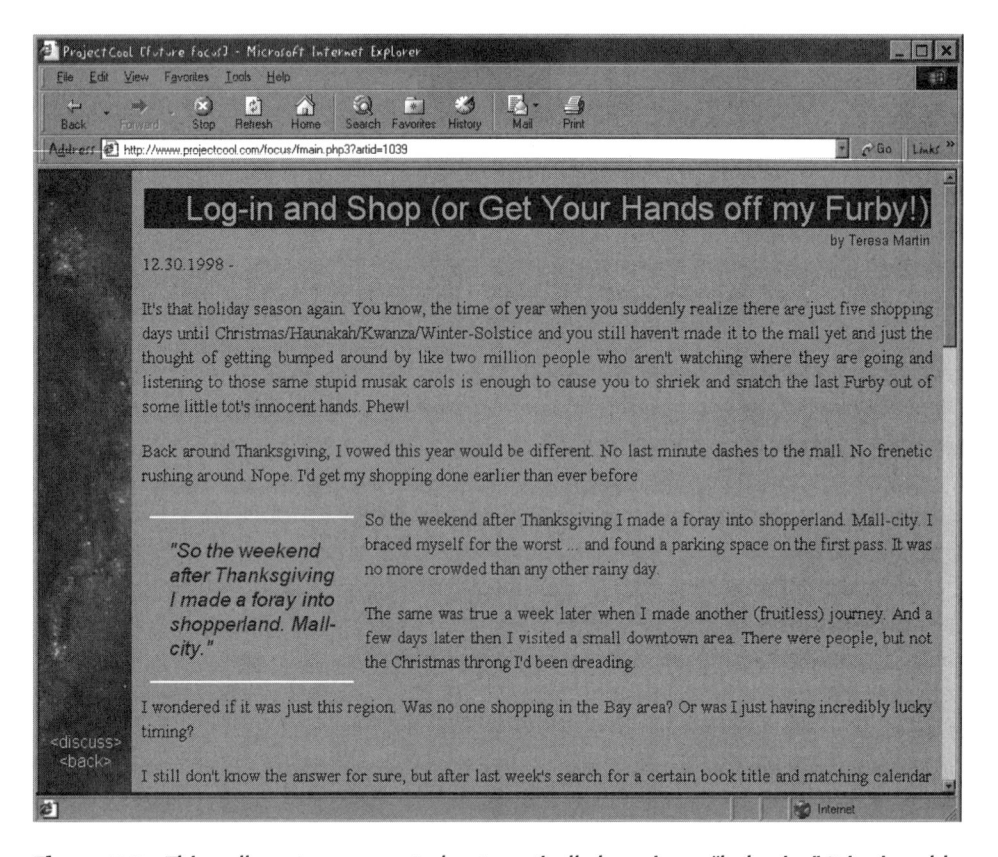

Figure 5.2 This pull quote was created automatically by using a "behavior." It is viewable only under IE 5.X and later browsers.

DOM. In straight English, DHTML lets you select an element on the page and change its display dynamically.

In the 4.X browsers, DHTML is handled differently under IE and Communicator, partly because the DOM spec had not been finalized as the browsers were being developed. The 5.X generation of browsers promises more consistent support for the DOM spec; we can only hope that DHTML will work more smoothly across platforms.

Structure Rule Sets

If the style standards turn XML into a displayable page, then the structure standards turn XML into a three-dimensional object, defining what elements make it up and what the relationships of those elements are to each other. They may also define what type of contents the elements are allowed to contain.

Structural Rules in SGML, XML, and HTML

With SGML, you must always have a formal external document, called a DTD. DTD stands for Document Type Definition; it defines the structural rules of the SGML document.

In XML you may have a DTD if you want, but you don't need one. Not needing a formal, external structural definition is one of the important differences between SGML and XML, and it is one of the factors that make XML easier to implement.

Creating a DTD can be a very complex process. This process makes SGML cumbersome and has been a barrier to the implementation of SGML in many applications. Removing the requirement makes XML worthwhile for a broader range of applications.

This external rule set also marks a difference between HTML and XML. HTML uses a DTD that is built into the browsers. You, the user or creator of a web page, never need to worry about it. This makes HTML easy to use and apply, but limits its flexibility. In contrast, XML allows you to create a DTD that is specific to your application. You don't need to do this, but you have the option to do so.

Here's how you might use a DTD with an XML document: Suppose you are creating a set of technical specifications. You will be using a series of XML tags that define the content of the documents. You would create a DTD that explains the relationship between the XML tags you are using. There will be certain required elements, certain elements that appear before or after other elements, and optional elements. You could use the external structure rules as a way of ensuring that each spec included a certain set of tags in a certain order. That way you wouldn't accidentally publish a critical spec that was missing a piece of necessary data.

The process of comparing the XML document to the external set of structure rules is called validation. A *parser* is a program that does the validation. A valid XML document is one that works with a DTD and complies with it.

DTDs remain the core system for defining the relationships of elements in a valid XML document. In addition to DTDs, a number of proposals on the table offer methods of validating data between the XML tags. For database applications especially, these additional proposals may be quite important.

It is likely to be late 1999 at the very earliest before these proposals solidify. In the meantime, DTDs as we know them today offer the means of defining the XML document's schema.

Schemas

A *schema* is a description of the rules for data. It does two things:

- It defines the elements in a data set and their relationship to each other.
- It defines the type and parameters of the content that can be placed within each element.

Right now, DTDs define how the different elements in an XML document are interrelated, but they offer very little control over what actual data can be allowed inside the tag. Some of the proposals in the structural area are looking to address this issue. The goal is to have one syntax, based on XML itself, that allows you to define elements and their relationships and to define what data can be placed within specific elements.

Here's an example (with thanks to Bruce Rosenblum of Inera Inc.) of how you might use a data schema to define a name and address list:

Rule 1. Exclude numbers from first and surnames and ensure that neither is more than 25 characters.

Rule 2. Ensure that a zip code in the United States has either five or nine digits while one in Canada has six characters—letters, and numbers—interspersed.

Rule 3. Ensure that a phone number in the United States has 10 digits. It may also allow delimiters such as -, ( ), and spaces while excluding everything else.

Schemas become particularly important for database work and for some applications such as e-commerce, in which you want to ensure that a price element, for example, doesn't have "Freddy Frog" for its value.

DTD

Document Type Definition, or DTD, is not a stand-alone standard; it is a term that describes a set of rules that define the structure of your SGML, HTML, or XML document.

Right now, the syntax and structure of a DTD is specified in the SGML standard and in the XML recommendation, and you need to follow these guidelines to create a DTD for SGML or XML. There is some variation between the two, so if you already have SGML DTDs, you'll need to do some reworking because you can't automatically use them for XML documents.

All SGML documents must have an associated DTD. The SGML DTD is very specific, defining what elements and attributes make up the document, the order in which they may appear, and their hierarchical relationship.

All HTML documents also have a DTD, although you don't need to create it. The HTML DTD is invisible to the end user but is implied in the browser. For example, the HTML DTD says paragraph elements are marked with the tag <p>.

If you're curious to see what the HTML DTD looks like, you can see several versions of it at the W3C website, <http://www.w3.org/TR/PR-html40/sgml/loosedtd.html>. One of the reasons so many people used HTML is that they could just start creating documents and using the HTML tags—they didn't have to spend the weeks of research and writing that it often takes to build a DTD. Heck, they didn't even have to know the phrase "DTD." Would you have built your first web page if you needed to understand code like that shown in Figure 5.3?

XML documents may or may not have a DTD. It depends on how strict you want your rules to be and how complex your documents are. That's one of the nice things about XML—you can create a DTD where it makes sense to have one, but you don't have to create one where it would be overkill. When you need to create and validate data, you'll probably want to build a DTD. When you want to present data, you probably won't need to worry about a DTD. Later in this book we'll talk about DTDs as they relate to XML documents.

DDML

Document Definition Markup Language (DDML) is a schema language for XML documents. Until January 1999 it was referred to as Xschema. DDML is a product of the XML-Dev mailing list. It was submitted to the W3C in January 1999, and its name changed from Xschema to Document Definition Markup Language.

DDML proposes a more XML-friendly way of specifying a DTD. It uses XML syntax to describe both the DTD and the allowable contents of data

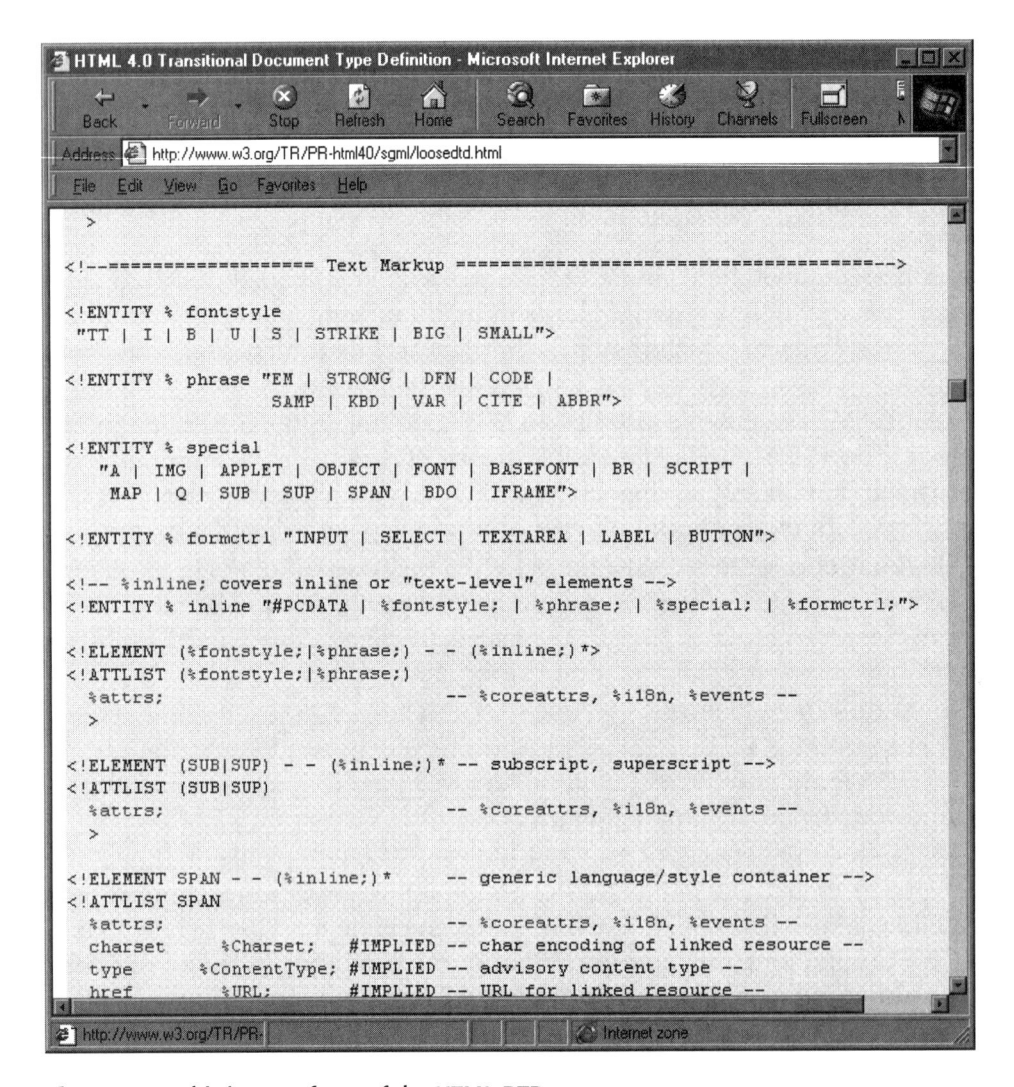

```
<!--================== Text Markup ======================-->

<!ENTITY % fontstyle
 "TT | I | B | U | S | STRIKE | BIG | SMALL">

<!ENTITY % phrase "EM | STRONG | DFN | CODE |
                   SAMP | KBD | VAR | CITE | ABBR">

<!ENTITY % special
   "A | IMG | APPLET | OBJECT | FONT | BASEFONT | BR | SCRIPT |
    MAP | Q | SUB | SUP | SPAN | BDO | IFRAME">

<!ENTITY % formctrl "INPUT | SELECT | TEXTAREA | LABEL | BUTTON">

<!-- %inline; covers inline or "text-level" elements -->
<!ENTITY % inline "#PCDATA | %fontstyle; | %phrase; | %special; | %formctrl;">

<!ELEMENT (%fontstyle;|%phrase;) - - (%inline;)*>
<!ATTLIST (%fontstyle;|%phrase;)
  %attrs;                       -- %coreattrs, %i18n, %events --
  >

<!ELEMENT (SUB|SUP) - - (%inline;)* -- subscript, superscript -->
<!ATTLIST (SUB|SUP)
  %attrs;                       -- %coreattrs, %i18n, %events --
  >

<!ELEMENT SPAN - - (%inline;)*   -- generic language/style container -->
<!ATTLIST SPAN
  %attrs;                       -- %coreattrs, %i18n, %events --
  charset    %Charset;    #IMPLIED -- char encoding of linked resource --
  type       %ContentType; #IMPLIED -- advisory content type --
  href       %URL;        #IMPLIED -- URL for linked resource --
```

Figure 5.3 This is part of one of the HTML DTDs.

within a tag in the XML document. Its proponents say that XSchema makes it easier to create and work with DTDs. For example, you can view the XSchema DTD with any XML-aware browser and edit, parse, and work with it using any XML-aware tool. SGML-styled DTDs do not offer that ease of viewing and editing.

The W3C also has a working group called XML Schema, which is studying the various schema proposals and options for XML. The working group's original proposal title (Xschema) and this group are unrelated. They just happen to share very similar names.

XML Data

XML Data was an early submission to the W3C, addressing the structural rules of an XML document. It described an XML vocabulary for defining data schemas, the descriptions of the rules for data. A *data schema* includes the names and order of data fields (the way a DTD does) along with rules for what can be inside those fields.

It would use the XML syntax to do this as well, both simplifying and extending the SGML style of DTD.

Companies behind the XML Data submission included Microsoft, ArborText, DataChannel, and Inso. It has since been superseded by the Document Content Description (DCD).

DCD

Document Content Description, or DCD, is a W3C note, published by the W3C in August 1998. It was submitted by Microsoft and IBM.

DCD is a structural schema facility. That means it lets you define the DTD for an XML document using the Resource Description Framework (RDF), an ongoing W3C effort for applying XML to metadata. In addition to structure, DCD will also let you do content typing, which means you can further define what sort of data is allowable inside an XML tag in a document that uses the particular DTD.

Essentially, DCD describes a way of making DTDs using XML instead of a non-XML syntax, and doing it in such a way that is machine-understandable, while adding some extra control and error-checking capabilities.

Processing

Now we have a way to identify data about data—XML. We have several proposals for applying formatting information to it—CSS, XSL. We have several proposed methods for setting up the rule sets that govern the data—DTDs, Xschema, DCD. What is still lacking are processing wrappers, the interface through which a program or script interacts with the underlying data.

DOM

The Document Object Model (DOM) specification is the standard that defines a specific document object model—in this case, the DOM that will be used with web pages. The term "document object model" is a broad phrase that encompasses many different types of specific DOMs.

The DOM gives you a standardized, interoperable way of manipulating individual pieces of the document. By having a standard DOM, you can control parts of the document—and you can have that control work across all platforms and browsers. By using a DOM, you can easily change just parts of your page, instead of sending a request back to the server for a full-page reload.

The DOM specification, which became a W3C recommendation in October 1998, does all three things:

- It defines a standard set of objects for displaying XML and HTML pages.
- It defines a model of how these objects work together.
- It defines a standard interface for accessing these objects.

By combining these three features, the DOM achieves its stated goal of "defining a programmatic interface for XML and HTML." That is, the DOM opens up the HTML and XML document for manipulation; it exposes the individual parts and tells you how to talk to each of them directly.

Chapter 3, "The Document Object Model," provides a full discussion of the DOM and how it applies to XML.

XML NS

XML Namespace (XML NS) lets you use tags with the same name in different ways in the same XML document. Why might you do this? Well, as XML becomes more common, you might find yourself using your industry's DTD as well as your own custom DTD. Namespaces make it clear that a tag belongs to a specific set of tags. You can use your version of *title* to mean the title of an article in a newsletter and your trade group's version of *title* to mean a book title in your inventory.

For example, suppose you have a site about used books and you are part of a used books consortium. The whole consortium might have decided to implement a bookstore DTD. All the sites about used books would use the same set of tags to describe the books they have in stock. This structure might allow the consortium to give book collectors an easy way to search for particular editions.

You'll be using the <title> tag to define the book's title because that's the tag the bookstore DTD says to use. You also have your own uses for your site, and you have your own DTD that describes those tags. With namespaces, you can use tags from both DTDs in the same documents, without confusion.

Here's how it would work: When you want to use one of the bookstore tags, you'd precede the name with the bookstore DTD Uniform Resource Identifier (URI), something like this:

```
<BOOKSTORE: TITLE, 1951, Signet, paper, good >The Catcher in the
Rye</BOOKSTORE: TITLE>
```

And when you wanted to use your tags that are part of the default DTD you specified in the document you could just use the tag, like this:

```
In our Winter/Spring edition article <TITLE>Classic Science
Fiction</TITLE>, we addressed this very issue.
```

You used the <TITLE> tag in both places, but with namespaces there was no confusion over which <TITLE> was really being used. You can be consistent with your industry DTD (or any other published DTD) and still use the tags you want for your own documents.

The Namespace proposal is a W3C recommendation, dated January 14, 1999.

Here's a response by Namespace editor Tim Bray to a question asked in an e-mail list. One member asked, "Could you give me a quick summary as to why this is useful to Web developers?"

Bray responded:

(a) the reason we put tags in documents is to mark up information for consumption and processing by computer programs

(b) in the web environment, you might commonly expect a document to contain tags that are designed for consumption by different computer programs; e.g., in an invoice from a wine store, some of the tags are going to be e-commerce/payment stuff, and some of them are going to be wine info: grape, year, country, etc.

(c) how can a computer program find the tags it's designed to process in an environment where a document can contain such a mixture?

(d) with namespaces, computer programs are given a canonical URI, and they know that they should deal with a certain set of tags that are associated (by namespaces) with that URI.

Linking

Linking, the connection of one point to another, is at the heart of HTML—it is the "hypertext" in HTML's very name. But the linking we see with HTML is just the start, just the tip of potential.

Under HTML, links are quite basic. One specified piece of text or graphic, when clicked, opens up the browser window into a second set of data. The link is one way: Once you've made the link you're there at the new page, and the link process is over. The links point to an absolute location. If that location changes, the link is dead. HTML linking is a good start, but XML provides a means for taking links to the next level.

Proposals related to XML will change the concept of linking, expanding it dramatically. Instead of being one-way, point-to-point links, the proposals offer the possibility of creating a menu of link choices from one link, as well as two-way links.

You might consider these link proposals applications of XML for a specific type of data—data about linking. As of this writing two proposals, XPointer and XLink, are under discussion. The two address different areas of the linking issue and are designed to work together. Both are being developed by the XML Linking Working Group under the W3C umbrella.

XPointer and XLink have some ancestral relationship with an ISO standard called ISO/IEC 10744, the Hypermedia/Time-based Structuring Language, or HyTime for short. If you've read much about SGML you have probably seen references to HyTime. You don't need to worry about HyTime, but if you hear the phrase now you will know what it means.

XPointer

XPointer is a way of identifying targeted data inside a link. You might think of XPointer as being a bit like an updated way of describing the URL inside an anchor tag.

Not all linked data is an XML document, an HTML file, an FTP location, or an e-mail address. Linked data could be an element that might be in a document or in a database. XPointer provides a way to specify a piece of data in a more specific way than the simple URL of an HTML file. It uses something called a *location term* to identify a data resource and a specific element. The targeted elements have been marked up in proper XML syntax.

Here's an important thing to remember when you begin to think about the next generation of links: A link isn't just a web page. When you think about links in XML, you'll need to think beyond a single, fixed HTML file. XPointer provides a way to specify exact data, not just a URL.

XPointer became a working draft of the W3C in March 1998. It is being developed by the XML Linking Working Group.

XLink

XLink describes a relationship between pieces of data. In the XLink spec, the term *link* means an explicit relationship between two or more data objects or portions of data objects. No longer is a link a pointer from one location to the next. XLink extends the concept of linking to be multi-ended, rather than linear.

XLink uses XML as its underlying syntax for describing data-to-data relationships. And it uses XPointer to describe the actual, targeted data. You might think of XLink as filling the role of the anchor tag.

Under XLink, you can have two basic types of links. The first, a simple link, is much like the link we know and love today: Data A is related to Data B. There are two locations and anchors; one is tied to the other.

The second is an extended link. This type of link can connect multiple locations, offering readers options of which to visit and allowing for links that go back and forth from various anchor points.

These link collections can include links with any number of endpoints and can include many different data elements. With XLink and XML, you can tie together different content in different locations and create a sort-of miniweb of interrelated data.

For example, if you're at a site that teaches you how to keep tropical fish and you click on the name "pelvicachromis taeniatus," an inline link might bring up a page with a picture of the pretty yellow East African River cichlad-family fish and a description of the species and its needs. Pretty much what you'd expect. But an extended link might bring up a menu choice letting you select one of four different links: a photo of the fish, a list of resources where you can order the fish, information about feeding the fish, and a cichlad breeder's page.

Another enhancement that XLink brings is the ability to create links either in-line or out-of-line. An in-line link is the sort of link we know today. It lives within one end of the link and is typically visually identified in some way. For example, in HTML, you may have placed an anchor tag around the words "more pictures here!". The words appear in a blue underline display style on the page. This is an in-line link.

In addition to in-line links, XLink allows out-of-line links, which live in a sort of external database. The out-of-line link is a bit analogous to the external style sheet or the external script set.

Querying

The term *query* is a phrase that means to ask the computer for information. One of the nice things about XML is that it makes it possible to search and ask questions about documents in more powerful and meaningful ways than are currently available with HTML documents.

Remember, XML lets you store metadata—that is, data about data. You might identify an element as a book title and also note the publisher and edition of that particular book. Suddenly your search options open. You can find the 1951 edition of *Catcher in the Rye*, not just any use of the phrase "Catcher in the Rye" or any use of the tag <booktitle>.

As with other XML-related topics, there are several standards in the works around the concept of query. Two of the proposals are XML-QL and XQL. The ideas in both are being explored, and the eventual solution will likely be neither one. By the time you read this, both may have changed dramatically. The ideas behind them—the need for a better way to query XML data and documents—are ones that will be addressed.

XML-QL

XML Query Language, or XML-QL, was proposed by Bell Labs as a solution to the issues of searching XML document.

There are two major elements to any language. First is semantics: what the language means and what it can express. Second is syntax: how it expresses what it means. XML-QL and XQL differ in both semantics and syntax.

Semantically, XML-QL models XML documents as graphs. An XML-QL query has two parts: a graph-matching clause and a graph-construction clause. This two-step process is important because it means XML-QL can both match queries and create a new XML document from the results. This means that you can search and display results between DTDs and across multiple sources.

For example, you might be able to query the Big Fish Database, the fish-list archives, and the Online Guide to Tropical Fish for "breeding needs of the pelvicachromis taeniatus" (our little yellow East African fish). Under an XML-QL approach, all of these results could be compiled into an XML document and presented to you.

In its syntax, XML-QL has its spiritual roots in SQL, the most common query language in use today.

XQL

Extensible Query Language, or XQL, is another proposal for querying XML documents. It was created by Microsoft.

Like XML-QL, XQL matches searches in the XML document. Unlike XML-QL, it cannot create new data from the results. This means it cannot integrate results across multiple sources and create a new XML document as the result.

For example, if you were looking for that fish breeding information, under the XQL approach you search and receive results from each source, one by one.

XQL uses XSL, the XML style application, as it syntax. Using a valid XML syntax is one of this approach's strengths.

Metadata

Metadata is data about data. It is information that describes the data in your document. It is a little like using the <META> tag in HTML to create descriptions, keywords, and abstracts, but magnified a few hundred times over.

Having a layer of information about the elements in your document makes it possible for you to do powerful searches, contextual displays of information, and secure forms processing.

XML itself is a metadata language in that it is a way of storing data about other data, including your documents. Most of the metadata initiatives are based on XML and are ways to apply XML for specific needs. XML is the base of a number of applications that offer a way to apply XML syntax and semantics to do a certain type of task.

XML enables you to add information about your data. You can describe where you found the data, you can quantify, you can qualify, you can further identify and define the data. With XML you no longer have to take data at face value—you can add all sorts of information about the data, information that can help you process and interpret the data, and you can make your presentation and understanding better and stronger.

As a designer, you may not be working directly with any of the proposed standards in this section, but you will likely hear the terms tossed around. They also give you an idea of the directions in which XML can drive the web.

One term you might hear about is RDF. RDF is an application of XML for making data machine understandable so that certain functions can be automated. RDF is being used in many applications of metadata. For example, one of the more interesting metadata initiatives under way is called the Dublin Core Initiative (<http://purl.oclc.org/dc/>). It is an international effort to create a structure for categorizing web pages, a sort of digital Dewey decimal system for a global digital library. It uses RDF (and therefore XML) as its descriptive language.

The W3C has set a number of goals for itself in its metadata work. First, it wants to create a machine-processable metadata language based on XML. RDF appears to be the solution of choice.

Second, it wants to create vocabularies for dealing with particular types of applications, such as forms or math. These vocabulary sets are called schemas. Remember, when we were talking about DTDs and structure rules sets we talked about schemas. A *schema* is a description of the rules for data. It defines the elements in a data set and their relationship to each other, and it defines the type and parameters of the content that can be placed within each element. These application-specific schema give you the "words" for working with certain types of data.

A third W3C goal is to create a language for querying information and filtering the results. We talked a bit about these efforts when we looked at XML query options, like XML-QL.

A fourth goal is to create a syntax for digital signatures. This ensures that the document is tamper-free and that the signature is authentic. This effort will help enable e-commerce.

RDF

RDF became a W3C proposed recommendation in January 1999. The Dublin Core project, the international effort to create a means of categorizing web pages so that they can be better searched, is using RDF as its language.

One of the biggest things that RDF does is to make data machine-understandable, thus enabling automation of certain processes.

The RDF Working Group explains it very nicely:

> The World Wide Web was originally built for human consumption, and although everything on it is machine-readable, this data is not

machine-understandable. It is very hard to automate anything on the web, and because of the volume of information the web contains, it is not possible to manage it manually. The solution proposed here is to use metadata to describe the data contained on the web. Metadata is 'data about data.'

"Resource Description Framework (RDF) is a foundation for processing metadata; it provides interoperability between applications that exchange machine-understandable information on the Web. RDF emphasizes facilities to enable automated processing of web resources. RDF can be used in a variety of application areas; for example, in resource discovery to provide better search engine capabilities, in cataloging for describing the content and content relationships available at a particular Web site, page, or digital library, by intelligent software agents to facilitate knowledge sharing and exchange, in content rating, in describing collections of pages that represent a single logical 'document,' for describing intellectual property rights of web pages, and for expressing the privacy preferences of a user as well as the privacy policies of a web site. RDF with digital signatures will be key to building the 'web of Trust' for electronic commerce, collaboration, and other applications.

The implementation of RDF has implications for the web. For example, the ability to automatically process and confirm certain types of transaction data will enable online commerce applications. The ability to automatically process data about digital signatures will make online contracts possible.

Application-Specific XML

Certain types of applications share specific requirements. All these applications share a need for a standard way of working with metadata, but they may use the metadata in specific ways or require a certain vocabulary. Forms, for example, need features that documents and databases don't. Multimedia integration has requirements that math does not.

As a result, we are beginning to see proposals for shared applications of XML. Many proposals are basically detailed DTDs or sets of structural rules for specific categories of applications.

Depending on the type of work you do, you may or may not encounter some of these applications. An increasing number of application-specific DTDs likely will be shared across an industry or industries.

XFDL

Extensible Forms Description Language, or XFDL, is an application of XML for digital forms. It lets you create and process complex forms, including digital signatures. It is a W3C note, as of September 1998.

XFDL makes it possible to create, manage, and use digital forms in a way that is both interoperable and legally binding.

SMIL

Synchronized Multimedia Integration Language, or SMIL (pronounced "smile"), is an application of XML that should make authoring audio and video within a web page easier.

With SMIL, you can describe the behavior of the multimedia object, you can describe its layout on the screen, and you can define its links.

Real Networks has introduced a player that can handle a SMIL document. Macromedia is also supporting this standard.

Ad Markup

The Ad Markup application of XML is being developed by the Newspaper Association of America (NAA). It is a way to allow for the submission of national newspaper advertising in digital format.

ICE

Information Content and Exchange Protocol (ICE) is a proposed XML-based solution for sharing data from site to site. It is designed with syndication relationships in mind, and its editors include Sun, Adobe, and web publishing vendor Vignette.

According to the proposal, ICE "manages and automates establishment of syndication relationships, data transfer, and results analysis. When combined with an industry-specific vocabulary, ICE provides a complete solution for syndicating any type of information between information providers and their subscribers."

Math ML

Mathematical Markup Language (Math ML) is an application of XML that describes mathematical notation. It is designed for describing mathematical and scientific content.

Much of what XML does for text, Math ML does for equations, creating a way to describe them by their structure and content, not just how to format them for display.

Summary

As you can see, a great many ideas for applications of XML are being tossed about. XML has a vibrancy that its original creators never expected. Because it combines extensibility with structure, it has become a possible solution for many problems.

The timing is right for an interoperable method of describing data. XML is the right tool, in the right place, at the right time.

CHAPTER 6

XML Document Basics

This chapter talks about how to create and tag a basic XML document. This is the easiest part of the process; if you've done any HTML tagging, doing XML tagging will feel very familiar.

Figure 6.1 shows what a very simple XML document looks like.

If you look at this example, you'll see that tags open and close using the familiar < and > delimiters. There is content between the open and close tags. The whole thing is an ASCII text file.

XML Alone Does Nothing

If you were to display this XML file in a web browser, you'd see just one long string of text. The XML tags would be ignored by the browser, just as the browser ignores any tags it doesn't understand.

This is a very important thing to remember about XML: It is a markup language. It identifies elements in your document. Period. It records that "this text" is a *book-title* element. Period. Unless you have style sheet data that tells the browser how to display different elements, the browser sees your XML file as one set of ASCII text.

You can do all the XML markup in the world, but unless you tie it into style sheets, it won't help you at all to display your page in a web browser.

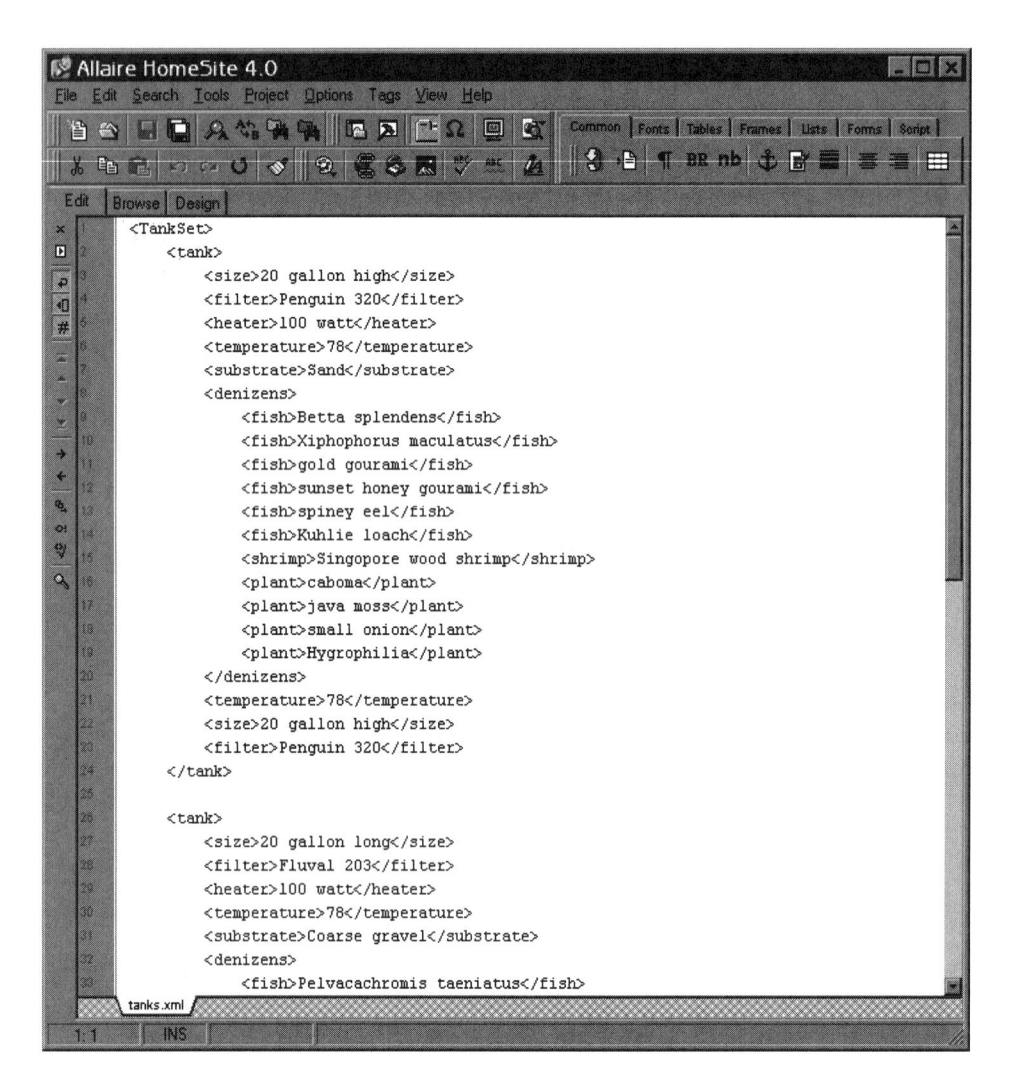

```
<TankSet>
    <tank>
        <size>20 gallon high</size>
        <filter>Penguin 320</filter>
        <heater>100 watt</heater>
        <temperature>78</temperature>
        <substrate>Sand</substrate>
        <denizens>
            <fish>Betta splendens</fish>
            <fish>Xiphophorus maculatus</fish>
            <fish>gold gourami</fish>
            <fish>sunset honey gourami</fish>
            <fish>spiney eel</fish>
            <fish>Kuhlie loach</fish>
            <shrimp>Singopore wood shrimp</shrimp>
            <plant>caboma</plant>
            <plant>java moss</plant>
            <plant>small onion</plant>
            <plant>Hygrophilia</plant>
        </denizens>
        <temperature>78</temperature>
        <size>20 gallon high</size>
        <filter>Penguin 320</filter>
    </tank>

    <tank>
        <size>20 gallon long</size>
        <filter>Fluval 203</filter>
        <heater>100 watt</heater>
        <temperature>78</temperature>
        <substrate>Coarse gravel</substrate>
        <denizens>
            <fish>Pelvacachromis taeniatus</fish>
```

Figure 6.1 A simple XML document.

This is one of the great strengths of XML. By separating structure and content from formatting you open up flexibility and freedom in your display options. You can easily display your data in different ways, without having to change your documents. You can make your book titles appear in italic, in purple, or in 24-point type, all without touching each book title in your document.

It can be a little disconcerting at first, though. You put all this effort into marking up a document—and it doesn't seem to have any effect on the document. You get no immediate, visual feedback to your work. But don't worry; that work does pay off. You just need to see it in context of the bigger picture.

XML Is Not about Display

Yes, you've heard many times in this book that XML separates structure and content from format. In your head you probably know this and can say it right back at us. For people who are accustomed to design and to working with printed and web page documents, however, internalizing this idea can be very difficult.

It is important to remember that XML has many uses in addition to web pages and many uses that are not about displaying data in a web browser at all.

You've probably seen tab-delimited text files, files that use the tab character to split data into pieces for use in a database application or to pull into a mail merge program. One use of XML is to mark pieces of data much like this, but to do it in a way that is cleaner and clearer and that enables you to add information about the data pieces as well.

For example, at Project Cool, we mark up our Sightings data with XML in a database and then export it to another publisher's database, where it is reused for another editorial product. (Sightings is our daily pointer to a website that shows good use of the web medium.)

XML is our common language of exchange that crosses computer platforms and applications while letting us retain structural information. We use an XML tag to identify the URL that was selected for that day's Sighting. We use another XML tag to identify the blurb we wrote about the URL. The fact that this bit of data is a URL and this bit of data is the blurb travels with the XML marked-up data wherever it goes. No one has to figure out what bit of data makes up the blurb. It is clearly marked as the blurb element.

This use of XML has everything to do with content and publishing—and nothing at all to do with displaying the Sightings data on the screen in a web page.

Well-Formed versus Valid Files

You can create two types of XML documents: well-formed and valid.

All *well-formed* means is that you have created an XML document that follows the XML syntax rules. In short, you've opened and closed all tags, you've used capitalization correctly, you've quoted all attributes, and you've nested cleanly. All the pieces are presented the way XML asks you to present them.

The well-formed document doesn't do anything—it just contains marked-up text. But it is cleanly marked up text that is ready for working with a style sheet or other style tool.

If you are using XML primarily for display, you will likely be creating well-formed documents. One of the nice things about XML is that you can create well-formed documents and not worry about DTDs if your application doesn't call for a DTD. This opens up XML to a wide range of uses by many levels of user skill.

Valid XML is an XML document that validates against DTD data. A *valid* document meets the syntax rules *and* it meets the rules of a DTD. By definition, all valid XML files are also well-formed, because they contain properly used XML tags.

If you are working with a set of documents, or working with documents that need to carefully conform to a certain structure, you will likely be creating valid XML documents. You will be running your documents through a validating parser to check your file's structure against your DTD rules.

Before You Create a Document

There are some things you need to do before you sit down to create an XML document.

Know Your Data

First, you need to know what tags you'll be using in your document. You need to look at your data and, with your team, decide what elements make up your document, how those elements are related to each other, and what attributes each element can have.

Even if you aren't going to be validating against a DTD, it is well worth your time to spend some thought cycles up front, before you start tagging files. Make yourself a little "cheat-sheet" listing your elements and when you use them. This list will also come in handy later when you create a style sheet file that describes how to display the elements.

Figure 6.2 shows a simple list of elements and how they relate to each other.

While XML allows you to create new elements on-the-fly, it's generally something you should avoid doing. That's one way to guarantee a messy, confusing, inconsistent document that will eventually come back to bite

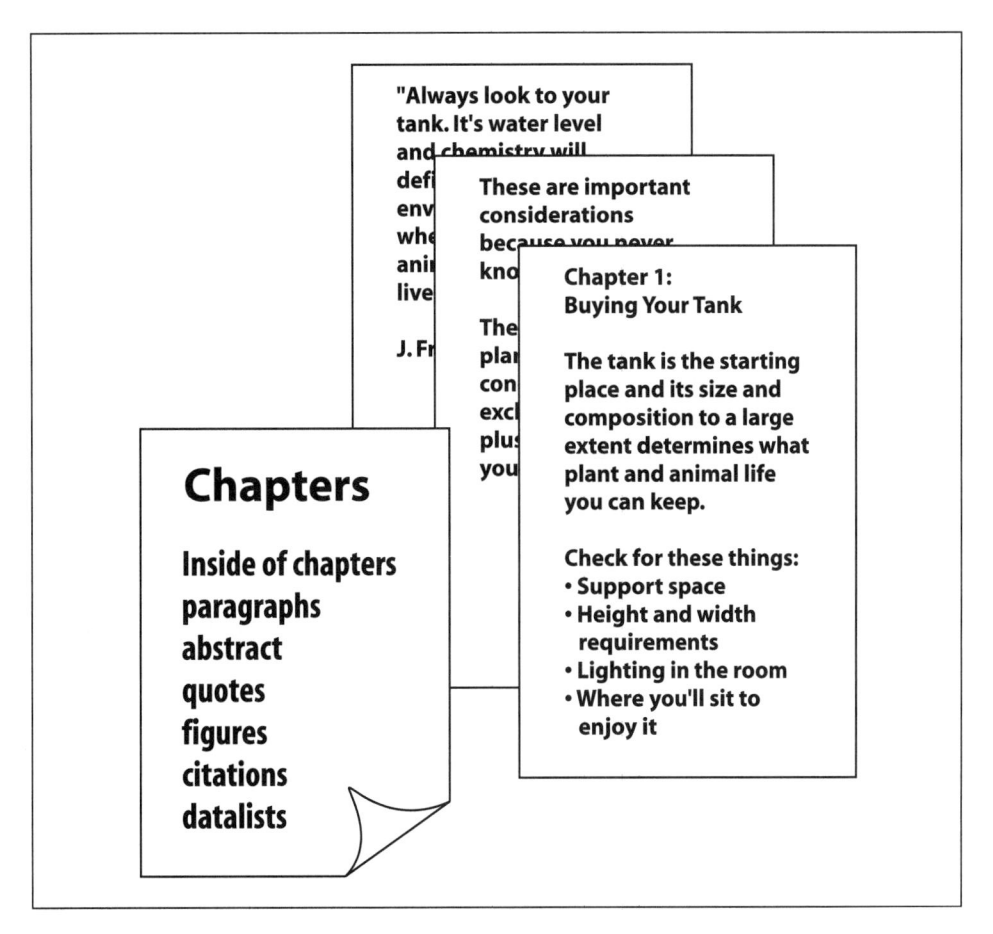

Figure 6.2 Make sure you know your data before you begin tagging files.

you. If you toss in a tag called <happy-talk>, are you going to remember that it is there? Will your style sheet deal with it? Will anyone else use it in any other document?

Know Your DTD

Next, you need to decide if you will be using an external DTD that already exists, creating your own external DTD, declaring your elements in your XML document, or avoiding DTDs altogether.

Remember, a DTD is a formal set of rules that describe the document. A DTD is not required for an XML document.

If you are using a DTD, you will be testing your document against this rule set to ensure that all elements were used correctly. Using a DTD is a way to check for errors and ensure that a document meets certain markup standards. If you are working collaboratively on many documents with many people, it is likely that you will be using a DTD. If you are using XML for display only, however, you may very well not be using a DTD.

If you will be using a DTD, you need to create your DTD. Or, if you are using a published one, you need to determine where you find it and what its rules say.

One place to check to see if your industry has a DTD you might want to use is the Graphic Communications Association (GCA) website, <http://www.gca.org>. In addition, the Organization for the Advancement of Structured Information Standards (OASIS), <http://www.oasis-open.org/>, announced in March 1999 that they were forming an XML Registry and Repository Technical Committee to find an industry-acceptable means of making XML DTDs findable and available. And, of course, don't forget to check your own industry associations' websites. In many cases, an existing DTD will fit your needs and there's no reason to reinvent the wheel. Many of the widely used SGML DTDs, such as DOCBOOK, are being converted to XML as well.

Elements

All XML documents are made up of different elements. The elements can be anything you want them to be. You don't have to use any predefined set of elements—unless, of course, you are working with a predefined DTD, then you'll want to follow that DTD's guidelines.

An element is a piece of data. For example, if you are creating a catalog of tropical fish, you might decide to make *scientific name* one of your elements. The scientific name of each fish referenced in your document could be marked up with the tag <SCI-NAME>, like this:

```
<SCI-NAME>Pangio kuhlii</SCI-NAME>
```

Elements can be nested within elements. The top-level element is called the *parent*. The nested elements are *children* of that parent.

For example, you might have an element called <SPECIES>. The SPECIES element comprises three other elements: a common name, <COM-NAME>, a scientific name, <SCI-NAME>, and a description, <DESCRIPTION>. Your marked-up document would look something like this:

```
<SPECIES>
<COM-NAME>Coolie loach</COM-NAME>
<SCI-NAME>Pangio kuhlii</SCI-NAME>
<DESCRIPTION>The Coolie Loach is a native of Thailand. It comes in two
```

```
color variations. Most are caught in the wild, and it is difficult to
breed.</DESCRIPTION>
</SPECIES>
```

<SPECIES> is the parent element. <COM-NAME>, <SCI-NAME>, and <DESCRIPTION> are all child elements of species.

You can use a DTD to create a structure that requires child elements to follow a parent element in a specified order. If you are creating documents that strictly require certain sets of information you can use validated XML to ensure that all the pieces are entered in the correct order.

For example, if you are creating an employee directory, you might want to mandate that all *name* elements have two child elements: *first* and *last*. And you'll be using a DTD to check that all "name" elements have both a "first" and a "last" child element.

This is quite different from HTML. In HTML you had a fixed set of elements you could use. You memorized the list and were ready to start. In XML the field is wide open. You can create elements and use tags that make sense for your data. Just be sure to plan which elements you are using and keep a reference list of them so that you have a record of what you have done.

Attributes

Attributes are a way to add more data about your elements. They are a little like adjectives in that they further define the element, the noun.

In HTML you often uses attributes to specify formatting information. For example, *align* is an attribute of paragraph. The tag <p align=center> creates a paragraph element and gives it an *align* attribute value of center.

Your XML elements use attributes to store data. For example, in that tropical fish guide, you could create a *year* attribute for the *SPECIES* element. You'd use the *year* attribute to store the year that species was first identified. Or, you might add a *region* attribute to record the region to which the species is native.

In this example, the first attribute, *region*, adds data to the *SPECIES* element, indicating the species' native region. The second attribute, *size*, adds information about the size of the species to the *DESCRIPTION* element.

```
<SPECIES region="asia">
<COM-NAME>Coolie loach</COM-NAME>
<SCI-NAME>Pangio kuhlii</SCI-NAME>
<DESCRIPTION size="8in">The Coolie Loach is a native of Thailand. It
comes in two color variations. Most are caught in the wild, and it is
difficult to breed in captivity.</DESCRIPTION>
</SPECIES>
```

When you define attributes for an element, you can also specify whether they are required and whether they have a default value.

You specify attributes through something called an ATTLIST. The process of specifying an attribute is described in more detail later in this chapter.

An important thing to remember about using element attributes in XML is that the attribute's value must always be surrounded by quotation marks. In HTML it was a mixed bag, but XML requires that you use quotes, like this:

```
<SPECIES region="asia">
```

Attributes, by defining metadata, give you many long-term options. The more you know about an element, the more flexible you are in what you do with it. For example, even though the attribute doesn't appear on your web page, you can sort or display elements based on a particular attribute. With our fish guide example, we could create custom web pages based on the regions of the world to which the fish is native, thus allowing a reader to see "The South American Tropical Fish List" or "Photos of North American Fish."

What Exactly Is an XML Document?

What is an XML document? First, it is nothing more than a text file with text and XML tags in it. The file is saved with a .xml extension, like this:

```
Mydocument.xml
```

Declarations

Every XML file begins with an XML declaration, which tells the processor, "Hey, here's an XML file." This is the first line in the file:

```
<?xml version="1.0"?>
```

If you are creating a valid XML file—that is, an XML file that uses a DTD—following your XML declaration is a doctype declaration. This lets the processor know the name of the type of document you are using. It states the name of the DTD to use. For example, if you're creating a fish type of document and using the "fish.dtd" DTD on the your server, the doctype declaration would look like this:

```
<!DOCTYPE fish SYSTEM "fish.dtd">
```

Marked-Up Text

After the declarations, you add the content of the file, text and markup tags. You'll need to follow proper XML syntax as you mark-up the text.

Comments

Comments are nondisplaying sections of your XML document where you can make notes to yourself or others. Comments are very important; they are a way explain what you've done in a certain place or to pass along information to someone who might be working on the document in the future.

You create comments just as you do in HTML. They begin with an open tag, exclamation mark, and two dashes, <!--, and close with two dashes and a close tag delimiter, -->. Between the markers is your comment.

For example, this comment notes that the following is an employee list:

```
<!-- Employee list contains names and phone extensions for everyone in
the XML development group -->
```

The parser ignores everything between the open and close of the comment. It doesn't parse it, it doesn't process it any way, it just skips over it.

That's all there is to an XML document. No mystery, just some simple tags applied to your data.

XML Syntax

Now you're on to the business of actually creating the document's contents. You'll need to follow the XML syntax rules as you do this. XML is fairly straightforward and applies a few basic rules across all tags.

XML Tags Begin with < and End with >, Just Like HTML

That's right. XML looks a lot like HTML. XML uses the same delimiters to mark the beginning and end of a tag. If you are using a species tag, it would look like this:

```
<SPECIES>
```

XML Tags Surround the Elements They Mark Up

XML elements begin with an opening tag. Then comes the content of the element, followed by an ending tag. The ending tag is a slash tag name, just like a closing HTML tag. For example, this creates an element named SPECIES. This species is the Spiny Eel:

```
<SPECIES>Spiney Eel</SPECIES>
```

All Tags Must Close

In HTML you can slip by without closing all the tags. For example, how often do you start a paragraph (<p>) tag without ending it (</p>)? I know we're all guilty of that.

Not so in XML! In XML all tags must close.

Empty Tags Must Close, Too

Some tags do not contain any content. In HTML, these are things like the IMG or BR tags. In HTML, these tags are used and not ended. You insert a break by typing <br>.

Not so in XML! Even empty tags must close. You can close them in one of two ways. You can enter a separate close tag, or you can combine the opening and closing tags into one tag. To create one combined tag, you type the tag and all of its attributes. Then, just before the closing delimiter, you type a slash to indicate that the tag ends.

For example, if you were putting a break tag into an XML file, it would look like this:

```
<br></br>
```

There is an end break tag, </br>.
Or it could look like this:

```
<br/>
```

See, there is a slash at the end.
Here's how an image tag entered into a well-formed XML file would look:

```
<img src="bigbluefish.gif" height="100" width="300" border="0" alt="a big blue fish"></img>
```

There is an end image tag, </img>.

Or it could look like this:

```
<img src="bigbluefish.gif" height="100" width="300" border="0" alt="a big blue fish"/>
```

See, there is a slash at the end, following all the tag's attributes and attribute values.

XML Is Case Sensitive

XML is case sensitive. This is a very important thing to remember! In XML, <TITLE>, <Title>, and <title> are three totally different element tags.

Some people recommend that you use ALL CAPS to avoid confusion when you are entering tags. Others recommend that you always use a first initial capital letter. Still others say that all lowercase is the way to go. It doesn't really matter what you do as long as you make your use consistent. It is very easy to get mixed up with capitalization, so make a decision on the way you and your team will use capitalization and stick with it.

Also, make sure your beginning and ending tags use the same capitalization. For example <AUTHOR> and </author> don't match—XML sees them as two different tags because they are capitalized differently; when the file is parsed you'll receive an error.

Nest Tags Properly

XML tags also need to nest properly. With HTML, you can get away with sloppy coding (and we've all been guilty of this!). You make an anchor tag, then you make something bold, then you end the anchor tag, and then you end the bold. The result is something that looks like this:

```
<a href="fishtank.html"><b>Building Your Tank</a></b>
```

You haven't neatly nested your tags. The anchor and bold opening and closing tags are intermingled.

With XML, you need matched pairs: beginning anchor tag, beginning bold tag, closed bold tag, closed anchor tag, like this:

```
<a href="fishtank.html"><b>Building Your Tank</b></a>
```

Quote Attribute Values

If you are using an attribute in your element tag, be sure that the attribute's value is surrounded by quotation marks. In HTML there was often confusion over when quotes were and were not required. In XML the rule is easy: All attribute values are enclosed in quotes.

If you follow all these rules, you will have a well-formed XML document.

You don't have to wait until you are working with XML to follow the rules for well-formed documents, either. Ending all tags, neatly nesting elements, quoting attributes, being consistent with capitalization—these are all things that make clean, neat HTML files also. They aren't required because HTML and the web browsers are fairly forgiving of not-so-neat code, but it doesn't hurt to start making all your documents well-formed—both HTML and XML.

XML Tools

We've been talking about the XML document as if the only way to create one is to code it by hand. In practice, however, you'll probably be using an XML editing tool to create and maintain your files.

An XML editor will handle some of the heavy work, such as entering declarations. Most editors will probably allow you to set lists of your elements, so that entering them will simply mean selecting them from a list, thus avoiding typographical errors and capitalization errors.

"Wow!" you say. "Let me at those editors!" Ah, there's a catch here. Editing tools are under development, but the technology is so new that no real XML-specific products are on the market as of this writing.

XML products are under way at traditional SGML vendors like ArborText, Inso, and Xyvision. Companies like SoftQuad Software, which has a foot in both SGML and HTML, have XML editors planned. Adobe's FrameMaker and FrameMaker+SGML is another SGML/HTML/print document publishing tool making the transition to XML. And web vendors, such as Macromedia, are said to be planning to support XML editing as well. For example, the next release of Dreamweaver is promising XML support. Even Office 2000 will be supporting XML and, much as there is an HTML extension to Word currently, there is rumored to be an XML extension to the next release of Word. The companion website to this book, <http://www.projectcool.com/guide/xml> contains links to vendors who have announced XML plans.

In the near future there will be options, quite a number of options, and that will make the process of creating XML documents much easier. But, right now, there are two options. First is hand coding. If you've been hand coding HTML you may want to continue the practice with XML. Second, is using an SGML editor, such as FrameMaker+SGML, and adapting it to your XML needs.

Summary

Creating an XML file is fairly easy; there is no mystery to it. Just enter text and tags, and follow a few basic syntax rules. The most important things are to use your element tags consistently and to follow the syntax rules carefully. That's one of beauties of XML. It was designed so that you could easily make use of it.

What's difficult is making sure the data is entered *correctly* and *consistently*. As anyone who has marked up data knows, this is much easier said than done. In the near future editing tools should be available that will help with this process.

Before you create even a single XML file, make sure you take some time to sit down with your data and understand what your documents are made of. The more time you spend planning your structure, elements, and attributes, the easier the data entry will be.

And take some time to consider display issues. Keep a list of the elements and their attributes, and refer to your list when you create style sheets to display the pages later on in a web browser.

CHAPTER 7

Creating Well-Formed and Valid XML Documents

You can create two types of XML documents: well-formed and valid.

A *well-formed* XML document conforms to the XML syntax rules. In short, you've opened and closed all tags, you've capitalized correctly, you've quoted all attributes, and you've nested cleanly. All the pieces are presented the way XML asks you to present them.

If you are using XML primarily for display, you will likely be creating well-formed documents.

A *valid* XML document conforms to the XML syntax rules also—but then it goes one step further. The valid XML document also conforms to DTD data. It meets all the XML syntax rules and all the DTD rules. This process of comparing the XML file to the DTD is called *validation*, hence the name "valid XML."

If you are working on a set of documents or on a document with specific structural requirements, you are likely to be creating a valid XML document.

Parsers

You've heard the term *parser* a number of times. The parser is the tool that error checks an XML file to be sure that it follows the rules and then creates a tree structure from the elements.

Parsers come in two flavors: nonvalidating and validating. A nonvalidating parser checks only that the document conforms to XML syntax rules. For example, it will flag an error if you have an opening tag without a matching closing tag. If you are creating well-formed documents, you'll need only a nonvalidating parser.

A validating parser checks both the XML syntax rules and the DTD rules, to be sure the document conforms to both syntax and DTD. It will display an error flag if any syntax or DTD rules are not followed. For example, if your DTD says that paragraphs can contain only text and you put a headline tag within a paragraph, the parser will note that there is an error.

If you are creating valid XML, you will want to find a validating parser to use to error check your documents.

As of this writing, parsers are mostly stand-alone tools that you can download and use. Most of them are written to run on PCs or Unix workstations. The companion website to this book (<http://www.projectcool.com/guides/xml>) has pointers to some of the different parsers available for download on the web. We can't guarantee any of them; your best bet is the look at some of the options and try a few until you find one that feels comfortable.

Later in this chapter we'll walk through the process of using one of the parsers, to give you a sense of what is involved.

In the future, a non-validating parser will be part of most applications that read an XML file. For example, the 5.X versions of web browsers will include non-validating XML parsers as part of their functionality. In addition, XML editing tools may contain either validating or non-validating XML parsers so that you can easily check your files as you are creating them. In the ideal world, you won't really have to be aware that a parser is running—you'll just know that you are checking your file to be sure it is correct and fixing errors as they are flagged.

Well-Formed XML

Well-formed XML is quite straightforward:

1. You create an ASCII text file with the extension .xml.
2. You enter the XML declaration.
3. You enter tags and data, following the rules for good XML syntax.
4. You can run it through a non-validating parser to check to be sure the syntax rules are applied appropriately.

Once you confirm that the syntax is correct, you have a well-formed XML document.

Creating a Well-Formed XML Document

To create a well-formed XML document, follow these steps:

1. Open an ASCII text file.

2. Type the XML declaration. The minimum declaration looks like this:

   ```
   <?xml version="1.0"?>
   ```

   This announces that the following data is XML version 1.0 marked-up data.

3. A well-formed XML document does not require a DOCTYPE definition. It does, however, require that there is a top-level element that contains all the content. The opening tag of this element will be the first tag in your file, and the closing tag of this element will be the last tag in your file. Type the opening top-level element tag. If the top-level element tag is BOOK, for example, you'd type this:

   ```
   <BOOK>
   ```

4. Begin entering the remainder of your content and marking it up. Remember to follow the XML syntax rules: Open and close all tags, use careful and consistent punctuation, and nest correctly.

5. Close your file with the ending tag for the top-level element. A very simple (and silly) XML file might look like this:

   ```
   <?xml version="1.0"?>
   <BOOK>
   <TITLE>When I Was A Tadpole</TITLE>
   <AUTHOR>Thadious J. Frog</AUTHOR>
   <CHAPTER>
   <P>
   I started out life as a tadpole.
   </P>
   <P>
   But I don't remember it at all.
   </P>
   </CHAPTER>
   </BOOK>
   ```

   That's all there is to it.

The Full XML Declaration

You need use only a minimum XML declaration at the beginning of your XML file. The declaration states that this is an XML version 1.0 document.

You may, if you choose, use a full XML declaration. The full declaration has three attributes and looks like this:

```
<?xml version="1.0" standalone="yes" encoding="UTF-8"?>
```

Version

The version attribute contains the value of the XML version you are using. Right now, the version is 1.0.

Standalone

The standalone attribute alerts the processor that this is or is not a document that requires the use of an external DTD file or an external entity file.

If you are making a well-formed XML document, you are not using an external DTD, so the value is most likely to be "yes." You can omit this standalone attribute from the declaration; when the processor finds no DTD specified it will assume this is a well-formed document and will not try to validate it.

Encoding

The encoding attribute declares how the file is encoded. The default encoding for XML is UTF-8. Use this attribute if you are using a different type of encoding.

Valid XML

A valid XML document is one that meets two criteria. First, it meets the rules for a well-formed file. That is, it follows all the syntax rules of XML: all tags started and ended, all attributes in quotes, careful nesting, and proper capitalization.

Then, it goes one step further. The valid XML document is compared against a specific DTD, and it must meet all the rules defined in that DTD as well. This process of comparing the XML file to the DTD is called *validation*. The validating parser is the tool that performs the validation task.

More about DTDs

A DTD is a set of rules about the elements you can use, the order in which you can use them, and the attributes the elements can or must have. The DTD is a formal description of the document tree, carefully defining the document and data structure.

After your XML document is complete, you will parse it. That is, you will use a tool that turns your XML tags into a structure and compares the structure to the rules specified in the DTD. This comparison process is called *validation*.

Validation is an error-checking process. If you are working on a document that is part of a larger set of documents, one that needs to conform to some industry rules, or one that you just want to be sure is created in a certain way, you'll probably be using a DTD.

The nice thing about XML is that you need to use a DTD only for applications for which it makes sense to use a DTD. You don't need to create a DTD for everything. You can have perfectly usable XML files by making them well-formed. The DTD is a way to ensure that your files follow a consistent set of rules.

DTDs come from several places:

There are public DTDs that anyone can use. HTML is a public DTD. You point to a public DTD in your XML file.

There are DTDs that you can use by permission. You point to the location of the DTD on a particular system in your XML file. Many industry groups are creating DTDs that others in the group can use. This will help create some standards in different content areas.

You can create your own external DTD. You will point to its location on your system in your XML file. Creating a DTD can be a complex task and is discussed later in this book.

You can embed simple DTD information in the file itself, as part of the DOCTYPE definition. You do this only for very simple DTD data.

One place to check for information about specific preexisting DTDs is the Graphic Communications Association (GCA) website, <http://www.gca.org>. In addition, the Organization for the Advancement of Structured Information Standards (OASIS), <http://www.oasis-open.org/>, announced in March 1999 that they were forming an XML Registry and Repository Technical Committee to find an industry-acceptable means of making XML DTDs findable and available. And, of course, don't forget to check your own industry associations' websites. In many cases, an existing DTD may fit your needs and there's no reason to re-invent the wheel. Many of the widely used SGML DTDs, such as DOCBOOK, are being converted to XML as well.

Creating a Valid XML Document

Creating a valid XML document isn't any more difficult than creating a well-formed one. You just need to be sure you follow the rules in your DTD. You need to be sure that elements are marked up in the specified manner and order and that they include attributes as defined in the DTD.

If your XML document meets *both* the XML syntax rules and the DTD rules for elements and attributes, then it is a valid document.

To create a valid XML file, follow these steps:

1. Open an ASCII text file.
2. Type the XML declaration. The minimum declaration looks like this:
   ```
   <?xml version="1.0"?>
   ```
   This announces that the following data is XML version 1.0 marked-up data.
3. Type the DOCTYPE definition. The DOCTYPE definition looks like this:
   ```
   <!DOCTYPE myfile SYSTEM "myfile.dtd">
   ```
   or
   ```
   <!DOCTYPE myfile PUBLIC "URI÷">@
   ```
4. Enter the tag that begins the top-level element.
5. Enter the rest of your content and mark it up. Remember to follow the XML syntax rules: Open and close all tags, carefully and consistently capitalize, quote all attributes, and nest correctly. Also, remember to use elements and attributes as specified in the DTD against which you will be validating.
6. At the end of your file, don't forget to close the top-level element.

The Full XML Declaration

You need use only a minimum XML declaration at the beginning of your XML file. The declaration states that this is an XML version 1.0 document.

You may, if you choose, use a full XML declaration. The full declaration has three attributes and looks like this:

```
<?XML version="1.0" standalone="no" encoding="UTF-8"?>
```

Version

The version attribute contains the value of the XML version you are using. Right now, the version is 1.0.

Standalone

The standalone attribute alerts the processor that this is or is not a document that requires the use of an external DTD file or an external entity file.

If you are making a valid XML document, you may choose to use an external DTD, so the value may be "no." You can omit this standalone attribute from the declaration; when the processor finds either a pointer to a DTD specified or embedded DTD data, it will assume this is a valid document and will validate it.

Encoding

The encoding attribute declares how the file is encoded. The default encoding for XML is UTF-8. Use this attribute if you are using a different type of encoding, such as UTF-16 for the full international set of characters.

The DOCTYPE Declaration

The DOCTYPE definition looks like this:

```
<!DOCTYPE myfile SYSTEM "myfile.dtd">
```

It tells the processor:

- That you are creating a certain type of document.
- The name of the document.
- The location of the DTD that defines this type of document. The DTD may be a URI on either a PUBLIC DTD or one that lives on a private server. Or, it may be defined within the DOCTYPE definition itself.

myfile

The first value in the DOCTYPE declaration is the name of the type of document you are creating. For example, if you are creating a book document, this would have the value "book."

SYSTEM or PUBLIC

The second value alerts the processor that the DTD is on a server. PUBLIC alerts the processor that you are using a PUBLIC DTD, while SYSTEM says that the DTD is on your local system.

myfile.dtd

The third value is the name of the DTD you want to use, or in the case of a public DTD, the URI that contains it.

Locally Defined DTD Data

The DOCTYPE definition can also include DTD data directly. The open brace indicates that data—typically either element and attribute definitions or entity definitions—are to follow and to be in effect for this document. For example, this is how a DOCTYPE declaration that includes element definitions looks. You'll see that instead of pointing to a public or system DTD, it actually defines the elements right there, within the DOCTYPE definition:

```
<?xml version="1.0" standalone="no"?>
<!DOCTYPE BOOK [
<!ELEMENT BOOK (TITLE, AUTHOR*, CHAPTER+)>
<!ELEMENT TITLE (#PCDATA)>
<!ELEMENT AUTHOR (#PCDATA)>
<!ELEMENT CHAPTER (P)*>
<!ELEMENT P (#PCDATA | QUOTE)*>
<!ELEMENT QUOTE (#PCDATA)>
]>
```

Putting DTD Data into the DOCTYPE Definition

Typically, you point to an external DTD in your DOCTYPE declaration. Having an external DTD makes it easy to maintain the DTD and to use it for multiple XML documents.

You can, however, specify elements and attributes in your DOCTYPE definition. Use this only for simple element and attribute definitions that you are unlikely to reuse.

Here's an example of simple DTD data. This declares six elements: the top-level book element, a title element, an author element, a chapter element, a paragraph element, and a quotation element. The tags are <BOOK>, <TITLE>, <AUTHOR>, <CHAPTER>, <P>, and <QUOTE>:

```
<!DOCTYPE BOOK [
<!ELEMENT BOOK (TITLE, AUTHOR*, CHAPTER+)>
<!ELEMENT TITLE (#PCDATA)>
<!ELEMENT AUTHOR (#PCDATA)>
<!ELEMENT CHAPTER (P)*>
<!ELEMENT P (#PCDATA | QUOTE)*>
<!ELEMENT QUOTE (#PCDATA)>
]>
```

You have just created a DTD that says the book element contains one title, followed by an optional one or more authors, followed by at least one chapter. Each chapter contains at least one paragraph. Each paragraph contains one or more of either textual data or a quote element, in any order. The quote element contains textual data.

Here's what a document using this DTD might look like:

```
<?xml version="1.0" standalone="no"?>
<!DOCTYPE BOOK [
<!ELEMENT BOOK (TITLE, AUTHOR*, CHAPTER+)>
<!ELEMENT TITLE (#PCDATA)>
<!ELEMENT AUTHOR (#PCDATA)>
<!ELEMENT CHAPTER (P)*>
<!ELEMENT P (#PCDATA | QUOTE)*>
<!ELEMENT QUOTE (#PCDATA)>
]>
<BOOK>
<TITLE>Cooking with Olive Oil</TITLE>
<AUTHOR>Olivia Vine</AUTHOR>
<CHAPTER>
<P>Adding olive oil to your regular cooking makes your food taste better
and lets you avoid other fatty products.
</P>
<P>There is a trend afoot today to label all oils as bad. But that's
just not fair. <QUOTE>"Olive oil is good for you!</QUOTE> says Annalisa
Huile, researcher at the Institute for Good Food.</P>
</CHAPTER>
</BOOK>
```

When the document is processed, the parser checks to see if you obeyed the rules outlined in our DOCTYPE definition—your internal DTD. It makes sure that there is just one title and that it contains text. It makes sure your chapter contains paragraphs. It makes sure the paragraphs contain either text or quote elements. It makes sure all tags, including the top-level <BOOK> tag, begin and end. It makes sure all nesting is correct.

As you can imagine, the DTD data can quickly become long and complex. If you are doing any complex specifications, you should be creating an external DTD instead of inserting the rules into your document.

Creating an external DTD makes it easier to update the DTD and reuse the DTD in other XML documents. Using the DOCTYPE definition to define the elements is a solution for simple declarations that you want permanently attached to this particular document.

To create elements within your DOCTYPE definition, follow these steps:

1. Start the DOCTYPE by typing:

   ```
   <!DOCTYPE
   ```

2. Type the name of the type of file you are creating:

   ```
   <!DOCTYPE myfile
   ```

3. Type an open square bracket:

   ```
   <!DOCTYPE myfile [
   ```

4. On the next line, start the first element definition:

   ```
   <!ELEMENT
   ```

5. Type the name of the element you are defining:

   ```
   <! ELEMENT BOOK
   ```

6. Enter what type of data the element can contain, surrounded by parentheses. (#PCDATA) means "parsed character data," which is essentially text and one of the most common types of data. There's more about element data in the next section. The element can also contain other elements, which you list by name. The element name alone means to use this element once and only once. A question makes the element optional. A plus means the element can be used more than once. Commas separating elements mean that they should be used in that particular order. Later sections in this chapter go into detail about how to set up element rules, and Chapter 9, "Understanding a DTD," provides additional details about creating a DTD and its rules:

   ```
   <!ELEMENT BOOK (TITLE, AUTHOR?, CHAPTER+)
   ```

7. End the element declaration:

   ```
   <!ELEMENT BOOK (TITLE, AUTHOR?, CHAPTER*)>
   ```

8. On the next line, end the DOCTYPE definition with a closing square bracket and a closing delimiter:

   ```
   ]>
   ```

Here's another example of how a very simple definition would look. This sets up an employee list. The parent element is called employee, and it has three child elements, first (first name), last (last name), and phone (phone extension):

```
<?xml version="1.0" standalone="no"?>
<!DOCTYPE EMPLOYEE[
<!ELEMENT EMPLOYEE (FIRST, LAST, PHONE)>
<!ELEMENT FIRST (#PCDATA)>
<!ELEMENT LAST (#PCDATA)>
<!ELEMENT PHONE (#PCDATA)>
]>
```

When the document is processed, the parser checks to be sure your structure looks like this—and that every element is present in the specified order:

```
<?xml version="1.0" standalone="no"?>
<!DOCTYPE EMPLOYEE[
<!ELEMENT EMPLOYEE (FIRST, LAST, PHONE)>
<!ELEMENT FIRST (#PCDATA)>
<!ELEMENT LAST (#PCDATA)>
<!ELEMENT PHONE (#PCDATA)>
]>

<EMPLOYEE>
<FIRST>Frances</FIRST>
<LAST>Jonek</LAST>
<PHONE>x346</PHONE>
</EMPLOYEE>
```

Types of Element Data

Your element can have five basic types of data:

- It can be empty.
- It can have text.
- It can have child elements arranged in a specific order.
- It can have any combination of child elements.
- It can have a combination of text and child elements.

Most elements contain either text or a mix of text and elements.

Empty

To make an empty element, use the value EMPTY, like this:

```
<!ELEMENT IMG (EMPTY)>
```

An empty element, as its name suggests, contains no content. It may, however, contain attributes and attribute values.

Text

Text is called "parsed character data" and is identified like this:

```
<!ELEMENT LAST-NAME (#PCDATA)>
```

A great many of the elements you create are likely to contain text as their content.

Child Elements in Specific Order

You can set up an element so that it contains other elements only. For example, if you are creating a type of list, the list might be a parent element that contains several child elements. You specify the order in which they should appear by the order in which you list them in the element definition. Separate each element with a comma:

```
<!ELEMENT EMPLOYEE (FIRST, LAST, PHONE)>
```

Child Elements in Any Order

You can set up an element so that it contains other elements. The elements don't need to be in a specific order, and they can be used more than once.

```
<!ELEMENT requirements (tank-size | temperament | food)>
```

Mixed Data

You can set up an element so that it can contain both text and other elements. If the elements can be in any order, separate each element name with a bar:

```
<!ELEMENT interview (#PCDATA | name | title | quote>
```

Note that in a mixed data element, #PCDATA must always come first.

Required, Optional, or Repeated Elements

Here's how to define how elements are used:

One use only. To set a rule that requires exactly one use of the element, use the element's name by itself, like this:

```
<!ELEMENT BOOK (TITLE)>
```

Optional. To make the element optional, follow its name with a question mark. The question mark means use this one time or no times:

```
<!ELEMENT BOOK (TITLE, AUTHOR?)>
```

Repeated and required. To allow many uses of the element, but to require at least one use of it, follow the element name with a plus sign:

```
<!ELEMENT BOOK (TITLE, AUTHOR?, CHAPTER+)>
```

Repeated and optional. To allow many—or no—uses of the element, follow the element with an asterisk:

```
<!ELEMENT BOOK (TITLE, AUTHOR*, CHAPTER+)>
```

Attribute Lists

As you define elements, you can also define attributes for the elements. You do this through attribute lists. Attribute lists define the name, data type, and default value (if any) of each attribute associated with an element.

In this very simple example, we're adding some attributes to the description element from our fish list. We want to be able to specify the size to which this fish grows and the region of the world from which this fish comes.

```
<?xml version="1.0" standalone="no"?>
<!--This defines a listing of fish-->
<!DOCTYPE FISH [
<!ELEMENT FISH (SPECIES+)>
<!ELEMENT SPECIES (COM-NAME, SCI-NAME, DESCRIPTION)>
<!ELEMENT COM-NAME (#PCDATA)>
<!ELEMENT SCI-NAME (#PCDATA)>
<!ELEMENT DESCRIPTION (#PCDATA)>
<!ATTLIST DESCRIPTION size CDATA #REQUIRED
continent (asia | africa | australia | europe | north-america | south-america | antarctica) "asia">
]>
```

Here's how this element would be used in a document. In the first species, we entered the continent because it was different from the default. In the second, the continent value is asia, so we didn't have to enter it; it will just be assigned the default value of asia.

```
<?xml version="1.0" standalone="no"?>
<!--This defines a listing of fish-->
<!DOCTYPE FISH [
<!ELEMENT FISH (SPECIES+)>
```

```
<!ELEMENT SPECIES (COM-NAME, SCI-NAME, DESCRIPTION)>
<!ELEMENT COM-NAME (#PCDATA)>
<!ELEMENT SCI-NAME (#PCDATA)>
<!ELEMENT DESCRIPTION (#PCDATA)>
<!ATTLIST DESCRIPTION size CDATA #REQUIRED
continent (asia | africa | australia | europe | north-america | south-
america | antarctica) "asia">
]>
<FISH>
<SPECIES>
<COM-NAME>Guppy</COM-NAME>
<SCI-NAME>Poecilia reticulata</SCI-NAME>
<DESCRIPTION size="2.5 in" continent="south-america">Guppies are live
bearers, easy to breed and easy to raise.</DESCRIPTION>
</SPECIES>

<SPECIES>
<COM-NAME>Cherry Barb</COM-NAME>
<SCI-NAME>Puntius titteya</SCI-NAME>
<DESCRIPTION size="2 in">This cheerful fish is best kept in a small
school.</DESCRIPTION>
</SPECIES>
</FISH>
```

To create an attribute list, follow these steps:

1. After the element definition, start an attribute list definition:

   `<!ATTLIST`

2. Type the name of the element for which you are creating the attribute list:

   `<!ATTLIST DESCRIPTION`

3. Type the name of the first attribute:

   `<!ATTLIST DESCRIPTION size`

4. Type the type of data that will go into the attribute. CDATA is character data and is one of the most common types of data. A list of allowable values surrounded by parentheses—(value1 | value 2 | value 3)—is another common data type.

5. If this attribute is required—that is, if you must always enter it as part of the element—type: #REQUIRED.

6. If you want to assign the attribute a default value that will be used if no other value is specified, enter that value in quotes.

7. Repeat for each attribute you want as part of the element.

8. End the attribute definition with a closing delimiter, >.

There is much more detail to creating a DTD than the rules we've just outlined. If you want to do more than this, you most certainly want to be creating an external DTD.

Parsing an XML File

Parsing is an important step in making sure your XML file is ready to use. There are so many little details and so many places you can make markup mistakes that parsing is an essential part of the XML file creation process.

There are many parsers, both validating and non-validating. Your XML creation tool may have one as part of the application. Your 5.X browser has a non-validating parser and will give you syntax errors if you try to view a document that is not correctly constructed.

This section walks you through a parsing process, using an online validating parser at Brown University's Scholarly Technology Group.

Here's how to try parsing XML data.

Go to <http://www.stg.brown.edu/service/xmlvalid/>. You will see a page that resembles Figure 7.1.

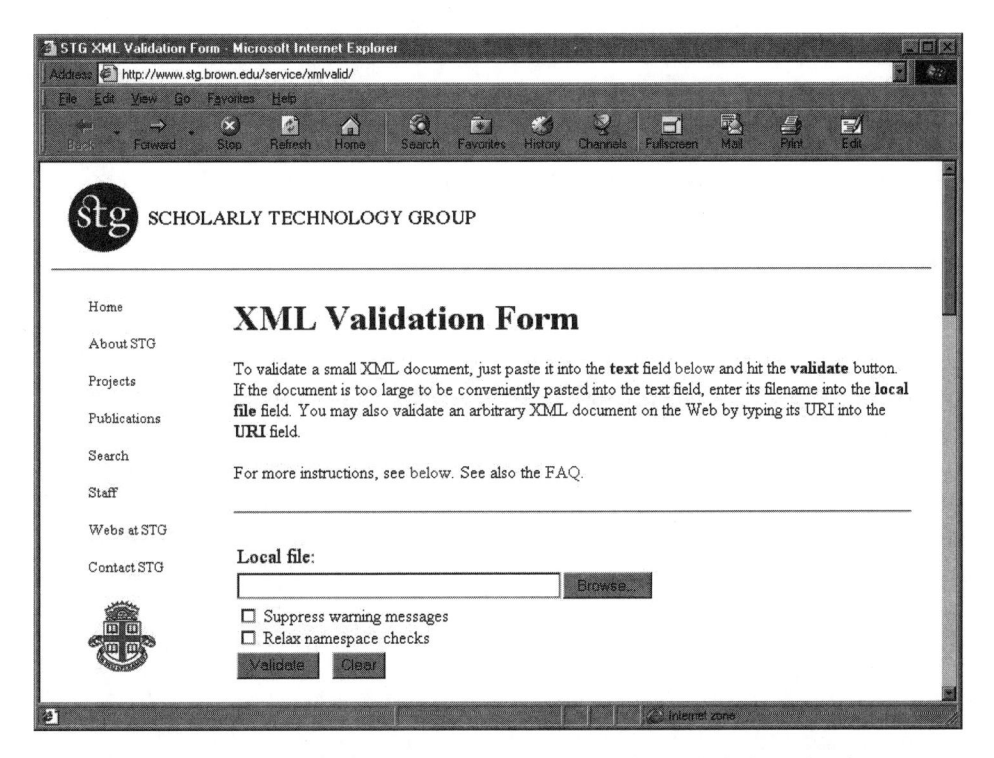

Figure 7.1 The online validating parser at Brown University's Scholarly Technology Group.

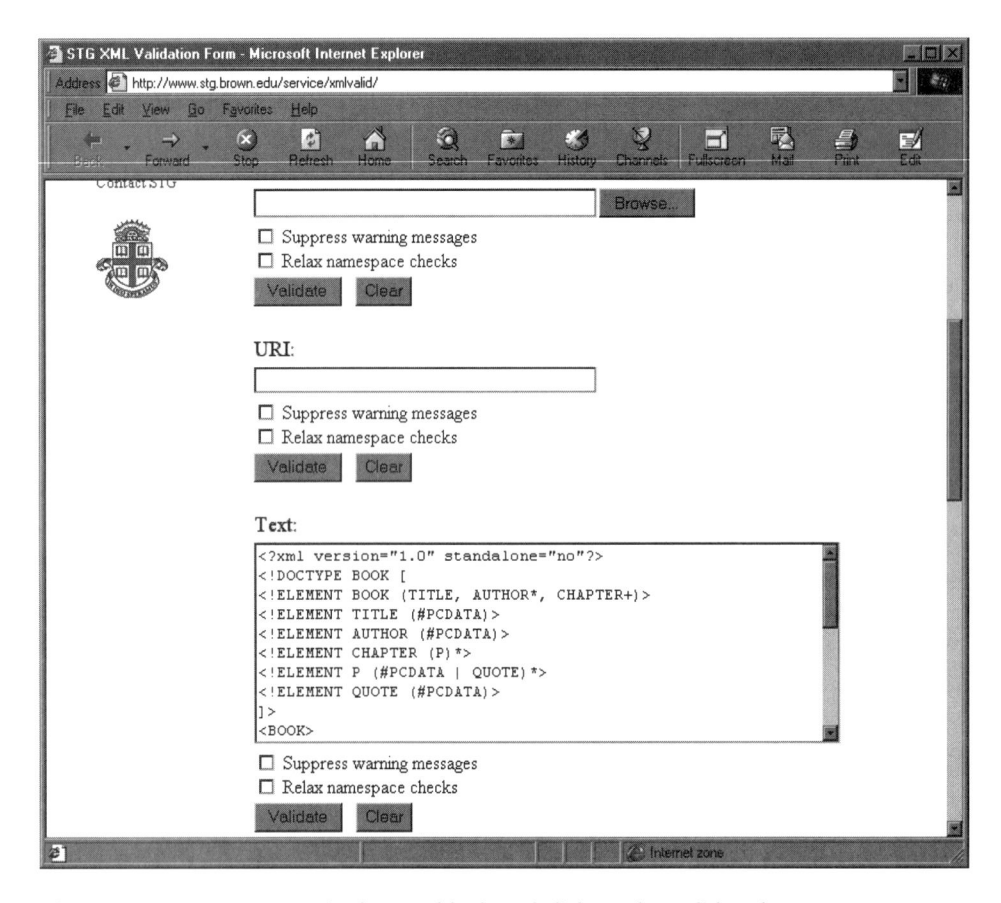

Figure 7.2 Enter your text in the text block and click on the Validate button.

The form lets you specify where the file you want to parse is located. You can pick a file from your local drive or network, from the web, or you may type in some text. We're going to type in a little simple text, so scroll down the page until you come to the text box.

Test the sample mini-XML document from earlier in the chapter. Type the following code into the online parser's text box (you'll end up with an entry that resembles Figure 7.2):

```
<?xml version="1.0" standalone="no"?>
<!DOCTYPE BOOK [
<!ELEMENT BOOK (TITLE, AUTHOR*, CHAPTER+)>
<!ELEMENT TITLE (#PCDATA)>
<!ELEMENT AUTHOR (#PCDATA)>
<!ELEMENT CHAPTER (P)*>
<!ELEMENT P (#PCDATA | QUOTE)*>
```

```
<!ELEMENT QUOTE (#PCDATA)>
]>
<BOOK>
<TITLE>Cooking with Olive Oil</TITLE>
<AUTHOR>Olivia Vine</AUTHOR>
<CHAPTER>
<P>Adding olive oil to your regular cooking makes your food taste better
and lets you avoid other fatty products.
</P>
<P>There is a trend afoot today to label all oils as bad. But that's
just not fair. <QUOTE>"Olive oil is good for you!</QUOTE> says Annalisa
Huile, researcher at the Institute for Good Food.</P>
</CHAPTER>
</BOOK>
```

Click on the Validate button. If there are any errors, you will see a report listing them by line number. Figure 7.3 shows the errors that would appear if you left off the question mark in the XML declaration. Figure 7.4 shows

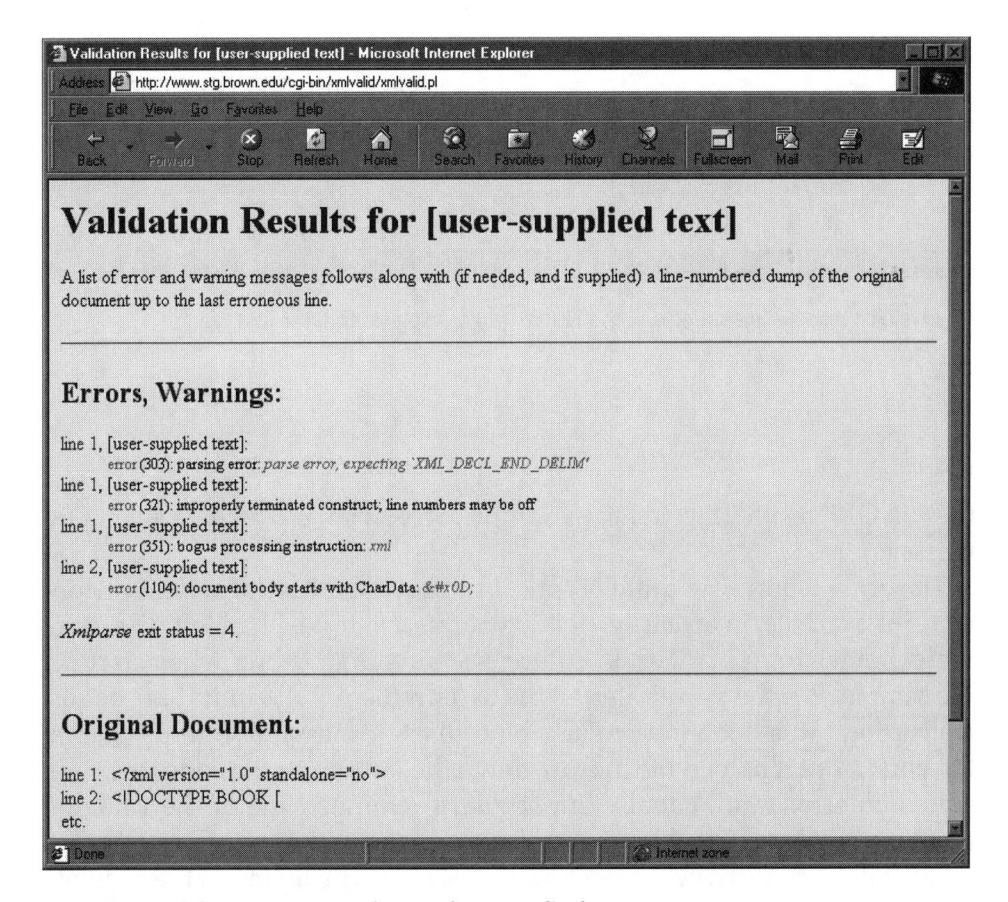

Figure 7.3 If there are errors, the results page displays error messages.

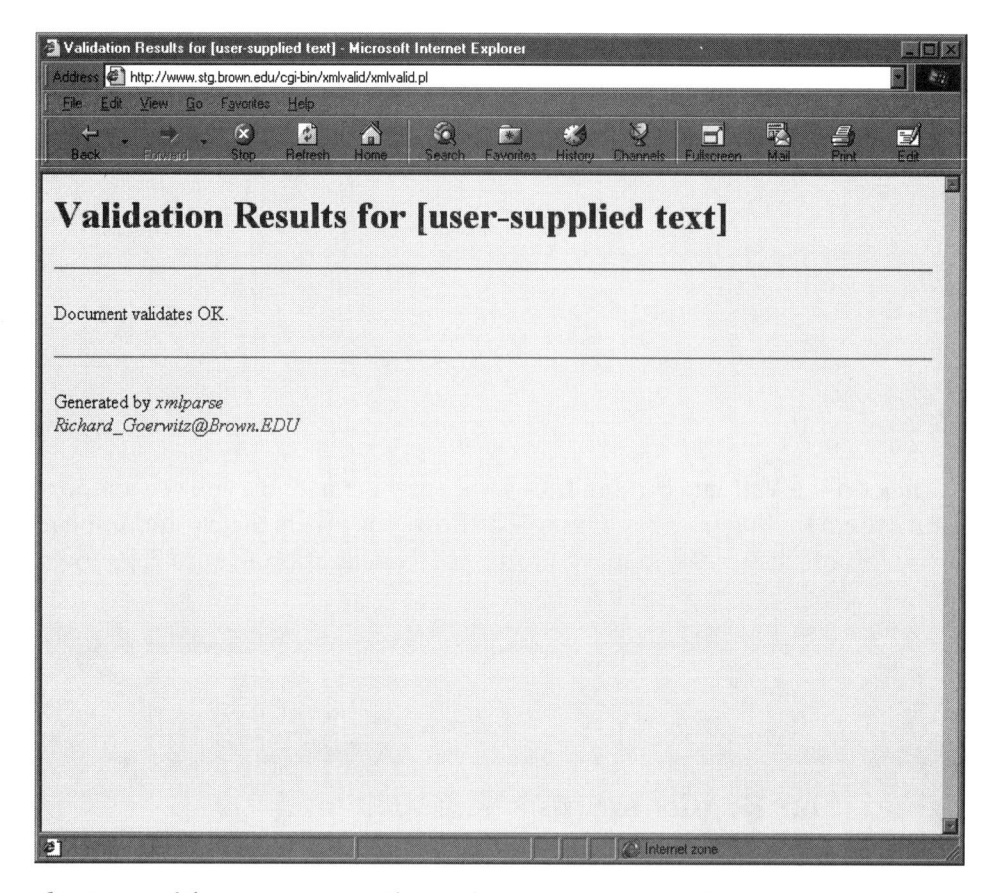

Figure 7.4 If there are no errors, the results page displays an OK message.

the "all OK" result. (I tested this example, so you should receive an all OK message).

The error reports are quite cryptic, but provide a hint of what is incorrect. For example, in an earlier version of this example, I had left off a closing delimiter from one tag. I couldn't see anything wrong when starting the sample. But the parser alerted me to a problem. I'll admit that "bogus instruction" was not a particularly helpful error message to receive from the parser, but it helped me narrow down the portion of the code that generated an error. And, equally important, it reminded me of the value of parsing and error checking everything—and of never assuming that I hand-coded correctly, no matter how careful I was in keying in the content.

Summary

You can create two types of XML documents. A well-formed document conforms to XML syntax rules. A valid document conforms to both syntax and DTD rules.

In both cases, the XML file is an ASCII text file with the extension .xml. It begins with an XML declaration.

After you create the file you need to process it, and assuming you want to see a web page, you need to tie it into a style sheet for display.

The parser is the name of the processor that checks an XML file for syntax and DTD structure.

CHAPTER 8

Other Pieces of an XML Document

In addition to document data, your XML document can contain a number of other pieces. These pieces can make creating and maintaining the file easier.

These pieces include comments, CDATA, entities, and namespaces.

Comments

Comments are nondisplaying sections of your XML document where you can make notes to yourself or others.

Comments are very important. They are a way to note and explain what you've done in a certain place or to pass along information to someone who might be working on the document in the future. Don't be afraid to use comments—people who must maintain your document will welcome the extra information and explanation.

Comments are created in the same way you create comments in HTML. They begin with an open tag delimiter, exclamation mark, and two dashes, <!--, and close with two dashes and a close tag delimiter, -->. Between the markers is your comment.

For example, this comment notes that this fish in the fish list was put into the document by Fred.

```
<!-- Fred inserted this fish. He says to double check its sci-name
because it might be changing.-->
```

The parser ignores everything between the open and close of the comment. It doesn't parse it; it doesn't process it; it just skips over it.

Be sure that you do not use two dashes, --, within your comment. XML will think the two dashes mark the end of your comment and may parse the material after the dashes.

CDATA

CDATA means "character data." Character data are letters, numbers, and punctuation that are used exactly as they are—they aren't parsed or processed.

CDATA in an Attribute List

One of the places you can use CDATA is as an attribute value type in an attribute list. Remember, an attribute list is the place where you define an element's attributes and the type of value each may contain. CDATA is one of those value types.

CDATA is used exactly as you enter it. If you type "145,873" as the value for an attribute that accepts CDATA values, that string of characters will be passed right along as is. Same with "happy-dogs" or "here&there." The processor doesn't check to see if the characters have special meaning, are used as programming values, or anything else. It just takes the data at face value.

For example, this attribute list definition says that the value for size is CDATA:

```
<!ATTLIST DESCRIPTION SIZE CDATA #REQUIRED
```

CDATA Sections in a Document

You might also want to use CDATA within your XML document.

Normally, a program called a parser looks at the contents of your XML document, checking it for syntax and, if you are using a DTD, comparing it to the DTD. Certain characters, like the < and > signs, have special meaning to an XML parser. When the document is parsed, the parser looks for these characters and, instead of treating them as less than and greater than characters, it treats them as the opening and closing of a tag.

What if you want to use a less than or greater than character as itself? A quick and easy way to do this is by using a CDATA section, which contains items that you don't want parsed—that is, for characters you want to use as themselves. For example, you can use a CDATA section for code examples.

You might think of CDATA as being somewhat like the <pre> tag in HTML.

It is quite easy to create a CDATA section. You simply declare the section as CDATA and then enter the content you want treated as unparsed characters.

To create a CDATA section, follow these steps:

1. Begin the declaration with the open tag sign and an exclamation mark, like this:

    ```
    <!
    ```

2. Type an open brace and the word CDATA in all caps, then another open brace, like this:

    ```
    <![CDATA[
    ```

3. Now, type the contents of your CDATA section. In this example, the contents are an example of XML code:

    ```
    <![CDATA[<NAME>Customer Name</NAME>
    ```

4. Finally, end the section with two closing brackets and a closing tag, like this:

    ```
    <![CDATA[<NAME>Customer Name</NAME>]]>
    ```

For example, here's how you would use a CDATA section in a tutorial about marking up customer data documents. This is a snippet of code from the XML file. We assume that the XML document uses a <P> tag to mark paragraphs and a <TOPIC> tag to mark the topic:

```
<TOPIC>
Customer Lists
</TOPIC>
<P>
```

Always make sure you identify the customer's name with the appropriate tag. The customer's name should appear first in the customer list, followed by his or her e-mail address, like this:

```
<![CDATA[<CUSTOMERLIST><NAME>Freda Elkhorn</NAME>
<EMAIL>freda@projectcool.com</EMAIL>
</CUSTOMERLIST>
]]>
</P>
```

```
<P>And don't forget to end your customer list!
</P>
```

Combined with some style data, Figure 8.1 shows how the CDATA section might display in a web browser. Notice that the CDATA section transfers exactly as typed.

Here's an example in which you want various character symbols to appear in the document as themselves:

```
<P>
And then the drunk tripped and smashed his bargain-bin bottle on the
concrete. <QUOTE><![CDATA[%!$###@@@%$!]]>! I lost my <![CDATA[%!$]]>
best drink I had all week.</QUOTE> And then he started to weep
pathetically.
</P>
```

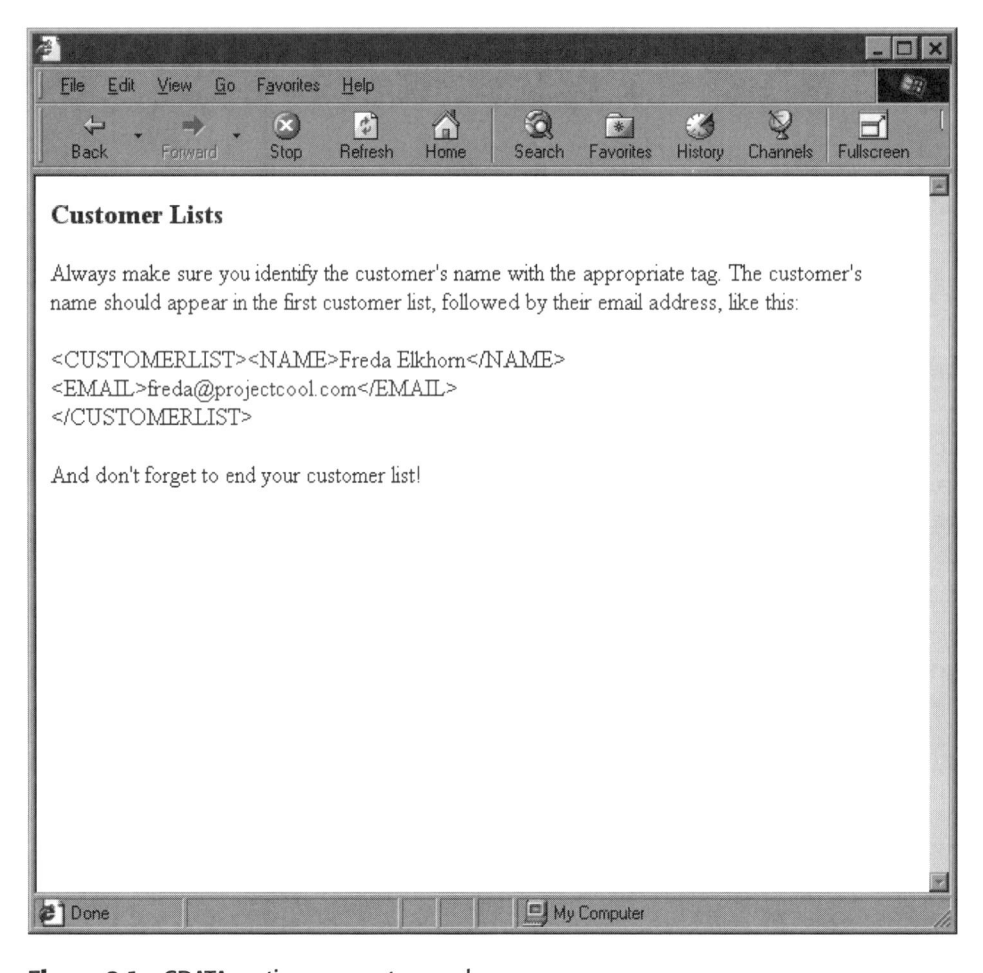

Figure 8.1 CDATA sections are not parsed.

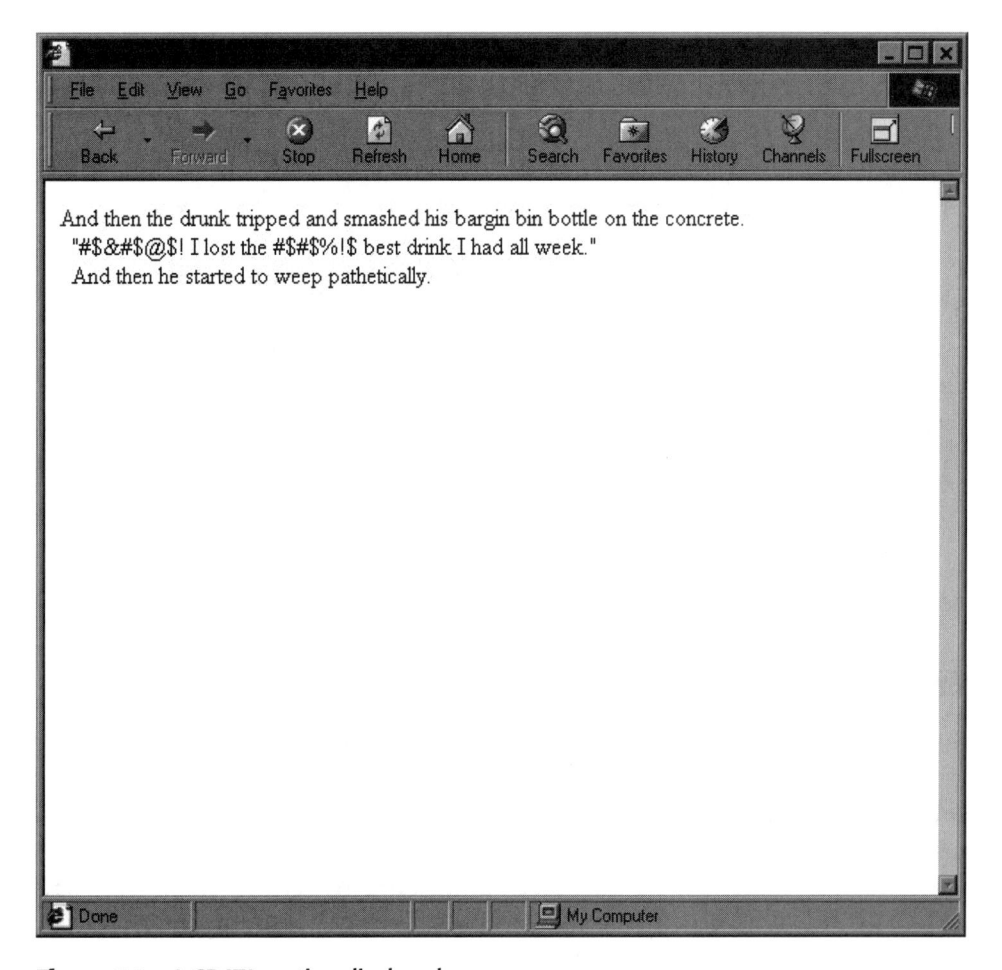

Figure 8.2 A CDATA section displayed.

Figure 8.2 shows how this might display when combined with style data. Notice again that the contents of a CDATA section are not parsed and are display as entered.

Entities

An entity is a shortcut that you can define and use. You might think of entities as being a little like programming macros—by typing one short phrase you're really inserting a larger amount of text into your document.

There are two types of entities. One type, the general entity, is used in an XML document. That's the type we'll discuss here. The other type, the parameter entity, is used in DTDs.

If you've ever used this code

```
&lt;
```

to create the < symbol in a web page, you've used an entity. This entity, lt, is a predefined shortcut for accessing a particular ASCII character. Instead of having to remember a character set number, all you need to remember—and use—is the logical abbreviation for less than, lt.

Entities begin with the ampersand symbol, contain the name of the entity, and conclude with a semi-colon. In addition to < you may have also used the entities > to produce the > symbol and & for the ampersand symbol (&).

You might want to create and use an entity in your document for a number of different reasons.

Entities Save Typing for Repeated Content

Suppose all your pages end with the same copyright statement. Instead of keying the entire statement into each document, you could create an entity called *copyright* and type that one word instead of the two-sentence statement.

Or, maybe you talk about carbon dioxide a lot. You could make an entity called *co2* that you could enter instead of typing the whole chemical name. Using an entity makes data entry quick and easy.

Entities Minimize Potential Errors

What if you have a phrase that is used repeatedly but is easy to mistype? Say the president of the company is named Thadious Panaloposlusa. That's one you wouldn't want to have a typo in! You could create an entity called *ph* and use it instead of typing the entire name.

Entities Are Easy to Update

Because entities are defined in one spot, they are easy to update. Remember that copyright notice example? Well, not only is "&copyright" easier to enter than two sentences, but if the dates change or the wording changes all you need to do is update the entity definition and all the uses of the entity now display the new information.

And what about our beloved Mr. PH, president? If we used an entity called *president* to refer to him, when the new president takes over you won't need to change all your document references. You can change your entity definition and your documents will refer to the current president by name.

Entities Can Be Placeholders

Sometimes you are working on a document in which a key bit of data is coming later—for example, the final name of the product you are documenting. You could enter the product code name and then go back later and do a search and replace when you have the real name. Or, you could create an entity called *product-name* and use that instead of typing a specific name. When the real name is chosen, you can just update the entity definition and your document is ready to go. And, when legal learns the name is already claimed by someone else—no problem! Just update that entity again and your document is still current.

Predefined Entities

The XML specification includes several predefined entities:

< Produces the < symbol.

> Produces the > symbol.

& Produces the & symbol.

" Produces the " symbol.

' Produces the ' symbol.

You can use these entities in an XML document without defining them.

Internal Entities

The content of your entities can live right there, in your XML document. These are called *internal entities* because they are completely within the document.

The internal entity is defined as part of the DOCTYPE declaration, like this:

```
<!DOCTYPE [
<!ENTITY copyright "This material is copyright MyCorp, 1999. All rights reserved.">
]>
```

External Entities

You can also set up an entity so that it points to information in another file. This type of entity is called an *external entity*.

For example, you might want to insert the same legal note into multiple documents. You could copy the entire note into each XML document as part of an entity declaration; you also could maintain the note in one location and point to that location in your entity declaration, like this:

```
<!DOCTYPE [
<!ENTITY legal SYSTEM "http://www.myurl.com/legal.xml">
]>
```

Nontext Entities

Your entities can contain text, as you've just seen. Your entities can also contain nontext files, such as GIF or JPG files. A nontext entity is identified by the keyword NDATA and a notation name, like this:

```
<!ENTITY logo SYSTEM "logo.gif" NDATA GIF>
```

Nontext entities are sometimes called "unparsed" entities because the material they reference isn't text, which means it isn't parsed.

Defining Entities

You define an entity in a DTD or within the DOCTYPE declaration of your XML document. When the processor validates your document it also reads the definition of your entities. Remember that entities are case sensitive, so as you create them, be consistent with your use of capitalization and be sure that your use of capital letters is what the people who will be using the entities expect. For example, don't try to be clever or unique and create an entity named "hellO" or "CopyRight." Odds are it won't be used correctly in the document.

You define an entity in much the same way you do an element, either in an external DTD or in a DOCTYPE declaration. To define an entity, follow these steps:

1. Start your DOCTYPE declaration as usual, like this:
   ```
   <!DOCTYPE [
   ```
2. Now, define your first entity. Begin the entity definition with an open tag symbol and exclamation point and the word ENTITY, like this:
   ```
   <!ENTITY
   ```

Other Pieces of an XML Document 157

3. Then, type a space and the entity name, like this:

   ```
   <!ENTITY copyright
   ```

4. Then, type the contents of the entity, surrounded by quote marks, like this:

   ```
   <!ENTITY copyright "This material is copyright MyCorp, 1999. All rights reserved."
   ```

5. Finally, end the entity definition with the closing tag mark, >, like this:

   ```
   <!ENTITY copyright "This material is copyright MyCorp, 1999. All rights reserved.">
   ```

6. You can define multiple entities. They can be fully defined within the entity definition, or the definition can point to an external file. When you have finished defining your entities (and your elements), end the DOCTYPE definition with a closing brace and a closing tag, like this:

   ```
   <!DOCTYPE [
   <!ENTITY copyright "This material is copyright MyCorp, 1999. All rights reserved">
   <!ENTITY co2 "carbon dioxide">
   <!ENTITY president "Francesa C.J. Underhill-Barkerman">
   <!ENTITY trademarks SYSTEM "http://www.bigcorp.com/docs/tms.xml">
   ]>
   ```

Using Entities

Although you define the general entities in your DTD or DOCTYPE declaration, you use them in the body of your XML document.

To use an entity within the content of your document, type an ampersand, the entity name, and a semi-colon.

Entities are case sensitive so you'll need to be sure you are using them exactly as they were defined. For example, &president; is not the same as &President;. For example, this code calls an entity named copyright:

```
&copyright;
```

This code is an example of how you might use several entities in your document.

```
<P>
We are carbon-based life forms. In this chapter we look at &co2; and
what it means for humanity-and the fiscal health of our company.
</P>
<P>
Developments that use &co2; are important to this company. Our
president, &president; has stressed this over and over again. Our work
```

```
in &co2; packaging has been vital to our success throughout history.
</P>
<P>
&copyright;
</P>
```

Figure 8.3 shows how the document, when combined with some style information, might display in a web browser. Note how the entities "expand."

Namespaces

An XML namespace is a collection of names, identified by a URI reference. Namespaces let you match a tag you are using with a particular set of tags.

Figure 8.3 Entities "call" expanded data.

For example, suppose you have a site about used books and you are part of a used books consortium. The whole consortium might have decided to implement a bookstore DTD. All the sites about used books would use the same set of tags to describe the books they have in stock. This structure might allow the consortium to give book collectors an easy way to search for particular editions.

You'll be using the <title> tag to define the book's title because that's the tag the bookstore DTD says to use. You also have your own uses for your site, and you have your own DTD that describes those tags. With namespaces, you can use tags from both DTDs in the same documents, without confusion.

Or, suppose you want to use HTML tags in your XML document. HTML is really a DTD, so you can just create a namespace called HTML and use the existing HTML tags without re-creating them. If you want tables, for example, you could create your own set of table elements, but why bother if HTML tables are already defined?

In the beginning of your document (or at the start of a particular element of your document), you identify the namespaces you'll be using. Then, when you use the tag to identify an element in your document, you precede it with the appropriate namespace name.

Declaring Namespaces

At the beginning of your document, you'll want to identify the namespaces you are using in your document. This process is called *declaring* the namespace.

To declare a namespace, follow these steps:

1. Type the open tag delimiter, <.
2. Type the name of your document type. This is the same name you used in your DOCTYPE declaration.
3. Type the phrase xmlns.
4. Type the name you are giving this namespace. This is the name you will use throughout your document when you want to refer to a tag in that namespace.
5. Type an equal sign, followed by the namespace to which you are pointing.

For example, this code creates a namespace called *ubi* (after a hypothetical Used Books Inc.):

```
<document xmlns:ubi='http://ubi.org/strucutres'>
```

This example creates a namespace called *html* and refers to the W3C.

```
<document xmlns:html='http://www.w3c.org/TR/REC-html40/'>
```

You can declare multiple namespaces in the same document and draw on multiple tag sets.

Using Namespaces

Once you've declared a namespace, you can then use it and its tags in your XML document. It's easy to use a namespace; you just make the name you've given the namespace be the first part of the tag, like this:

```
<UBI:TITLE>My Life: A Biography of Sorts</UBI: TITLE>
```

This announces that the tag belongs to the UBI namespace.
Here's another example. This one uses the HTML namespace:

```
<HTML:IMG src="underwater.gif" border="yes"/>
```

(Notice that we ended the empty tag with a slash, thus closing it.)
You type the namespace, a colon, and the tag–that's all there is to it.

Namespaces are a straightforward way of using multiple tag sets in the same document, without confusion. The rules are simple: If the processor sees a phrase followed by a colon at the beginning of a tag, it knows the tag refers to a namespace. If it sees just the tag, it knows it does not refer to a namespace.

Namespaces raise an important note about naming your elements. Because XML treats a colon as a call to a namespace, make sure you don't create element names that contain colons. For example, if you tried to use an element named <FIRST:NAME>, the XML processor would assume you are trying to use a namespace called FIRST and a tag called NAME.

Summary

In its most simple form, an XML document contains elements and data. You can add other items to the file.

- Comments are a way of adding notes for others working on the file to see and use.
- CDATA is a way of putting data that will be displayed but not parsed into the file.

- Entities are shortcuts for entering larger or more difficult-to-enter pieces of data.
- Namespaces are a way of using multiple tag sets in the same XML document.

You don't need to use any of these items in your document, but they are available to you and extend the power and usefulness of XML.

CHAPTER 9

Understanding a DTD

This chapter talks about how to read an existing DTD, which stands for Document Type Definition. A DTD is a set of rules about a particular type of XML document.

The DTD defines the elements that are allowed in the document, the relationship between the elements, and the attributes that are part of the elements.

When you are using a DTD, the processor will compare your use of elements in your XML document with the rules outlined in the DTD and alert you to any possible errors.

DTDs can be very complex and powerful. This chapter is not designed to make you a DTD god or goddess, but to enable you to read and understand an existing DTD and how it defines the way you mark up your XML document.

Document Trees

The term *document tree* has been used several times in this book. If you read other material about structured documents, XML, or SGML, you'll encounter it again and again.

The document tree is the way people in the structured document world describe the hierarchy of elements in a document.

At the very base is the root element. This is the type of document you are creating. If your document type is "menu," then the menu element is your root element. If your document type is "fish-guide," then the fish-guide element is your root element. Everything else in the document "sprouts" from the root.

After the root element, you have a number of branches. Each branch is a child element of the root and has child elements of its own. For example, *dessert* might be a branch element in our menu document. *Fishlist* might be a branch element in our "fish-guide" document. In each case, the branch

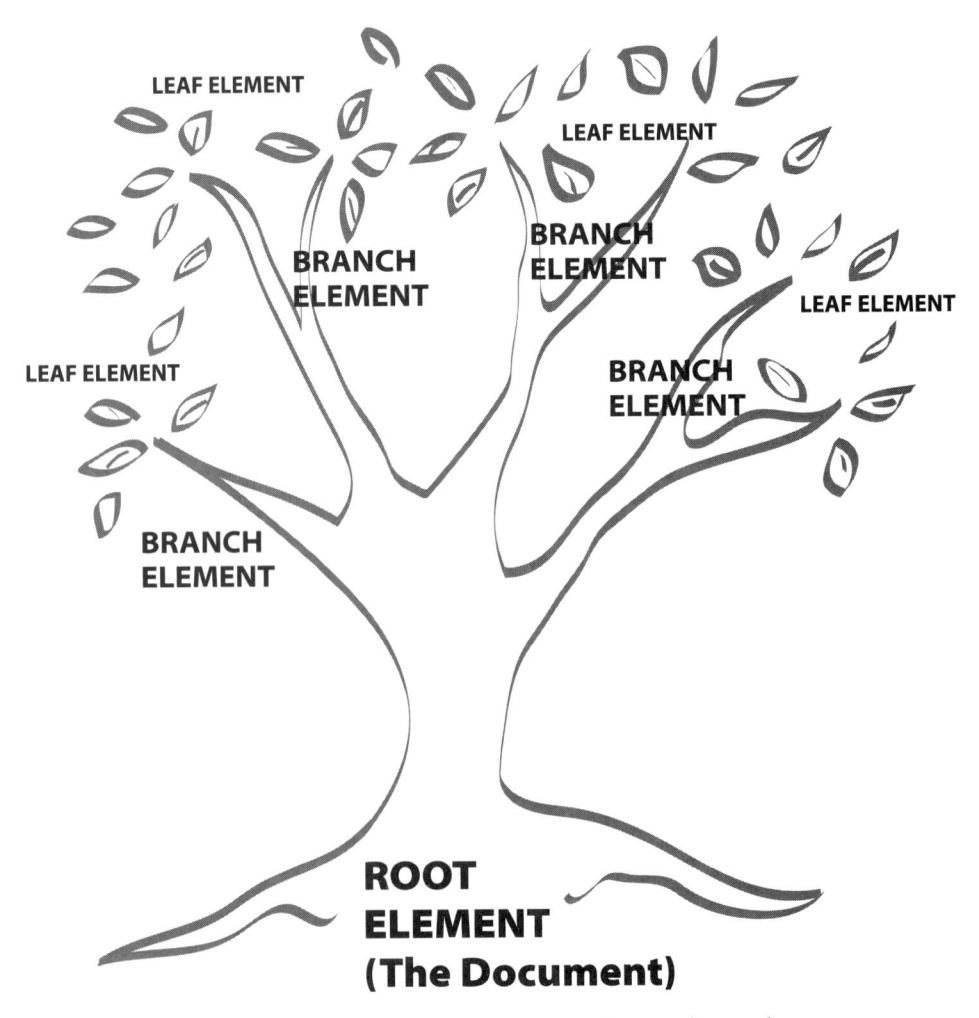

Figure 9.1 A document tree has one root, many branches, and many leaves.

element is a subset of the root element, and it has child, or branch, elements of its own.

At the very tip, after a series of one or more branches, are the leaf elements. These elements are child elements, but they have no children of their own. For example, "quantity" might be a leaf in our menu document tree. It is a child of the dessert element, and it contains only textual data and no other elements. "Scientific-Name" might be a leaf in our "fish-guide" document. It is a child of the *fishlist* element, and it contains text—a Latin name—and no other elements.

Figure 9.1 shows a document tree, with many leaves and branches. Figure 9.2 shows a more traditional representation of the document tree, as a hierarchical flowchart.

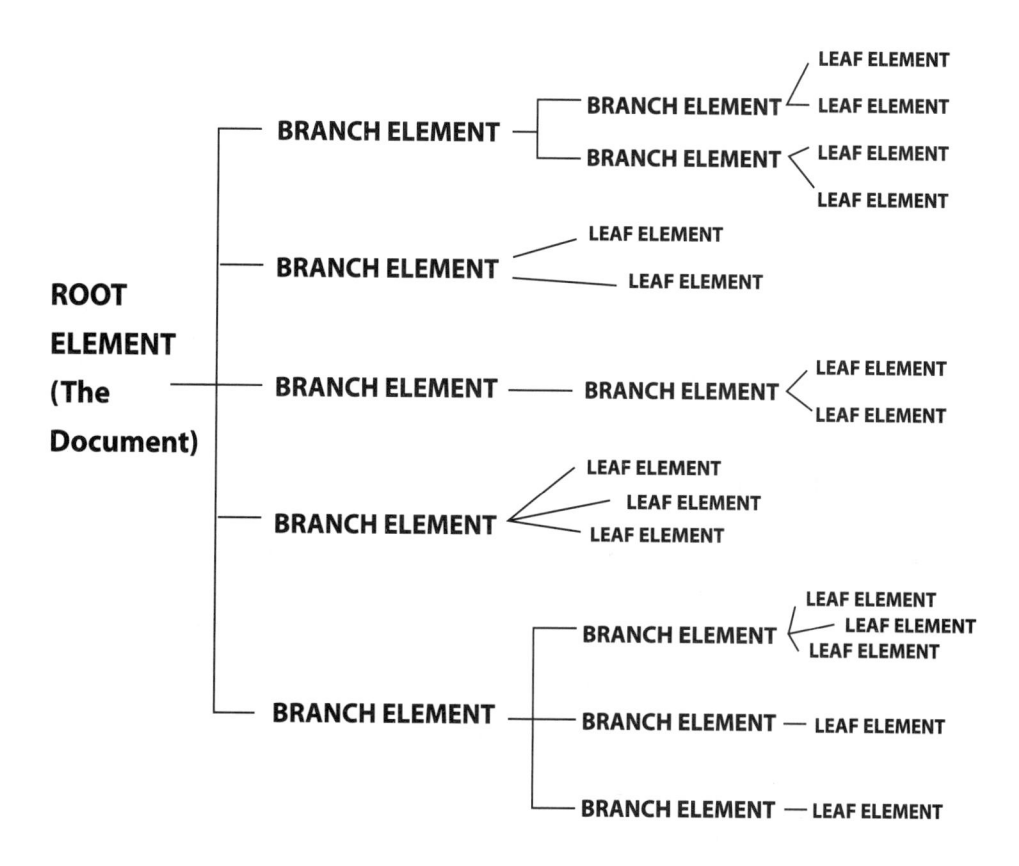

Figure 9.2 Parent and child elements make up the document hierarchy.

There is nothing especially technical about the root, branch, and leaf elements—these names are just the accepted terminology for structured documents. The terms help make the idea of hierarchical relationships clearer.

Parsers and Applications

The parser is the tool that interprets the contents in your XML file and passes the information along to an application. The application is the tool that does something with that XML data.

The XML parser can do three things:

First, it checks the file to be sure it conforms to XML syntax and is a well-formed document.

Second, it compares the XML file to a DTD and validates it against the DTD rules.

Third, it builds a "tree" (there's that word again!) from the elements and passes this information on to an application.

Some parsers just check the syntax and build the tree. Other parsers check the syntax, compare the document to the DTD rules, and build the tree. Parsers that do the latter are called *validating parsers* because they validate the XML file.

You can find parsers that stand alone and parsers that are part of an application. For example, you could have a web browser with a built-in parser. It parses the XML file and then passes the information along to the rest of the browser application. (The 5.X browsers are expected to include an XML parser.) You might have a parser as part of an XML editor; as you create the XML document, it checks for syntax and DTD rule errors.

As a designer, you tend to think of the application as something that does a visible action, like displaying a page. However, an application can be something that is machine-to-machine also, such as sending information to a database. Because a driving force in XML is metadata, many times the word "application" refers to something not visible or managed by a human.

Parts of a DTD

A DTD is used to define several things.

It always defines elements. The element is the basic unit of data in a document.

It always defines the relationship between elements. The DTD creates parent-child relationships between different elements.

In addition to elements, it usually defines attributes. An attribute is additional data about the characteristics of an element.

It may define entities. An entity is a sort of programmer's shortcut or macro that points to other data. For example, you might define an entity that contains the corporate motherhood clause for your press releases. In your document, you can use that clause just by typing the entity name.

It may define notations. A notation is a definition of how the innards of a piece of content should be interpreted by a processor. Through notations you can narrow down the allowable content of an attribute, for example.

To DTD or Not to DTD?

In SGML, a DTD was required. You couldn't do anything with SGML unless you had a corresponding DTD for the document. DTDs can be very complex and challenging to create, so this requirement became a huge barrier to the widespread use of SGML. It made SGML palatable only for large document sets, large documents, or very specialized documents that required error checking. That's why, for example, SGML is used most often in applications such as aerospace documentation or financial data publishing.

With XML, you don't need to have a DTD. This is an important distinction between XML and SGML.

The beauty of XML is that you can use a DTD and create a valid document when it makes sense—and you can avoid DTDs and create a well-formed document when that approach makes sense.

Typically, you'll use a DTD as a way to error check your file, to be sure that all elements and attributes are entered correctly.

For example, if you are creating the online documentation for your product, you will probably want to create a DTD. You'll want to be sure that the tutorial step lists are used correctly and that each section includes a topic tag that describes the task being taught. If you are using XML to create an IE 5 behavior about pullquotes, however, you probably won't want to create a DTD; it would be overkill.

Here are some questions to ask yourself as you think about DTDs, to help you determine whether you might want to use one.

Large Document Set?

Is your document part of a larger document set? If so, you might want to consider creating a DTD for the set. The DTD will ensure that whoever creates the XML files uses the tags in the same way. It will ensure consistency across all documents.

For example, if you are creating a series of 50 online product spec sheets, you might want to consider creating a *specsheet* DTD that defines all the elements and attributes—that way, you'll know that all the sheets have the same elements and attributes and will use them correctly.

Very Specific Needs?

Does your document need to contain very specific data? Data that must appear in a certain order? Or data that must be part of the document? If so, you might want to consider using a DTD as a way to ensure that nothing is accidentally left out or misused.

For example, if you are creating an online financial report, you might want to ensure that certain sub-summaries always precede certain totals and that lists of categories always have data in them.

Industry Needs?

Are you creating a document that needs to match other documents created by people across your industry? If so, you might want to use your industry's DTD so that your documents are consistent with other people's documents.

For example, if you are part of a network of antique dealers, everyone might agree to use the same set of tags in the same way so that potential customers can search all documents for the item they are seeking. You'll want to error check your document against the DTD to be sure you conform to your industry's standard tag use.

Small Set, Single Creator?

Are you creating a document specifically for display on the web? Are you using just a few tags to create this document? Will you be the only page creator? If so, you might not want to use a DTD. Creating a well-formed document might be the perfect use of XML for this application.

For example, if you are creating a personal home page, you are likely to be the only one building the pages. You don't need to error check someone else's coding work. You probably work with a relatively small set of tags, and you can probably trust yourself to use those tags in the way you intend them to be used. You probably don't need a DTD; you can go directly to work building your pages.

Finding a DTD

You've looked at your application of XML, and you've decided that you do want to use a DTD and create valid XML files. The next question is this: Where does that DTD come from?

Share Existing DTDs

Using a DTD doesn't necessarily mean that you have to create it. Increasingly, DTDs will be available that can be used by groups of people with similar document needs. Why re-create the wheel when one already exists?

For example, if you want to use data entry forms, you could create your own tags or you could use existing HTML form tags. Because HTML is a DTD, you could simply point to that existing DTD and use the HTML tags.

If you are exploring XML for your document set, ask around and see if anyone has created a DTD that might do the job for you. If you work in a larger company, check with your MIS department and any other departments that create documents. You might find that by pooling your efforts you can create a DTD that is useful beyond your immediate needs.

Other places to look for existing DTDs are trade associations, like the Graphic Communications Association (GCA) (its website is <http://www.gca.org>), the Organization for the Advancement of Structured Information Standards (OASIS) (its website is <http://www.oasis-open.org/>), or even the W3C. And, of course, don't forget to check your own industry associations' websites. In many cases, an existing DTD will fit your needs and there's no reason to re-invent the wheel. Many of the widely used SGML DTDs, such as DOCBOOK, are being converted to XML as well.

Roll Your Own

Another option is create your own DTD. DTDs are a series of definitions and statements stored in an ASCII text file with a .dtd extension.

The complexity of your DTD depends on your needs and inclinations. You can create a fairly straightforward DTD with a little thought and planning. You can also create a very complex DTD that nests data and even calls other DTDs.

Creating a DTD is a little like creating an HTML table—the basic table is quite easy to build and understand, but the application of tables can quickly grow complex and confusing to anyone but its creator.

Internalize

If you want to error check and create a valid XML document, but you have a very simple set of tags and attributes, you can place the DTD data inside your XML file instead of in a separate external file.

You can also use internal DTD data to override information in an external DTD. For example, suppose you want to require the use of an attribute for an element and the external DTD makes the attribute optional. You can create internal DTD data for that element. Your document will use the external DTD data—except for the element that you specify internally.

Reading a DTD

Even if you don't plan to build a DTD from scratch, being able to understand one is helpful. This section walks you through the process of reading a DTD.

DTDs typically contain elements and attributes. They may also have entities and notations. Sometimes you will also see marked sections which tell the parser to ignore or include certain sections of the DTD. This is a handy way to test DTDs or to use parts, but not all, of an existing DTD.

The best way to understand a DTD is to break it down into bite-sized pieces. The rules in this section can sound more complex than they actually are. Just remember to break everything down into its component parts; it then becomes easier to understand.

Read the Comments

Comments are non-displaying sections of a DTD. In a comment, the person who created the DTD left notes to make the DTD easier to understand.

Comments are very important! Take the time to read them. They can often help you make sense of what is going on. When you create a DTD yourself make sure to include them as well. They can help you remember what you've done and make it possible for others to follow your work more easily.

Comments begin with an open tag delimiter, exclamation mark, and two dashes (<!--) and close with two dashes and a close tag delimiter (-->). Between the markers is the comment.

For example, this comment notes what the element does:

```
<!-- The entree element describes the dish and what ingredients you need
to make it -->
```

The parser ignores everything between the open and close of the comment. It doesn't parse it; it doesn't process it in any way. It just skips over it.

Look for Basic Elements

An element is a piece of data within an XML file. In your XML file, you identify elements with tags. In a DTD you define what those elements are, giving them names and establishing relationships with other elements.

Elements can contain textual data, other elements, or both. Sometimes elements can be empty. Your element definition gives the element a name and describes what it can contain.

Each element in the DTD is defined through an element declaration. The element declaration is easy to find. It begins like this:

```
<!ELEMENT
```

Read the Element Declarations

The element declaration looks like this:

```
<!ELEMENT ENTREE (#PCDATA) >
```

It has three possible parts.

The first part—the open tag, exclamation mark, and word ELEMENT—announces that this statement defines an element.

The middle part—the name—is the name of the element. This is also the name of the tag that you enter in your XML document. Make sure you notice the capitalization of the name. XML is case sensitive, so you'll need to enter the tag in the XML document exactly as it is named in the DTD.

The last part—the information inside the parentheses or the keyword—is the data that the element contains. PCDATA means "parsed character data," which is basically textual information. This is a common type of data.

When you use this element in an XML document it will look like this:

```
<ENTREE>Pasta with sauteed eggplant and roasted garlic in a rich tomato
base</ENTREE>
```

Look for Parent/Child Relationships

When you set up rules for an element, you create a hierarchy. Some elements are at the top level; others are contained within elements. A top-level element is called a *parent element*. An element that is contained within the parent is called a *child element*.

In this element declaration, the food and quantity elements are children of the ingredients element:

```
<!ELEMENT INGREDIENTS (FOOD | QUANTITY)*>
```

This is how you would use it in an XML document:

```
<INGREDIENTS>
<FOOD>Flour</FOOD>
<QUANTITY>2 cups</QUANTITY>
</INGREDIENTS>
```

Look for the Element's Data

Elements may contain five types of data:

- They may contain any mix of content in any order.
- They may contain other elements in a particular order.
- They may contain textual data.
- They many contain text and specific elements.
- They may be empty.

Is It a Free-for-All Element?

The keyword ANY in an element declaration means that this element can contain literally anything. That anything could be text, elements, or totally random characters. As long as there is something between the open and close tags in the file, the ANY element meets the rule requirement.

You will seldom see ANY used in a finished DTD. Its primary use is as a placeholder for an element, when a DTD is being developed and tested.

For example, the <ABOUT> element can contain whatever you want to place between the open and close <ABOUT> tags:

```
<!ELEMENT ABOUT ANY>
```

Does the Element Contain Text?

If you see the keyword #PCDATA in the element description, you know that this element contains normal text. PCDATA means "parsed character data." Many elements fall into this category.

For example, the <FOOD> element must contain text between the open and close <FOOD> tags:

```
<!ELEMENT FOOD (#PCDATA)>
```

How Are Elements within Elements Related?

Some elements contain other elements. For example, lists typically don't contain text—they contain list elements.

If the elements are separated by commas, it means "use these child elements in this exact order." For example, the *foodlist* element must contain two other elements, *food* and *quantity*:

```
<!ELEMENT FOODLIST (FOOD, QUANTITY)>
```

Every time you use the tag *foodlist*, it will contain the *food* and *quantity* tags, like this:

```
<FOODLIST>
<FOOD>olive oil</FOOD>
<QUANTITY>3 tablespoons</QUANTITY>
</FOODLIST>
```

If the elements are separated by a bar it means you can use either of the elements. For example, this definition means that the *excuse* element contains either the *why* element or the *whynot* element:

```
<!ELEMENT EXCUSE (WHY | WHYNOT)>
```

Every time you use the tag in an XML file, it contains either why or why not, like this:

```
<EXCUSE>
<WHY>Because I said so.</WHY>
</EXCUSE>

<EXCUSE>
<WHYNOT>You'll shoot your eye out.</WHYNOT>
</EXCUSE>
```

When child elements are part of an element's data, the children are called by name inside the parent element's declaration, as you've just seen.

In addition, the child elements might also have symbols—an * or a + or a ?—next to them. These symbols define how many times the child element can be used within the parent element.

The element by itself. This means "use this element once and only once." For example, this declaration says that *foodlist* will contain only one use of the *food* element and nothing else:

```
<!ELEMENT FOODLIST(FOOD)>
```

It is used like this in an XML file:

```
<FOODLIST>
<FOOD>Cream cheese</FOOD>
</FOODLIST>
```

The plus sign (+) after an element. This means "use this element at least once, or as many times as you want." For example, this declaration says that *foodlist* must contain at least one—but maybe more—*food* elements.

```
<!ELEMENT FOODLIST (FOOD+)>
```

It is used like this in an XML file:

```
<FOODLIST>
<FOOD>Cream cheese</FOOD>
<FOOD>Confectioners sugar</FOOD>
</FOODLIST>
```

The question mark (?) after an element. This means "use this element once or don't use it at all." For example, this declaration says that *foodlist* must contain either exactly one *food* element and one *quantity* element or it may contain one *food* element and no *quantity* element.

```
<!ELEMENT FOODLIST (FOOD, QUANTITY?)>
```

It can be used like this in an XML file:

```
<FOODLIST>
<FOOD>Cream cheese</FOOD>
<QUANTITY>6 oz</FOODQUANTITY>
</FOODLIST>
```

Or, it can be used like this:

```
<FOODLIST>
<FOOD>Cream cheese</FOOD>
</FOODLIST>
```

The asterisk (*) after an element. This means "use this element as many times as you want, or omit it if you want." For example, this declaration says that *foodlist* may contain exactly one *food* element and any number of *comment* elements, from none to as many as the creator wants to put in:

```
<!ELEMENT FOODLIST (FOOD, COMMENT*)>
```

It can be used like this in an XML file:

```
<FOODLIST>
<FOOD>Cream cheese</FOOD>
<COMMENT>Use only real cream cheese</COMMENT>
<COMMENT>We recommend Philly brand</COMMENT>
<COMMENT>You'll get runny results if you use one of those weirdo low-fat varieties.</COMMENT>
</FOODLIST>
```

Or, it can be used like this:

```
<FOODLIST>
<FOOD>Cream cheese</FOOD>
</FOODLIST>
```

How Are Elements Grouped?

Remember high school algebra and how you thought you'd never find a use for it? If you are exploring DTDs, it is back in your life and it even has a purpose!

Yup, element declarations use groups, in combination with the comma, bar, asterisk, question mark, and plus sign, to create specific use rules. Look for the use of the parenthesis to indicate groups and the placement of declaration punctuation to define what the groups mean.

Here are some examples:

```
<!ELEMENT FOODLIST ((FOOD, QUANTITY)+)>
```

The foodlist element must have at least one, but maybe more, sets of *food/quantity* element combinations, like this:

```
<FOODLIST>

<FOOD>Cream cheese</FOOD>
<QUANTITY>6 oz</QUANTITY>
```

```
<FOOD>Confectioners sugar</FOOD>
<QUANTITY>2 cups</QUANTITY>

<FOOD>Vanilla</FOOD>
<QUANTITY>1 tsp.</QUANTITY>

</FOODLIST>
```

or like this:

```
<!ELEMENT FOODLIST ((FOOD, QUANTITY) | COMMENT)>
```

The *foodlist* element must have either one *food/quantity* combination or one *comment* element, like this:

```
<FOODLIST>

<FOOD>Cream cheese</FOOD>
<QUANTITY>6 oz</QUANTITY>

</FOODLIST>

<FOODLIST>
<COMMENT>These ingredients can be found in any grocery store's baking
section. Make sure you select only quality ingredients. </COMMENT>

</FOODLIST>
```

or like this:

```
<!ELEMENT FOODLIST ((FOOD, QUANTITY, COMMENT*)*)>
```

The *foodlist* element must may have at least one set of child elements. There could be many more. Each set must have one food child and one quantity child. It may also have none, one, or many comments, like this:

```
<FOODLIST>

<FOOD>Cream cheese</FOOD>
<QUANTITY>6 oz</QUANTITY>
<COMMENT>Don't use the low fat variety; the recipe won't work
correctly.</COMMENT>

<FOOD>Confectioners sugar</FOOD>
<QUANTITY>2 cups</QUANTITY>

<FOOD>Vanilla</FOOD>
<QUANTITY>1 tsp.</QUANTITY>
<COMMENT>Use real vanilla</COMMNENT>
<COMMENT>You may substitute 1/2 teaspoon orange extract if you
prefer.</COMMENT>

</FOODLIST>
```

As you can see, you can create some fairly specific rules. Don't be overwhelmed; just break the element declaration into small pieces, starting at the center of the group and working your way out. You might feel that you're back in Mr. King's ninth-grade algebra class, but you'll also be able to figure out how the author of the DTD wants you to use the elements.

Does the Element Use Both Text and Child Elements?

Elements can contain a mixture of text and child elements. Element declarations that contain both an element name and the keyword #PCDATA do exactly this. In a mixed content element, the keyword #PCDATA will always be the first item in the list of content.

For example, you could allow an element to mix text and multiple uses of the *quote* element:

```
<!ELEMENT COMMENTARY ((#PCDATA | QUOTE)*)>
```

You could use the *commentary* element like this in an XML document:

```
<COMMENTARY>The ride to Estes Park takes about two hours from Denver,
but it is a pretty ride. <QUOTE>Make sure you notice the snow in the
front range, off to your left</QUOTE>, says local tour guide Sam Long.
<QUOTE>And sometimes you can even see the snow swirling around on the
mountain tops!</QUOTE> he adds.
</COMMENTARY>
```

Is the Element Empty?

If you see the keyword EMPTY you know that this element does not contain data. The declaration for an empty element looks like this:

```
<!ELEMENT IMAGE EMPTY>
```

Typically, an empty element will get its values from attributes. For example, in HTML the src attribute gives a value to the empty <img> tag.

Look for Element Attributes

Attributes are a bit like adjectives, in that attributes modify elements. An attribute contains metadata about your element. This is information that may not actually be displayed, but that gives further meaning to the content of the element.

For example, you might have an element named *recipe*. You want to know who created the recipe, and you might want to sort the recipes by chef or to display only those recipes created by a certain chef. *Chef* is an attribute that further defines the element *recipe*, and it is entered as part of the element tag in the XML file:

```
<RECIPE chef="Rosalind Martin">BRAISED VEAL SHANKS</RECIPE>
```

The information contained in the *chef* attribute travels with that *recipe* element, across platforms, systems, and applications.

Attributes are created using attribute lists, which are part of a DTD. They typically follow the element declaration.

You can identify an attribute list by looking for this:

```
<!ATTLIST
```

Read the Attribute Lists

The attribute list looks like this:

```
<!ATTLIST element-name attribute-name attribute-type default-data >
```

It has five parts.

First is the declaration <!ATTLIST that starts every attribute list.

Second is the name of the element to which the attribute belongs.

Third is the name of the attribute.

Fourth is the type of attribute, which identifies the type of data it can contain.

Fifth is the default information, which tells what happens if no attribute value is specified.

This is what an attribute list looks like. In this example, it follows the element declaration for RECIPE. It creates three attributes. The first is *chef*; *chef* contains a text value and is not required. The second is *servings*; it may be one of the listed values, and if it is not entered it will take on a default value of "4–6." The third is *calories*; it contains textual data and is required.

Remember that attribute names are also case sensitive, so be sure to note the capitalization of the names in the ATTLIST. Keywords, such as CDATA and #REQUIRED must always be in all capital letters. In these examples, we are making the attribute names all lowercase.

```
<!ELEMENT RECIPE (FOODLIST | DIRECTIONS)*>
<!ATTLIST RECIPE chef CDATA #IMPLIED
                 servings (1-2|2-4|4-6|6-8|many) "4-6"
                 calories CDATA #REQUIRED>
```

What Element Does It Define?

Right after the ATTLIST declaration is the name of an element. This is the element that the attribute list defines.

Most DTDs will have one attribute list with multiple attributes for each element that has attributes. Typically the ATTLIST follows the element declaration. Look at the attribute list carefully to see what it defines and how many attributes are defined in the same declaration.

What Is the Attribute's Name?

Following the element name is the name of the first attribute declared in this list. This is the attribute name you type into the element tag in the XML file.

For example, this declares an optional attribute named *chef*:

```
<!ATTLIST RECIPE chef CDATA #IMPLIED>
```

What Is the Attribute Type?

Attributes can be one of several different types. The type describes the value that the attribute can contain.

Here are the most common types and what they mean:

- **CDATA.** CDATA means "character data." The value of this type of attribute can be any normal letter, number, or punctuation symbol. Many attributes are of the CDATA type.
- **NMTOKEN.** NMTOKEN means "name token." It is like CDATA, except a little more restricting. An NMTOKEN type attribute can have a value that is any combination of letters, numbers, and the symbols _, -, ., and :. It cannot begin with the letters "xml."
- **A list of options (option1 | option2 | option3).** The attribute must contain one of the listed values.
- **ID.** The keyword ID means that this attribute has an ID value that serves as a marker for this element.

IDREF. This keyword means that this attribute tells the element to refer to a pre-existing ID value in another element's attribute. ID and IDREF work together to let you do things like cross-reference elements.

ENTITY. This keyword says that the value of the attribute is an entity, rather than text. An entity is a value that has been defined elsewhere to have a particular meaning.

NOTATION. This keyword says that the value of the attribute is a notation. A notation is a description of how information should be processed. You could set up a notation that allows only numbers to be used for the value, for example.

The majority of the attributes you encounter, however, are likely to be either CDATA or a value list.

What Is the Attribute's Default?

It is important to notice the default value of the attribute. The default value has a strong effect on how the attribute is used and what values it might have if you don't use it in the XML tag.

#REQUIRED. This keyword says the attribute is mandatory. If you see the keyword #REQUIRED at the end of the ATTLIST definition, you know that this attribute must always be entered as part of the element tag. For example, the calories attribute must always be entered as part of the *recipe* element tag. If you omit the attribute, the parser will give you an error message:

```
<!ATTLIST RECIPE calories CDATA #REQUIRED>
```

#IMPLIED. This keyword says the attribute is optional. If you see the keyword #IMPLIED, you know that this attribute will be ignored unless it is included in the element tag. It won't take on any default values. For example, the *calories* attribute can now be used or not used at the document creator's option:

```
<!ATTLIST RECIPE calories CDATA #IMPLIED>
```

#FIXED. This keyword says the attribute is optional, but if it is used, it must always have a certain value. If you see the keyword #FIXED, you know that this attribute will always have the specified value when it is entered. For example, if calories is not used in the tag, the *calorie* attribute will not have any value for that instance of the element, but if it is used, its value will be "hundreds".

```
<!ATTLIST RECIPE calories "hundreds" #FIXED>
```

"value". If you see a value in quotation marks at the end of the definition, that value is the attribute's default value. If you don't enter the attribute in the element tag, the processor will assume this value for it. For example, the default value for the *servings* attribute of the recipe element is "4–6." Unless you specify otherwise, the processor will assume that the attribute has this value.

```
<!ATTLIST RECIPE servings (1-2|2-4|4-6|6-8|many) "4-6"
```

Explore an Example

Let's pause for a moment and examine what we've learned about elements and attributes. This is a relatively simple DTD.

The document type is "menu," and its structure resembles Figure 9.3. If you were to create its hierarchy, it would resemble Figure 9.4 and have these characteristics:

- MENU is the root element.
- MENU has multiple instances of the *meal* element.
- Each MEAL must include at least one of the following elements: APPS, ENTREE, DESSERT, BEVS, but it may include several. It could also include a COMMENT.
- Each MEAL also has an attribute named *type*, that can have a value of breakfast, lunch, dinner, brunch, or other.
- Each of the MEAL child elements includes a DESCRIPTION and/or a RECIPE element.
- The DESCRIPTION element contains text.
- Each RECIPE includes a TITLE, followed by a FOODLIST, followed by a STEP and/or a COMMENT.
- The FOODLIST includes a FOOD element, repeated one or more times.
- The FOOD element includes text and an optional QUANTITY element, repeated one or more times.
- The STEP and COMMENT elements contain text.
- The BEVLIST contains one or more BEV elements.
- The BEV element contains text.

```
MENU
  MEAL
    ENTREE                    DESERT
      DESCRIPTION               DESCRIPTION
      RECIPE                    RECIPE
        TITLE                     TITLE
        FOODLIST                  FOODLIST
          FOOD                      FOOD
          QUANTITY                  QUANTITY
          FOOD                      FOOD
          QUANTITY                  QUANTITY
        STEPS                     STEPS
        STEPS                     STEPS
        COMMENT                   COMMENT
        STEPS                     STEPS
        COMMENT                   COMMENT
        STEPS                     STEPS

  MEAL
    APPS                      ENTREE
      DESCRIPTION               DESCRIPTION
      RECIPE                    RECIPE
        TITLE                     TITLE
        FOODLIST                  FOODLIST
          FOOD                      FOOD
          QUANTITY                  QUANTITY
          FOOD                      FOOD
          QUANTITY                  QUANTITY
        STEPS                     STEPS
        STEPS                     STEPS
        COMMENT                   COMMENT
        STEPS                     STEPS
        COMMENT                   COMMENT
        STEPS                     STEPS
```

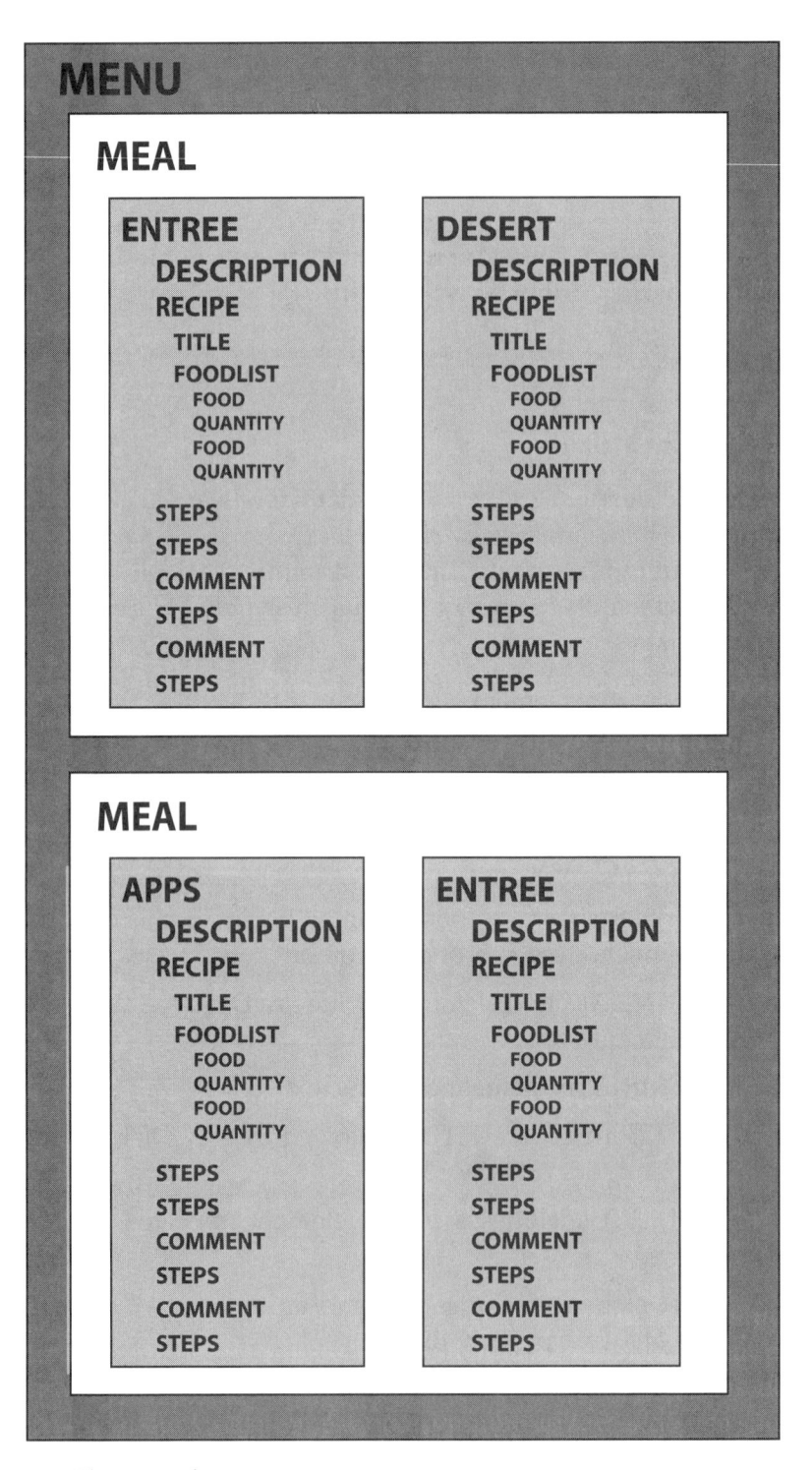

Figure 9.3 The menu document.

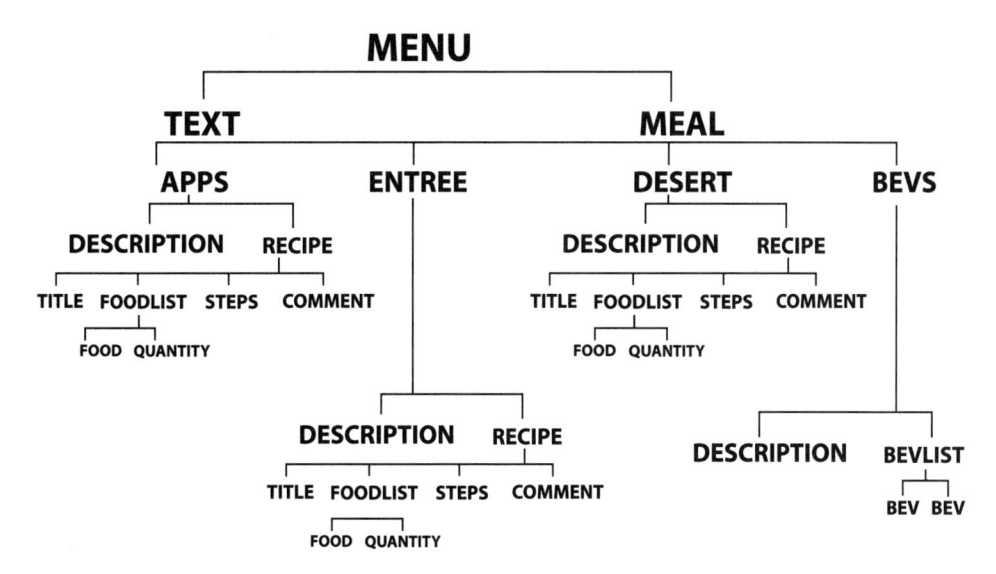

Figure 9.4 The menu document tree.

Here's the DTD:

```
<!-- The doctype is menu. Menu is the root element-->
<!ELEMENT MENU (MEAL*)>

<!-- each meal set might include appetizers, entree, dessert, and
beverage options, as well as a comment. The meal's type attribute
describes the meal as breakfast, lunch, dinner, or brunch.-->

<!ELEMENT MEAL ((APPS | ENTREE | DESSERT | BEVS)+ | (COMMENT)*)*>
<!ATTLIST MEAL type (breakfast | lunch | dinner | brunch | other)
"other">

<!ELEMENT APPS (DESCRIPTION | RECIPE)*>
<!ELEMENT ENTREE (DESCRIPTION | RECIPE)*>
<!ELEMENT DESSERT (DESCRIPTION | RECIPE)*>
<!ELEMENT BEVS (DESCRIPTION | BEVLIST)*>

<!-- The description contains a textual description of the meal course -
->
<!ELEMENT DESCRIPTION (#PCDATA)>

<!-- each recipe has a title, foodlist, steps, and comments and an
attribute value that contains the creating chef's first and last names -
->

<!ELEMENT RECIPE (TITLE, FOODLIST+, (STEP | COMMENT)*)>
```

```
<!ATTLIST RECIPE chef-first-name CDATA "firstname"

chef-last-name CDATA "lastname">

<!-- the recipe has a title, a foodlist, and several steps and comments
-->

<!ELEMENT TITLE (#PCDATA)>

<!ELEMENT FOODLIST (FOOD*)>

<!ELEMENT FOOD (#PCDATA | QUANTITY)*>

<!ELEMENT QUANTITY (#PCDATA)>

<!ELEMENT STEP (#PCDATA)>

<!ELEMENT COMMENT (#PCDATA)>

<!ELEMENT BEVLIST (BEV+)>

<!ELEMENT BEV (#PCDATA)>
```

Here is what an XML file using this DTD might look like:

```
<?xml version="1.0" standalone="no"?>
<!DOCTYPE MENU SYSTEM "menu.dtd">

<MENU>

<MEAL type="dinner">

<ENTREE>
<DESCRIPTION> Prime Rib with baby carrots in honey glaze.</DESCRIPTION>
<RECIPE chef-first-name="R" chef-last-name="Martin">
<TITLE>Prime Rib and Glazed Carrots</TITLE>
<FOODLIST>
<FOOD>
Cuts of Prime Rib
<QUANTITY>12 oz each</QUANTITY>
</FOOD>
<FOOD>
Baby carrots
<QUANTITY>10 per serving</QUANTITY>
</FOOD>
<FOOD>Butter</FOOD>
<FOOD>Honey</FOOD>
</FOODLIST>
<COMMENT>Prepare steak first. As steak is cooking stir fry
```

```
carrots.</COMMENT>
<STEP>Heat heavy flat bottom pan.</STEP>
<STEP>Season steak with salt or pepper to taste.</STEP>
<STEP>Immediately sear steak, 6 minutes on each side.</STEP>
<STEP>Meanwhile, melt butter in small heavy bottom pan.</STEP>
<STEP>When butter bubbles, add washed carrots and fry until tender,
about 4 minutes.</STEP>
<STEP>Add honey, 1 tsp for each serving of carrots.</STEP>
<COMMENT>You can vary the amount of honey for individual
tastes.</COMMENT>
<STEP>Stir until coated. Keep warm until turning out onto plate.</STEP>
</RECIPE>
</ENTREE>

</MEAL>

</MENU>
```

Check for Entities

In addition to elements and attributes, you may see items in the DTD that look like this:

```
%meal;
```

These are entities. An entity is a way of storing a set of data and then reusing it throughout the DTD. For example, many elements may use the same set of attributes. You could type the full ATTLIST for each element, or you could create the ATTLIST once and store it in an entity. Then, you would use the much shorter and easier-to-type entity instead of listing out the many different attribute definitions.

Entities inside a DTD look a little different from the entities you might have used in an XML file. In the XML file, the entities begin with an ampersand and end with a semi-colon (&entity;); in the DTD, they begin with the percent sign (%).

An entity definition looks like this:

```
<!ENTITY %  meal
"type (vegan | veggie | meat | other) #REQUIRED">
```

One odd thing about entities in a DTD is that when they are defined they include a space between the percent sign and the entity name— but when the entity is used, there is no space between the percent sign and the name.

Here's how an entity might look in use:

```
<!ATTLIST APPS %meal;>
<!ATTLIST ENTREE %meal;>
<!ATTLIST DESSERT %meal;>
```

The DTD creator could have typed the same attribute definition three times. Instead, with the entity, he or she just had to type it once and then refer back to it. When the document is processed, the entity will "expand" and the ATTLIST will have this meaning, as the contents of the entity replace the entity name:

```
<!ATTLIST APPS type (vegan | veggie | meat | other) #REQUIRED>
<!ATTLIST ENTREE type (vegan | veggie | meat | other) #REQUIRED>
<!ATTLIST DESSERT type (vegan | veggie | meat | other) #REQUIRED>
```

It makes for easier updating also. For example, to change the list of type values, you need only change it in one location and it will be in effect through all the ATTLIST declarations:

```
<!ENTITY % meal "type (vegan | veggie | meat | lo-fat | other)
#REQUIRED">
```

It will create this when processed, without requiring someone to edit every ATTLIST declaration.

```
<!ATTLIST APPS type (vegan | veggie | meat | lo-fat | other) #REQUIRED>
<!ATTLIST ENTREE type (vegan | veggie | meat | lo-fat | other)
#REQUIRED>
<!ATTLIST DESSERT type (vegan | veggie | meat | lo-fat | other)
#REQUIRED>
```

A heavy use of entities can make reading a DTD difficult at first glance, but once you understand how the entities are used, it can actually end up being cleaner, neater and an easier to read. If you're trying to decipher a DTD with a lot of entities, print out all the entity definitions, so you can have them in front of you as you figure out what the DTD says.

Check for Notations

In addition to elements, attributes, and entities you may see the keyword NOTATION or a <!NOTATION declaration.

The notation can be used for several different things. One of its uses is to point to some external file that might be used for processing a certain non-textual element, such as the location of a plug-in player. Another use is to point to external data processing definitions, such as one that defines a number set or a date use.

Summary

DTDs can very quickly become complex. Focusing on your needs and how to meet them can help you keep that complexity under control.

When you read a DTD, don't be overwhelmed by its scope. Break it down into portions and make sense of each, one by one. Sketch out the tree as you go if visual representations help you.

Keep lists of entities and externally referenced files.

Above all, don't let DTDs intimidate you. Although they may seem very complex, by breaking them down into understandable pieces you can turn them into a set of elements and a plan for your XML documents.

CHAPTER 10

Creating a DTD

A DTD is a set of rules about the elements you can use, the order in which you can use them, and the attributes the elements can or must have.

After you have completed your XML document, you will parse it. That is, you will use a tool that turns your XML tags into a structure and compares the structure to the rules specified in the DTD. This comparison process is called *validation*.

You can link your XML file to an external DTD file as part of the DOCTYPE definition. This external file is an ASCII file with the extension .dtd, like this:

```
menu.dtd
```

This chapter walks you through the technical process of creating a DTD—what code to use and how to build it. The next chapter, Chapter 11, "Under the Hood: A Simple XML Example," walks you through an example of the important thought process behind building a DTD—how to think about element and attribute names, how to create a DTD that is easy to use in production, and how to test a DTD.

The DTD Process

The process of creating a DTD can take days, weeks, or even months, depending on the complexity of the document structure. This sometimes painful DTD process is one reason that SGML was implemented in limited types of applications—the up-front effort just wasn't justified unless the project was big enough, complex enough, or specialized enough.

The XML DTD does not need to be nearly that complicated, however. Depending on your application, the DTD might be straightforward with a dozen or so tags—or it might have a hundred tags. Because XML extends to meet your needs, the complexity of the DTD is really up to you.

Sketch Out Your Structure

It is very helpful to sketch out your structure and make notes about your DTD plans *before* you start creating the DTD.

This up-front time is the most important part of the process.

- Look at your documents and understand what elements constitute them.
- Think about what attributes those elements might have and what sorts of values will fill the attributes.
- Think about how you want the elements to be used, when they should be required, and when they should nest within other elements.
- Think about what you want to name the elements—what will help with data entry, and what will make the tagging process easier.
- Look to see if portions of the DTD are repeated, such as sets of attributes. You might want to consider making entities for those sections.

The more time you spend understanding your data, the better your DTD will work.

Anyone can learn the mechanics of writing a DTD; the difficult part of the process is planning a meaningful, useful, and usable DTD.

Don't skimp on the time you spend exploring and understanding your data, your documents, and your document needs.

Start the File

The DTD is a basic ASCII text file. You can create it with any text editing tool.

Give the filename a .dtd extension.

Use Comments

DTDs can quickly become complex. That's why the comment is your friend. A comment is an area of the DTD that is not processed.

Comments begin with an open tag, an exclamation point, and two dashes, like this:

```
<!--
```

Then, you type the comment:

```
<!-- This is my comment about the element that follows
```

Finally, you close the comment with two dashes and an end tag, like this:

```
<!-- This is my comment about the element that follows -- >
```

You'll typically want to include a comment at the beginning that provides identification of the DTD, along with notes about any changes that may have been made to it. You'll note that in this example, the comment is many lines long, but it still begins and ends with the open and close comment markers:

```
<!--    World Science Full Length Article DTD version 2.1.0

     Copyright (c) World Science 1999-1999
     Permission to copy and distribute verbatim copies of this document
is granted, provided this notice is included in all copies, but changing
it is not allowed.

     Typical invocation:
     <!DOCTYPE art PUBLIC "-//ES//DTD full length article DTD version
2.1.0//EN" []>
-->

<!-- Revisions -->
<!-- 5/13/98     BDR          Add <abs> to Letter; version to 2.1.1 -->
<!-- 6/4/98      BDR          Added url tag to <cor>; version to 2.1.2 --
>
```

Set the Doctype Declaration

You'll begin and end the contents of the DTD with a DOCTYPE declaration, like this:

```
<DOCTYPE doctypename [
all the elements and other defintions go here
]>
```

Create Elements

To create your elements, some people suggest placing them in the DTD from the root to the leaf. That is, begin your DTD with the root element and define elements outward. This lets you build in a logical manner and refine elements later on in the same logical manner.

Other people suggest putting your elements in alphabetical order. This makes it quick and easy to find any given element at a later date.

Each organizational approach has its strengths. What is most important is not which organizational approach you take, but that you be consistent in what you do and organize your DTD in a way that is most comfortable for both you and your coworkers to follow and understand.

To create an element, follow these steps:

1. Begin the element declaration:

   `<!ELEMENT`

2. Type the element name. Remember, XML is case sensitive. The way you type the name here is the way you'll need to type it when you use it elsewhere in the DTD and in an XML document. Be sure to be consistent in the way you capitalize your element names. It doesn't matter if you use all lowercase, all uppercase, or some other combination. Just be sure you are consistent and that the case will make sense for the people who are creating the XML documents with these elements.

   `<!ELEMENT FOODLIST`

3. Enter the type of content that can be part of the element (there's more detail about this later):

   `<!ELEMENT FOODLIST (FOOD, QUANTITY)`

4. End the declaration with a closing tag:

   `<!ELEMENT  FOODLIST(FOOD, QUANTITY)>`

You see, creating the declaration is a straightforward process!

Element Rules

When you specify the content of the element, you create a rule for how that element is used.

Elements may contain five types of data:

- They may contain any mix of content in any order.
- They may contain other elements in a particular order.

- They may contain textual data.
- They many contain text and specific elements.
- They may be empty.

Free-Form Elements

Use the keyword ANY to make a rule that says an element can contain literally anything. That anything could be text, elements, or totally random characters. As long as there is something between the open and close tags in the file, the ANY element meets the requirement.

For example, the <ABOUT> element can contain whatever you want to place between the open and close <ABOUT> tags:

```
<!ELEMENT ABOUT ANY>
```

Although ANY is an option, it is unlikely that you will be using this keyword in your real DTD. After all, a DTD is about defining an element and if the element can contain anything, what is the point of defining it? The one time you might use ANY is when you are building and testing a DTD. For example, you might set all your elements to ANY and then focus on creating and testing them one at a time. You won't get any error messages with ANY, so you'll be able to focus on getting the element under construction nailed down just right.

Textual Elements

You can create elements that contain any combination of text. They cannot, however, contain other elements. Specify the use of textual content by giving the element a #PCDATA data value. Many elements fall into this category of rule.

For example this creates an element named DESCRIPTION that contains text:

```
<!ELEMENT DESCRIPTION (#PCDATA)>
```

In an XML document, <DESCRIPTION> can contain either text or be left empty, like this:

```
<DESCRIPTION>This breed of dog has hair that grows instead of fur that sheds.</DESCRIPTION>
```

Elements within Elements

Some elements contain other elements. For example, lists typically don't contain text; they contain list elements. The top-level element is the parent element. The elements contained with the parent are called child elements.

For example, the *employee* element can contain three child elements, *first-name*, *last-name*, and *phone*. It cannot contain textual content or any elements other than the ones specified:

    <!ELEMENT EMPLOYEE (FIRST-NAME, LAST-NAME, PHONE)>

As you can see, you specify child elements by calling them by name in the parent element declaration.

Element within Element Rules

Within DTDs you can make some rudimentary rules about how child elements are used.

You can define how often the child elements may be used, and you can specify the order in which they may be used.

Table 10.1 summarizes the different rules you can make about elements.

Use This Element Once and Only Once: (Element)

You can require that an element contain exactly one use of another element. You do this by listing that element as the data, like this:

    <!ELEMENT FOODLIST(FOOD)>

This sets a rule that says the element named *foodlist* can contain only one element, the element *food*. <FOOD> must always be the only content of <FOODLIST>. See Table 10.2 for some valid and invalid examples of (element).

Use This Element at Least Once or as Many Times as You Want: (Element+)

You can allow the same element to be used several times within the parent element. You do this by putting a plus sign after the child element.

    <!ELEMENT FOODLIST (FOOD+>

Now the <FOODLIST> element can contain multiple uses of the <FOOD> element. See Table 10.3 for some valid and invalid examples of (element+).

Table 10.1 Element Rules

MEANING	HOW TO SAY IT	VALID EXAMPLE OF USE	INVALID EXAMPLE OF USE

Use this element once and only once.	List the element by name:
	`<!ELEMENT EXAMPLE (SAMPLE)>`
		`<EXAMPLE>`
		`<SAMPLE>Green Tea</SAMPLE>`
		`</EXAMPLE>`
			`<EXAMPLE>`
			`<SAMPLE>Green Tea</SAMPLE>`
			`<SAMPLE>Black Tea</SAMPLE>`
			`</EXAMPLE>`

Use this element at least once or as many times as you want.	List the element, followed by a plus sign:
	`<!ELEMENT example (SAMPLE+)>`
		`<EXAMPLE>`
		`<SAMPLE>Green Tea</SAMPLE>`
		`<SAMPLE>Black Tea</SAMPLE>`
		`</EXAMPLE>`
			`<EXAMPLE>`
			`</EXAMPLE>`

Use this element once or don't use it at all.	List the element, followed by a question mark:
	`<!ELEMENT EXAMPLE (SAMPLE?)>`
		`<EXAMPLE>`
		`</EXAMPLE>`
		or
		`<EXAMPLE>`
		`<SAMPLE>Green Tea</SAMPLE>`
		`</EXAMPLE>`
			`<EXAMPLE>`
			`<SAMPLE>Green Tea</SAMPLE>`
			`<SAMPLE>Black Tea</SAMPLE>`
			`</EXAMPLE>`

Make this element optional or use it as many times as you want.	List the element, followed by an asterisk:
	`<!ELEMENT EXAMPLE (SAMPLE*)>`
		`<EXAMPLE>`
		`</EXAMPLE>`
		or
		`<EXAMPLE>`
		`<SAMPLE>Green Tea</SAMPLE>`
		`</EXAMPLE>`
		or
		`<EXAMPLE>`
		`<SAMPLE>Green Tea</SAMPLE>`
		`<SAMPLE>Black Tea</SAMPLE>`
		`</EXAMPLE>`
			`<EXAMPLE>`
			`<FRED>Green Tea</FRED>`
			`</EXAMPLE>`

continues

Table 10.1 Element Rules *(Continued)*

MEANING	HOW TO SAY IT	VALID EXAMPLE OF USE	INVALID EXAMPLE OF USE

Use the elements in this specific order.	List the elements, separated by commas, in the order in which they must appear:
	
	`<!ELEMENT EXAMPLE (SAMPLE, DESCRIPTION)>`
		`<EXAMPLE>`
		`<SAMPLE>Green Tea</SAMPLE>`
		`<DESCRIPTION>The essential element of tea, gently steeped.</DESCRIPTION>`
		`</EXAMPLE>`
			`<EXAMPLE>`
			`<DESCRIPTION>The essential element of tea, gently steeped.</DESCRIPTION>`
			`<SAMPLE>Green Tea</SAMPLE>`
			`</EXAMPLE>`

Use one or the other of the elements in the list.	List the possible allowed elements, separated by a bar:
	
	`<!ELEMENT EXAMPLE (SAMPLE | DESCRIPTION | COMMENT)>`
		`<EXAMPLE>`
		`<DESCRIPTION>The essential element of tea, gently steeped.</DESCRIPTION>`
		`</EXAMPLE>`
		
		or
		
		`<EXAMPLE>`
		`<SAMPLE>Green Tea</SAMPLE>`
		`</EXAMPLE>`
		
		or
		
		`<EXAMPLE>`
		`<COMMENT>Tea tastes good!</COMMENT>`
		`</EXAMPLE>`
			`<EXAMPLE>`
			`<SAMPLE>Green Tea</SAMPLE>`
			`<SAMPLE>Black Tea</SAMPLE>`
			`</EXAMPLE>`

Use elements this many times, in this order.	Combine order rules and number of use rules. For example, to make a list with many uses of one element and only one use of another, follow this convention:
	
	`<!ELEMENT example (sample+, description)>`
		`<EXAMPLE>`
		`<SAMPLE>Green Tea</SAMPLE>`
		`<SAMPLE>Black Tea</SAMPLE>`
		`<DESCRIPTION>Green tea and Black tea are two preparations of the same plant.</DESCRIPTION>`
		`</EXAMPLE>`
			`<EXAMPLE>`
			`<SAMPLE>Green Tea</SAMPLE>`
			`<DESCRIPTION>Green tea is gently steeped.</DESCRIPTION>`
			`<DESCRIPTION>Green tea is very common in Japan.</DESCRIPTION>`
			`</EXAMPLE>`

Table 10.2 Valid and Invalid Examples of (Element)

VALID EXAMPLE OF USE	INVALID EXAMPLE OF USE

`<FOODLIST>`
`<FOOD>Pound Cake</FOOD>`
`</FOODLIST>`
	`<FOODLIST>`
	`<FOOD>Pound Cake</FOOD>`
	`<FOOD>Stawberry Glaze</FOOD>`
	`</FOODLIST>`

Use This Element Once or Don't Use It at All: (Element?)

You can create a rule that allows an element to contain a child element one time or to omit the child element totally. You do this by putting a question mark after the optional element, like this:

```
<!ELEMENT FOODLIST (FOOD, QUANTITY?)>
```

In use, the <FOODLIST> element must contain one <FOOD> element and it may or may not contain one <QUANTITY> element. See Table 10.4 for some valid and invalid examples of (element?).

Make This Element Optional or Use It as Many Times as You Want: (Element)*

You can make a child element optional and allow it to be repeated. Do this by putting an asterisk after the child element:

```
<!ELEMENT FOODLIST (FOOD*)>
```

The <FOODLIST> element may have zero, one, or many <FOOD> elements. See Table 10.5 for some valid and invalid examples of (element*).

Use the Elements in This Specific Order: (Element1, Element2)

In your DTD, you can use the element declaration to define the order in which elements must appear.

Table 10.3 Valid and Invalid Examples of (Element+)

VALID EXAMPLE OF USE	INVALID EXAMPLE OF USE

`<FOODLIST>`
`<FOOD>Pound Cake</FOOD>`
`<FOOD>Stawberry Glaze</FOOD>`
`</FOODLIST>`
	`<FOODLIST>`
	`</FOODLIST>`

Table 10.4 Valid and Invalid Examples of (Element?)

VALID EXAMPLE OF USE	INVALID EXAMPLE OF USE

`<FOODLIST>`
`<FOOD>Pound Cake</FOOD>`
`</FOODLIST>`
or
`<FOODLIST>`
`<FOOD>Pound Cake</FOOD>`
`<QUANTITY>2 slices</QUANTITY>`
`</FOODLIST>`
	`<FOODLIST>`
	`<QUANTITY>2 slices</QUANTITY>`
	`</FOODLIST>`

If you want them to appear in a specific order, list them in order separated by commas.

```
<!ELEMENT FOODLIST (FOOD, QUANTITY)>
```

In this example, the *food* element must always come first. The *quantity* element must always come second. If your XML document lists them in the reverse order, you'll see an error when you validate your file. See Table 10.6 for some valid and invalid examples of (element1, element2).

Use One or the Other of the Elements in the List: (Element1 | Element2 | Element3)

You can allow any of the elements from a list to be used by listing the elements and separating them with bars.

```
<!ELEMENT FOODLIST (FOOD | QUANTITY | COMMENT)>
```

Table 10.5 Valid and Invalid Examples of (Element*)

VALID EXAMPLE OF USE	INVALID EXAMPLE OF USE

`<FOODLIST>`
`<FOOD>Pound Cake</FOOD>`
`</FOODLIST>`
or
`<FOODLIST>`
`<FOOD>Pound Cake</FOOD>`
`<FOOD>Ice Cream</FOOD>`
`</FOODLIST>`
	`<FOODLIST>`
	`We all like to eat food.`
	`</FOODLIST>`

Table 10.6 Valid and Invalid Examples of (Element1, Element2)

VALID EXAMPLE OF USE	INVALID EXAMPLE OF USE

`<FOODLIST>`
`<FOOD>Pound Cake</FOOD>`
`<QUANTITY>2 slices</QUANTITY>`
`</FOODLIST>`
	`<FOODLIST>`
	`<QUANTITY>2 slices</QUANTITY>`
	`<FOOD>Pound Cake</FOOD>`
	`</FOODLIST>`

The *foodlist* element must contain a single use of one of the following: the *food* element, the *quantity* element, or the *comment* element. See Table 10.7 for some valid and invalid examples of (Element1 | Element2 | Element3).

Use Elements This Many Times, in This Order: (Element1, Element2)*

Group items, and add the repeat symbols to the group to create rules that repeat sets of child elements.

For example:

```
<!ELEMENT FOODLIST (FOOD, QUANTITY)*>
```

The *foodlist* element may contain multiple sets of *food* and *quantity* child elements. See Table 10.8 for some valid and invalid examples of (Element1, Element2)*.

Group Elements (Group)

You can group elements in various ways to create the rules you want. You use parentheses to define the groups.

Table 10.7 Valid and Invalid Examples of (Element1 | Element2 | Element3)

VALID EXAMPLE OF USE	INVALID EXAMPLE OF USE

`<FOODLIST>`
`<FOOD>Pound Cake</FOOD>`
`</FOODLIST>`
 	
`<FOODLIST>`
`<COMMENT>Yum, Yum. Strawberry shortcake!</COMMENT>`
`</FOODLIST>`
	`<FOODLIST>`
	`<FOOD>Pound Cake</FOOD>`
	`<COMMENT>Yum, Yum. Strawberry shortcake!</COMMENT>`
	`</FOODLIST>>`

Table 10.8 Valid and Invalid Examples of (Element1, Element2)*

VALID EXAMPLE OF USE	INVALID EXAMPLE OF USE

`<FOODLIST>`
`<FOOD>Milk</FOOD>`
`<QUANTITY>1 cup</QUANTITY>`
`<FOOD>Brown sugar</FOOD>`
`<QUANTITY>1 tsp, or to taste</QUANTITY>`
`</FOODLIST>`
	`<FOODLIST>`
	`<QUANTITY>1 cup</QUANTITY>`
	`<FOOD>Milk</FOOD>`
	`</FOODLIST>`

For example, this lets you use one or more food elements, followed by a single comment. You can repeat this combination over and over:

```
<!ELEMENT FOODLIST (FOOD+, COMMENT)*>
```

It might be used like this in an XML file:

```
<FOODLIST>
<FOOD>Milk</FOOD>
<FOOD>Oatmeal</FOOD>
<FOOD>Dried cranberries</FOOD>
<FOOD>Brown sugar</FOOD>
<COMMENT>Put oatmeal into a bowl, then add warm milk. Stir in a small
handful of dried cranberries. Sprinkle with brown sugar to
taste.</COMMENT>
</FOODLIST>
```

For example, the *foodlist* element must have either one *food/quantity* combination or one *comment* element.

```
<!ELEMENT FOODLIST ((FOOD+, QUANTITY) | COMMENT)>
```

In an XML file, either of these examples would be acceptable:

```
<FOODLIST>
<COMMENT>This is an empty dish so there is no food.</COMMENT>
</FOODLIST>

<FOODLIST>
<FOOD>Milk</FOOD>
<FOOD>Oatmeal</FOOD>
<QUANTITY>1/2 cup</QUANTITY>
</FOODLIST>
```

Table 10.9 Valid and Invalid Examples of Mixing Text and Elements

VALID EXAMPLE OF USE	INVALID EXAMPLE OF USE

`<ENTREE>`
`And for tonight's dining`
`pleasure we bring you glazed ham.`
`</FOODLIST>`
or
`<ENTREE>`
`<FOOD>Baked honey ham</FOOD>`
`<QUANTITY>3 slices</QUANTITY>`
`</FOODLIST>`
	`<ENTREE>`
	`And for tonight's dining pleasure`
	`we bring you this meal.`
	`<FOOD>Baked honey ham</FOOD>`
	`<QUANTITY>3 slices</QUANTITY>`
	`</FOODLIST>`

Mixing Text and Specific Elements

Using the rules for elements, you can specify a mixture of text and element data within a parent element.

For example, you could allow an element to contain either text or a combination of two elements:

```
<!ELEMENT ENTREE (#PCDATA | (FOOD, QUANTITY))>
```

See Table 10.9 for some valid and invalid examples of mixing text and element data within a parent element.

In this example, you could mix many uses of text and the *quote* element. See Table 10.10 for some valid and invalid examples of this.

```
<!ELEMENT MENU ((#PCDATA | QUOTE)*)>
```

Table 10.10 Valid and Invalid Examples of Mixing Text and the Quote Element

VALID EXAMPLE OF USE	INVALID EXAMPLE OF USE

`<MENU>`
`Let's start at the very beginning.`
`And what would a meal be without a`
`starting course? <QUOTE>A lite`
`bite to whet the appetite,</QUOTE>`
`says our chef-in-residence, who`
`brings you today's menu.`
`</MENU>`
	`<ENTREE>`
	`And for tonight's dining pleasure`
	`we bring you this meal.`
	`<FOOD>Baked honey ham</FOOD>`
	`<QUANTITY>3 slices</QUANTITY>`
	`</FOODLIST>`

Empty Elements

You can specify that an element is empty by using the EMPTY keyword, like this:

```
<!ELEMENT IMAGE EMPTY>
```

Empty elements typically have attributes that receive a value. The value might be a nonbinary value, like a .gif file, or simply some data that you want to be able to record and work with later.

Create Attribute Lists

As you define elements, you can also define attributes for the elements. You do this through attribute lists.

Attribute lists define the name, data type, and default value (if any) of each attribute associated with an element.

This is what an attribute list looks like. This example defines two attributes for the element *entree*.

```
<!ELEMENT ENTREE ((#PCDATA), FOOD, QUANTITY)>
<!ATTLIST ENTREE meal (breakfast|lunch|dinner|brunch) "dinner"
          chef (#CDATA) #REQUIRED>
```

To create an attribute list, follow these steps:

1. After the element definition, start an attribute list definition:
   ```
   <!ATTLIST
   ```
2. Type the name of the element for which you are creating the attribute list. Remember to use the same capitalization for the element name that you used when you created the element:
   ```
   <!ATTLIST ENTREE
   ```
3. Type the name of the first attribute. Attributes are also case sensitive. In this example we are making all attribute names lowercase:
   ```
   <!ATTLIST ENTREE meal
   ```
4. Type the type of data that will go into the attribute. CDATA is character data and is one of the most common types of data. A list of allowable values surrounded by parentheses—(value1 | value 2 | value 3)—is another common data type.
5. Determine this attribute's default information. For example, if the attribute is required—that is, if you must always enter it as part of the element—type the keyword #REQUIRED. If you want to assign the attribute a default value, which will be used if no other value is specified, enter that value in quotes.

6. Repeat for each attribute you want as part of the element. You can string together many attribute definitions as long as they are all assigned to the same element. In addition, you can use the same attribute name on different elements. For example, the ENTREE and the APPS element could both have a *type* attribute where you can give the dish a vegetarian or meat value.

7. End the attribute definition with a closing delimiter, >:

    `<!ATTLIST ENTREE meal (breakfast|lunch|dinner|brunch|other) "other">`

Attribute Values

Attributes may have a number of different value types. Table 10.11 summarizes the different value types you can define for an attribute.

Make This Attribute Contain Anything (CDATA)

You can require that an attribute's value be any unparsed character data. Do this by entering the keyword CDATA to define the attribute type.

Table 10.11 Attribute Values

MEANING	HOW TO SAY IT
Make this attribute contain anything.	Use the keyword CDATA: `<!ATTLIST EXAMPLE name CDATA>`
Make this attribute contain only common letters and numbers and the symbols _, -, ., and :. Do not let the value begin with the letters XML.	Use the keyword MNTOKEN: `<!ATTLIST EXAMPLE name MNTOKEN>`
Make this attribute contain one of a set of predefined values.	Include the group of possible values: `<!ATTLIST EXAMPLE name (value1 | value2 | value3)>`
Make this attribute contain a unique ID value.	Include the keyword ID: `<!ATTLIST EXAMPLE name ID>`
Make this attribute reference an existing unique ID value.	Include the keyword IDREF: `<!ATTLIST EXAMPLE name IDREF>`
Make this attribute contain an entity.	Include the keyword ENTITY: `<!ATTLIST EXAMPLE name ENTITY>`
Make this attribute contain a value that refers to a notation.	Include the keyword NOTATION: `<!ATTLIST EXAMPLE name NOTATION>`

This is one of the most common types of attributes.

With CDATA, the value can even be empty—you could enter an attribute like this, and it would be considered valid:

```
<FOOD type="">
```

Make This Attribute Contain Almost Anything (NMTOKEN)

You can narrow the range of allowable values a little by using the name token, NMTOKEN value.

The attribute's value can be any combination of letters, numbers, and the symbols _, -, ., and :. It cannot begin with the letters "xml," and it cannot be empty.

Make This Attribute Contain a Predefined Set of Values (value1|value2|value3)

You can require that an attribute's value be one of a specified set of values. Enter each value, separated by a bar. The entire set should be surrounded by parentheses, like this:

```
<!ATTLIST FOOD type (protein|dairy|carbo|sugar)>
```

This is the second of the most common types of attribute.

When you are creating a predefined list, it is always a good idea to have "other" as one of the options. That way, you'll always have a graceful way to mark the unexpected exception.

Make This Attribute Contain a Unique ID Value (ID)

You can use the attribute to assign the element a unique ID value. This value can be referenced later by other elements or other applications, such as style sheets.

Do this by using the keyword ID:

```
<!ATTLIST FOOD name ID>
```

ID and IDREF work together to create intradocument linked references.

Make This Attribute Contain a Reference to an ID Value (IDREF)

You can use the attribute to refer to another element's ID value. Do this by using the keyword IDREF:

    <!ATTLIST FOOD name IDREF>

ID and IDREF work together to create intradocument linked references.

Make This Attribute Contain an Entity Value (ENTITY)

You can require that the attribute value contain an entity. Do this by using the keyword ENTITY:

    <!ATTLIST FOOD warning ENTITY>

Make This Attribute Contain a Notation Value (NOTATION)

You can require that the attribute value contain a notation value. Do this by using the keyword NOTATION:

    <!ATTLIST FOOD image NOTATION>

Attribute Defaults

You can set a number of default values when you define an attribute list. Table 10.12 summarizes the different defaults you can define for an attribute.

Make This Attribute Required (#REQUIRED)

You can require that an attribute be included as part of the element. You do this by appending the keyword #REQUIRED at the end of that attribute's definition:

    <!ATTLIST FOOD category (meat|fish|dairy|grain|veggie|fruit|sweets)
    #REQUIRED>

This requires that every use of the food element includes a category attribute, like this:

    <FOOD category=fish>Salmon</FOOD>.

Table 10.12 Attribute Defaults

MEANING	HOW TO SAY IT
Make this attribute required.	Include the keyword #REQUIRED: `<!ATTLIST example attribute name (CDATA) #REQUIRED>`
Ignore this attribute if it isn't included.	Include the keyword #IMPLIED: `<!ATTLIST example attribute name (CDATA) #IMPLIED>`
If this attribute is used, it must have this value.	Include the keyword #FIXED and the required values: `<!ATTLIST example attribute name #FIXED value>`
If this attribute is not used, assume it has this value.	Include the default value after the allowable data: `<!ATTLIST example attribute name (coffee|tea|milk) "coffee">`

Ignore This Attribute if It Is Not Included (#IMPLIED)

You can tell the processor to ignore this attribute unless it is included in the element. You do this by appending the keyword #IMPLIED:

```
<!ATTLIST FOOD category (meat|fish|dairy|grain|veggie|fruit|sweets)
#IMPLIED>
```

If you don't include the category attribute, no default value will be automatically assumed. It will be as if the attribute just doesn't exist for that element.

If This Attribute Is Used, It Must Have This Value

You can set a single predefined value for an attribute. If the attribute is used, it must have this value. You do this by appending the keyword #FIXED:

```
<!ATTLIST FOOD category CDATA#FIXED "now due">
```

If This Attribute Is Not Used, Assume It Has This Value ("XXX")

You can set a default value for an attribute. If the attribute is not specified otherwise, it is assumed to have this value. You do this by appending the value to the end of the attribute's definition:

```
<!ATTLIST FOOD form (fresh | frozen| canned) "fresh">
```

This will assign the value "fresh" to the form attribute of the food element unless you specify otherwise.

Entities

An entity is a short word that refers to other data. It is a bit like a macro.

Instead of entering the other data, you can simply enter the entity; when the document is processed, the processor replaces the entity with the data it represents.

Entities are convenient ways to use a shortcut for repeatedly entering data, for inserting data whose value might change over time, or for inserting data that might be difficult or awkward to type. For example, in an XML document you might use an entity for an ASCII key series. It is far easier to remember & for ampersand, than a number code.

There are two types of entities: general and parameter. You use a general entity in an XML document; these were discussed in Chapter 8, "Other Pieces of an XML Document."

You use parameter entities in a DTD. Parameter entities may be either internal or external. That is, the replacement text can be stored in the DTD or in some other file.

In addition, parameter entities must be parsed and cannot be unparsed. That is, they must contain textual data that is processed rather than a GIF or other nontextual data type.

Declaring Entities

Before you can use an entity you must first declare it. Declaring an entity assigns the entity a name and value.

A parameter entity can contain either information you define in the DTD or information from an external file. For example, you could point from one DTD to another to reuse the same entity.

An entity declaration can define the entity as either a text or a nontext file, such as a .JPG or .GIF file.

To declare an entity, follow these steps:

1. Type the entity declaration:
   ```
   <!ENTITY
   ```
2. Type a space, followed by a percent sign:
   ```
   <!ENTITY %
   ```
3. Type another space, followed by the name of the entity:
   ```
   <!ENTITY % info
   ```
4. Type the value of the entity, surrounded by quotation marks:
   ```
   <!ENTITY % info
   "name CDATA #REQUIRED
   gender (m | f) "f"
   color (red | fawn | merle | black)"
   ```
5. End the declaration with an end tag symbol:
   ```
   <!ENTITY % info
   "name CDATA #REQUIRED
   gender (m | f) #REQUIRED
   color (red | fawn | merle | black |other) #REQUIRED"
   ```

One thing to notice about entities in a DTD is that when they are defined there is a space between the percent sign and the entity name—when the entity is used, though, there is no space between the percent sign and the entity name.

If your entity refers to data that is outside the DTD, the definition will include a pointer to the other data, like this:

```
<!ENTITY % para SYSTEM "http://myurl.com/common.dtd">
```

Using Entities

It is quite simple to use an entity. Simply enter the entity name, preceded by a percent sign and followed by a semi-colon, like this:

```
<HOUND (NAME)>
<!ATTLIST HOUND %info;>

<WORKING (NAME)>
<!ATTLIST WORKING %info;>

<COMPANION (NAME)>
<!ATTLIST COMPANION %info;>
```

When the DTD is processed, the entity will be expanded. In this example, %info; will be replaced with a set of attribute data, which was defined in the *info* entity declaration.

```
<HOUND (NAME)>
<!ATTLIST HOUND breed CDATA #REQUIRED
gender (m | f) "f"
color (red | fawn | merle | black | other) "other">

<WORKING (NAME)>
<!ATTLIST WORKING breed CDATA #REQUIRED
gender (m | f) "f"
color (red | fawn | merle | black | other) "other">

<COMPANION (NAME)>
<!ATTLIST COMPANION breed CDATA #REQUIRED
gender (m | f) "f"
color (red | fawn | merle | black | other) "other">
```

Notations

A notation can be used for several things. Often it describes a particular type of data. It can also be used to provide processing information.

To declare a notation, follow these steps:

1. Begin the declaration like this:
   ```
   <!NOTATION
   ```

2. Enter the name of the notation:
   ```
   <!NOTATION JPG
   ```

3. Enter information about where additional data for this notation is found and close the tag:
   ```
   <!NOTATION JPG SYSTEM "jpgview.exe">
   ```

Ignore and Include Sections

You can turn "on" and "off" sections of the DTD. When the processor encounters an *ignore* section it skips over it. This can be a handy way to test a DTD.

To create an *ignore* section, place this notation around the section you want marked as *ignore*:

```
<![IGNORE [the section you want ignored]]>
```

The same structure is used for sections you want to mark as *include*:

```
<![INCLUDE[the section you want to mark as include]]>
```

Creating an Internal DTD

Most of this chapter has focused on reading and creating an external DTD. You can, however, make DTD declarations directly inside your XML file. You do this as part of your DOCTYPE declaration.

Example

Here's an example of simple DTD data; it declares one root element, named *recipe*, and five child elements: *title, comment, foodlist, food*, and *quantity*. It also contains one attribute, *chef*.

```
<!ELEMENT RECIPE (TITLE?, COMMENT?, FOODLIST)>
<!ELEMENT TITLE (#PCDATA)>
<!ATTLIST TITLE chef CDATA #IMPLIED><!ELEMENT COMMENT (#PCDATA)>
<!ELEMENT FOODLIST (FOOD, QUANTITY)*>
<!ELEMENT FOOD (#PCDATA)>
<!ELEMENT QUANTITY (#PCDATA)>
]>
```

Here's how your document might look using this structure:

```
<?xml version="1.0"?>
<RECIPE>
<TITLE chef="Rosalind Martin">Holiday Turkey Broth</TITLE>
<COMMENT>What a great use for your Thanksgiving or Christmas
bird!</COMMENT>
<FOODLIST>
<FOOD>
Turkey carcass
</FOOD>
<QUANTITY>
One
</QUANTITY>
<FOOD>
Water
</FOOD>
<QUANTITY>
12 cups or enough to cover carcass.
</QUANTITY>
</FOODLIST>
</RECIPE>
```

When the document is processed, the parser checks to see if you obeyed the rules outlined in the DOCTYPE definition—your internal DTD. It makes sure that *title* tags contain text. It makes sure your *foodlist* contains at least one if not more pairs of *food* and *quantity* tags.

Using the DOCTYPE Declaration

You can specify DTD data inside your DOCTYPE declaration in your XML file. It is a good idea to do this only for simple element, attribute, and entity declarations. If you are creating complex definitions, it is better to create and manage them in a separate DTD file.

To create elements, attributes, and entities within your DOCTYPE declaration, follow these steps:

1. Start the DOCTYPE by typing:

   `<!DOCTYPE`

2. Type the name of the type of document you are creating:

   `<!DOCTYPE myfile`

3. Type an open square bracket:

   `<!DOCTYPE myfile [`

4. On the next line, start the first element or entity declaration:

   `<!ELEMENT`

5. Complete the element or entity.

6. When you are done, end the DOCTYPE definition with a closing square bracket and a closing delimiter:

   `]>`

Summary

DTDs can very quickly become complex. Focusing on your needs and how to meet them can help keep that complexity under control.

When you build a new DTD, make sure you budget time to do the critical up-front research. Determine the needs of your documents, your data, and your process. Don't start the mechanics of creating the DTD until you understand what you need from the document structure. Get input from other people who will be using or creating your documents.

As you make the DTD, use comments to note what you are doing. Someone else is likely to be reading your DTD, and comments are a good way to help them understand what you've done and to document your work.

Above all, don't let DTDs intimidate you. With some planning, you can make them manageable, not something that manages you.

Under the Hood: A Simple XML Example

This section walks you through the thought process of turning document data into an XML file displayed in a web page. The example is a very, very simple set of information, but we will use it to discuss the thought that goes into planning a set of XML tags and/or creating a DTD, and into creating a CSS file for displaying the data.

Our Example

Our example is an online newsletter called *The Community Cooker*. (In case you haven't gathered by now, the author of this book enjoys cooking . . . and eating!) Figure 11.1 shows what one displayed issue might look like.

Understanding Your Data

The very thing you need to do is scope out your data. Take a look at the type of document you want to produce and explore the different pieces that combine to create the document.

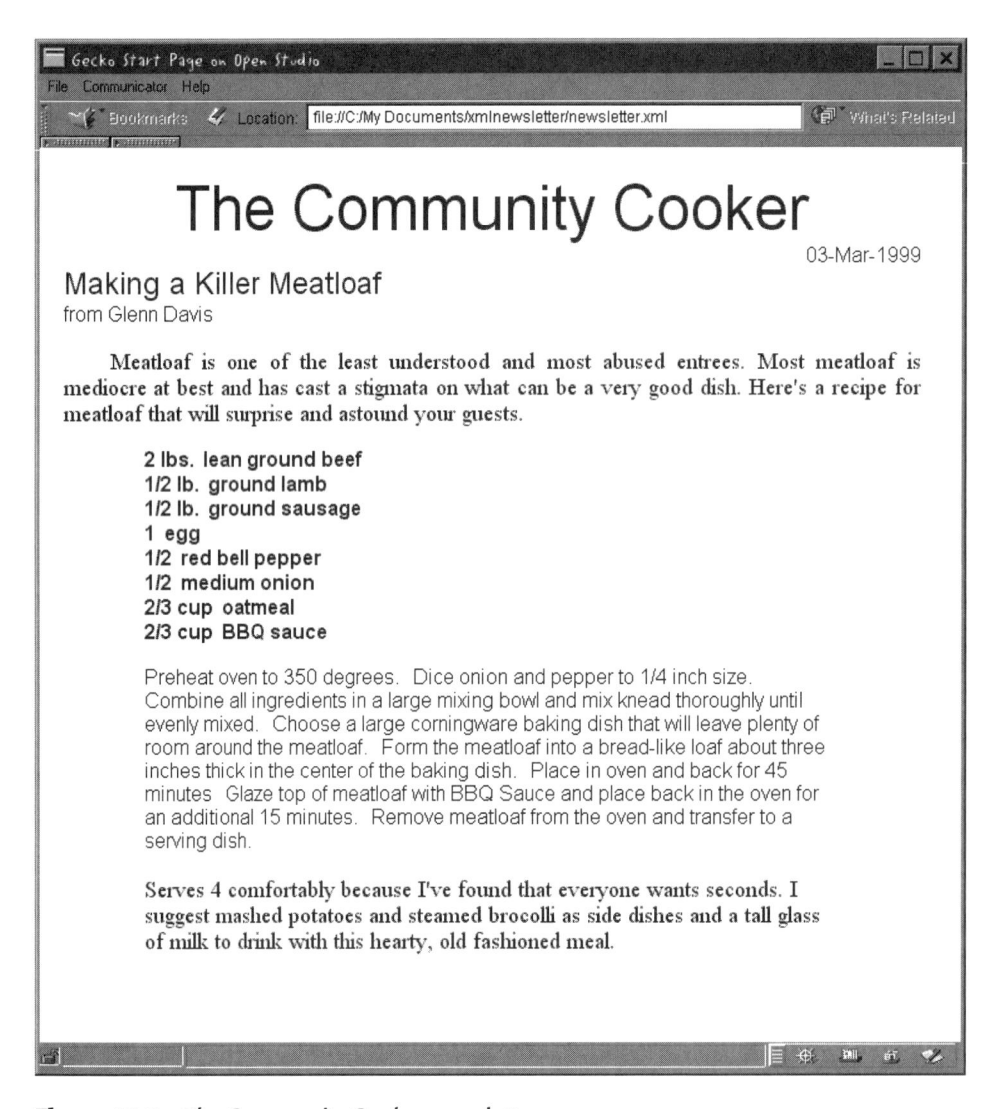

Figure 11.1 *The Community Cooker* newsletter.

This isn't always an easy task nor one that can be done in a few short minutes. Factor in time to spend looking at your documents and talking to the people who create and use them.

Ask yourself these questions:

- What big pieces appear in all documents?
- What smaller pieces appear in each of the bigger pieces?
- Do similar subsets appear in each bigger piece?

- What options do the pieces have?
- What sort of information would you like to store about each piece?
- Do you want to require that this piece always be part of the document?
- How many times do you want this piece to appear?

What Top-Level Pieces Appear?

In our make-believe newsletter, *The Community Cooker*, we always have three major pieces: a masthead that contains the name of the newsletter, a date that contains the issue number, and an article. These three pieces are top-level elements. We can start to draw the tree as shown in Figure 11.2.

What Smaller Pieces Appear?

Now that we know the big picture, we start to dig a little deeper. Remember, this is a very simplistic example, and your own applications will likely be more complex than this.

We examine each of the top-level elements to determine what they contain. In our example, we find that *masthead* contains some text that is the name of the newsletter. We find that *date* contains some text that describes the date of the newsletter. And we find that *article* has a headline, a byline, some paragraphs, and some recipes.

We end up with a tree like the one shown in Figure 11.3.

Exploring a little deeper, we see that the *recipe* element contains additional elements. Each recipe element has a *title, foodlist, steps*, and *comments*. And, going one step further, we see that the *foodlist* element contains *food* elements, and *food* elements contain *text* and *amount* elements, and finally, *amount* elements contain *text*. Figure 11.4 shows the tree with branches and leaves.

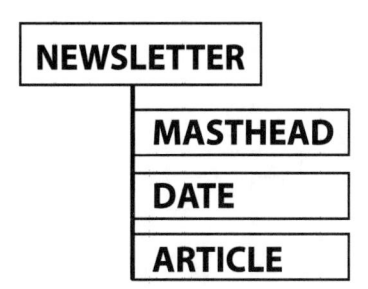

Figure 11.2 Top-level elements.

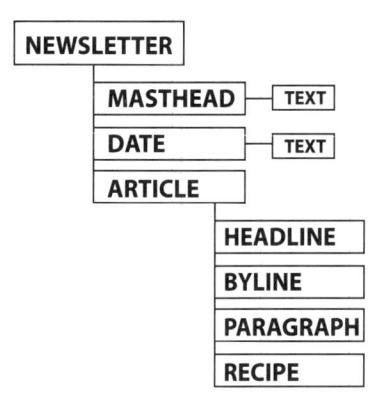

```
NEWSLETTER
    ├── MASTHEAD ── TEXT
    ├── DATE ── TEXT
    └── ARTICLE
            ├── HEADLINE
            ├── BYLINE
            ├── PARAGRAPH
            └── RECIPE
```

Figure 11.3 Next-level elements.

Do Similar Subelements Appear?

As you look at your data, are there similar subelements? For example, do you have subheads within three different types of elements? Identify the similar elements.

In our mythical newsletter, we have a headline in the article and a title in the recipe that are similar. And we have paragraphs that are similar to comments.

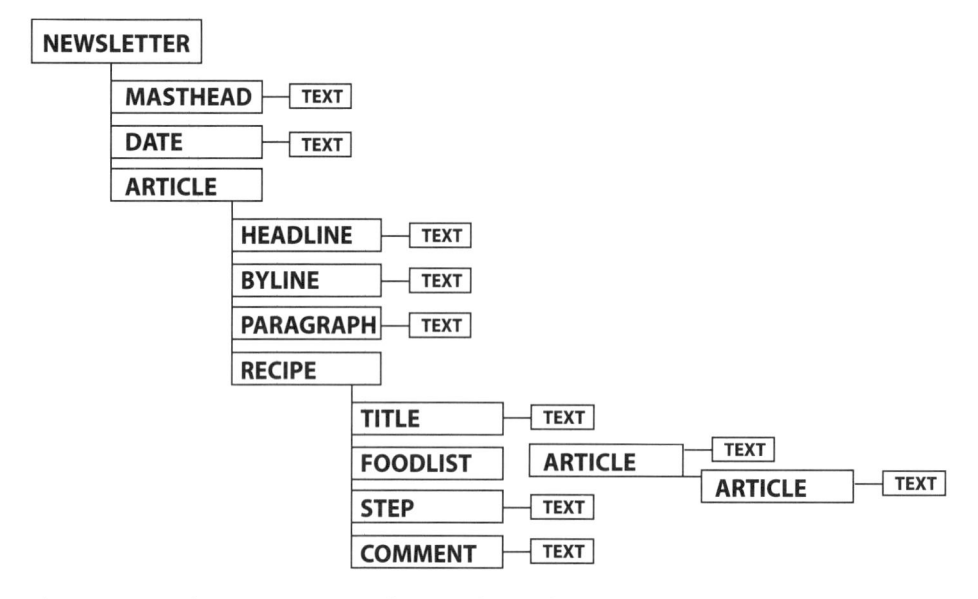

```
NEWSLETTER
    ├── MASTHEAD ── TEXT
    ├── DATE ── TEXT
    └── ARTICLE
            ├── HEADLINE ── TEXT
            ├── BYLINE ── TEXT
            ├── PARAGRAPH ── TEXT
            └── RECIPE
                    ├── TITLE ── TEXT
                    ├── FOODLIST ── ARTICLE ── TEXT
                    │                  └── ARTICLE ── TEXT
                    ├── STEP ── TEXT
                    └── COMMENT ── TEXT
```

Figure 11.4 *The Community Cooker* newsletter document tree.

Ask yourself if any of these subelements are really the same thing, but just appear as branches from a different parent element. You can have one *paragraph* element and use it in different places in your document tree.

What Information Do You Want to Know about the Element?

Look at each of your elements and ask yourself what sorts of additional data you want to collect about the element. For example, do you want to know its type or its author or its date of creation or its place of origin? As you think about this additional data, you are exploring the attributes that you want to give each element.

In our newsletter, we will keep it simple and give an attribute to just one element, *recipe*. That attribute will be *type,* and there will be seven possible answers: *meat, eggs/dairy, bread, cookie, dessert, veggie,* and *other*. It is always a good idea to have an *other* option to cover any contingency.

Do You Want to Require That the Element Be Used?

Look at the different child elements you have defined, and ask yourself which of these must be in each and every parent element, and which you may or may not use depending on the circumstances.

For example, every single newsletter must have a masthead, a date, and at least one article. Every article must have a headline and paragraphs, but it may or may not have a byline.

How Many Times Do You Want This Piece to Appear?

How many times can each child appear in the parent element? Can it appear only once? Can it appear many times? You have four choices for the frequency at which an element can appear:

- Once and only once (name)
- Either not at all or only once (name?)
- At least once, but maybe many times (name+)
- Not at all, only once, or many times (name*)

In our newsletter, there must be exactly one use of the masthead. There may be multiple uses of the article. An article can have either one or no bylines.

DTD Building

Now you have some sense of your data and a working list of the elements that make up your document. You are beginning to understand the relationship between those elements and how the elements are used in the document.

The next step is to codify those elements into a DTD.

Even if you are not planning to create a DTD, read this section anyway. The thought you give to naming elements will apply to either a well-formed or a valid XML document.

Understand the People

To create a good DTD you, of course, need to understand your data. That alone won't make a usable and useful DTD. You also must understand the people who will be creating your documents and what they need and expect in their document production processes.

You can make all the DTDs in the world and each might be an incredible creation, worthy of high praise. If they are too difficult to learn, too complex to implement, or just too much of a pain, though, no one will use them well and correctly—or they may not even use them at all. If a DTD is only half applied, or if it is ignored, all your work is in vain.

That's why it is critical to look at your authoring and production processes and prepare a DTD and/or a set of element tags that make sense not only for your data but also for your staff.

A number of groups will be part of the process:

- The authors who create the content
- The editors who mark it up
- The designers who plan how to display it
- The programmers who might process it in different ways

Each of these groups has a set of expectations, some guidelines that they are accustomed to following, and some ways of working. Take time to understand what is used and what does and doesn't work. Incorporate that information into your decisions on document structure and element and attribute naming conventions.

For example, do your editors use cryptic, but very short, tags? Or do they prefer descriptive terms? Are there industry-specific phrases already in use to describe elements? Byline, masthead, and cutline might make sense to someone with a newspaper background but feel alien to someone with a mathematical text background. Are certain sections treated as separate elements already? Are people using comment lines to add data about elements? If so, that data might become an attribute of the element instead.

Use the existing culture where it makes sense, and see if a structured approach can also fix problems and frustrations. Don't foist a different perspective on people. Or, if you do, prepare yourself for a long learning curve as people adjust not only to XML elements, but also to alien, nonintuitive names.

Look also at the tools being used—what programs do the authors create in? In what programs does the markup happen? (The companion website to this book, <http://www.projectcool.com/guide/xml>, contains links to some of the vendors who are working in the XML production space.) Different programs offer different options that might shape your approach.

Here's a very important item to remember when you're preparing to implement an XML solution: XML isn't about creating a single document once—it is about having a whole system that works well, consistently, and repeatedly.

The more intuitive you can make the DTD, the easier it will be for people to use and the better it will be applied to your documents.

Learning Curve

The size of a DTD is less important that how quickly and easily people can learn to use it. This is one of the lessons taught by SGML: It was so difficult to master, and its DTDs were so complex, that it was never deployed in the larger publishing market. HTML, in contrast, had a fairly short learning curve and could be implemented immediately.

As you think about your document structure, make sure you aren't creating such a complex beast that it will drown in its own juices!

You can do a number of things to help the learning curve.

Be Logical

In defining your structure, your element, and your element's attributes, add a dollop of common sense. Create logical units that hold together as a whole.

Be Consistent

Use naming conventions consistently. If you have three distinct types of lists, use the word list as part the name of each. Which is easier to remember, a series of list elements like this:

```
Foodlist
Shoppinglist
Guestlist
```

or a set of words that don't give you any clue that each element is a list:

```
Foods
Thingstobuy
People
```

Words that might or might not end in an "s" can be a special problem—is it <food> and <guests>? Or <foods> and <guests>? Or <foods> and <guest>? Pick one approach and use it throughout.

Here's a place where case sensitivity comes into play as well. As with plural/singular choices, follow one rule for using lowercase and uppercase in all your names. Make all your element names begin with a capital letter. Or make them all uppercase. Or make them all lowercase. Don't mix and match, making some names all uppercase and others uppercase and lowercase. If you do that, you'll end up with people spending lots of time trying to remember if it should be <FOOD> or <Food> or <guests> or <GUEST>.

It is easier for people to memorize one specific rule that applies to 15 tags than it is to memorize variations on 6 different but similar tags.

Be Clear

There's really no need to be cryptic. Create element names that make sense to the people who will be using them. Don't arbitrarily assign new names to things—if people call a headline a hed, use *hed* as your tag. If they call headline a heading, use *heading*.

Don't Create Typing Bears

In the quest to be clear, don't create long things to type. Try to use names that are easy to remember, make sense, and don't add extra keystrokes.

Use Attributes Carefully, Defaults Well

Don't create endless attribute lists for your elements. First, if you need 10 attributes it probably indicates that something is off-kilter with your document structure and that perhaps some of those attributes should really be treated as elements. Second, no one is going to remember 10 different attributes.

For example, in our newsletter, we could have made <AMOUNT> an attribute of <FOOD>. But when we looked at it more closely, we realized that amount is really a separate element, not just something that modifies food. It is a child of <FOOD>, but we might want to work with <AMOUNT> separately. It is also easier to enter as a separate element and easier to create a display style for it as an element.

Be especially consistent in your naming of attributes. For example, if you want to allow for several types of recipes and several types of articles and several types of steps, don't give recipe the attribute *type* and article the attribute *kind* and step the attribute *variety*. All that will do is ensure that no one ever gets the attribute right. Use *type* or *kind* or *variety* throughout. And make attribute values consistent, too. Have you ever wavered over whether HTML table data is valigned *middle* or *center*? We have, too. (It's valign="middle" and align="center".)

Use defaults in ways that help the production process. If the value is almost always "yes," then create a default that is "yes." Don't force people to think about the attribute except for the exceptions.

Document What You've Done

Documenting your work sounds obvious, but it is often a forgotten step. You write your DTD. You move on to other things. Who outlines the entry process for the authors? Who creates the tag list for the editors? Who tells the designer what the style sheet needs to support? Who lets the database folks know what elements they may need to process?

Take the time, either as you build your DTD or after it is complete and tested, to record what you've done. List the elements in use, when they are used, and what their attributes are.

Our Example DTD

This code shows what a simple DTD for *The Community Cooker* newsletter might look like. The comments help document its structure and use.

```
<!-- Newsletter for Community Cooker DTD version 1.1.0

     Copyright (c) Food Folks 1999
     Permission to copy and distribute verbatim copies of this document
is granted, provided this notice is included in all copies. Please do
not change this document.

     Typical invocation:
     <!DOCTYPE newsletter SYSTEM "newsletter.dtd">
```

```
-->

<!DOCTYPE newsletter [

<!ELEMENT NEWSLETTER (masthead, date, article+)>

<!-- each newsletter must include exactly one masthead and one date
element. It must include at least one article. It may include more-- >

<!ELEMENT MASTHEAD (#PCDATA)

<!ELEMENT DATE (#PCDATA)>

<!ELEMENT ARTICLE (HEADLINE, BYLINE?, (PARA | RECIPE)*>

<!-- Each article must have one headline. It has an optional byline. It
may have any number of paragraphs and/or recipes -- >

<!ELEMENT HEADLINE (#PCDATA)>

<!ELEMENT HEADLINE BYLINE (#PCDATA)>

<!ELEMENT PARA (#PCDATA)>

<!ELEMENT RECIPE (TITLE?, FOODLIST, (STEP | COMMENT)*>
<!ATTLIST RECIPE type (meat | eggs/dairy | bread | cookie | dessert |
veggie | other) "other">

<!-- the recipe has an optional title, a foodlist, and several steps
and/or comments. It has one attribute called type, and type can be one
of the seven choices. If the value isn't entered it will use the default
value, other-->

<!ELEMENT TITLE (#PCDATA)>

<!ELEMENT FOODLIST (FOOD+)>

<!--the foodlist has at least one but possibly more food elements>

<!ELEMENT FOOD (#PCDATA | AMOUNT)*>

<!-- the food element has text and the amount element uses zero, one, or
multiple times in any order>

<!ELEMENT AMOUNT (#PCDATA)>

<!ELEMENT STEP (#PCDATA)>

<!ELEMENT COMMENT (#PCDATA)>
]>
```

Making the XML Document

Now you have the DTD ready. You've documented it and have a list of every element and how each is used. The next step is to begin to apply the DTD to documents.

Some XML editors let you define element tags so that entering them becomes a simple exercise in picking the tag name from a list. You can also hand code XML. However you do it, you'll end up with a document that resembles the following code.

Notice how the element tags are used. Note also that the XML file is connected to both a DTD and a style sheet.

If you don't want to validate your document—that is, if you don't want to error check it against a DTD—you can create a well-formed document without the DTD reference.

The exercise you went through in thinking about elements, attributes, and tag names is still important, however. Just because you won't be validating against a DTD doesn't mean you can enter random, unplanned tags and expect to get a good result.

Here's a sample issue of *The Community Cooker*, in its XML file. The indents just make it easier to see the elements and the document tree:

```xml
<?xml version="1.0" standalone="yes"?>
<?xml-stylesheet href="newsletter.css" type="text/css"?>

<!DOCTYPE newsletter SYSTEM "newsletter.dtd">
<NEWSLETTER>
      <MASTHEAD>The Community Cooker</MASTHEAD>
<DATE>03-Mar-1999</DATE>
<ARTICLE>
<HEADLINE>Making a Killer Meatloaf</HEADLINE>
<BYLINE>from Glenn Davis</BYLINE>
<PARA>Meatloaf is one of the least understood and most abused entrees.
Most meatloaf is mediocre at best and has cast a stigma on what can be a
very good dish. Here's a recipe for meatloaf that will surprise and
astound your guests.
</PARA>
<RECIPE>
<FOODLIST>
<FOOD>
<AMOUNT>2 lbs.</AMOUNT>lean ground beef
</FOOD>
<FOOD>
<AMOUNT>1/2 lb.</AMOUNT>ground lamb
</FOOD>
<FOOD>
```

```
<AMOUNT>1/2 lb.</AMOUNT>ground sausage
</FOOD>
<FOOD>
<AMOUNT>1</AMOUNT>egg
</FOOD>
<FOOD>
<AMOUNT>1/2</AMOUNT>red bell pepper
</FOOD>
<FOOD>
<AMOUNT>1/2</AMOUNT>medium onion
</FOOD>
<FOOD>
<AMOUNT>2/3 cup</AMOUNT>oatmeal
</FOOD>
<FOOD>
<AMOUNT>2/3 cup</AMOUNT>BBQ sauce
</FOOD>
</FOODLIST>
<STEP>Preheat oven to 350 degrees.</STEP>
<STEP>Dice onion and pepper to 1/4 inch size.</STEP>
<STEP>Combine all ingredients in a large mixing bowl and knead
thoroughly until evenly mixed.</STEP>
<STEP>Choose a large Corningware baking dish that will leave plenty of
room around the meatloaf. </STEP>
<STEP>Form the meatloaf into a bread-like loaf about three inches thick
in the center of the baking dish.</STEP>
<STEP>Place in oven and bake for 45 minutes</STEP>
<STEP>Glaze top of meatloaf with BBQ sauce and place back in the oven
for an additional 15 minutes.</STEP>
<STEP>Remove meatloaf from the oven and transfer to a serving
dish.</STEP>
<COMMENT>Serves 4 comfortably because I've found that everyone wants
seconds. I suggest mashed potatoes and steamed broccoli as side dishes
and a tall glass of milk to drink with this hearty, old-fashioned
meal.</COMMENT>
</RECIPE>
</ARTICLE>
</NEWSLETTER>
```

Parsing the Document

Now you're ready to test your document and see if it has been formed correctly. In the future, the parser will likely be part of your XML file creation tool, and parsing may take place as you create the document. For example, Figure 11.5 shows how *The Community Cooker* looks in a simple shareware editor from Microsoft called XML Notepad. It has been parsed (using a

Under the Hood: A Simple XML Example **225**

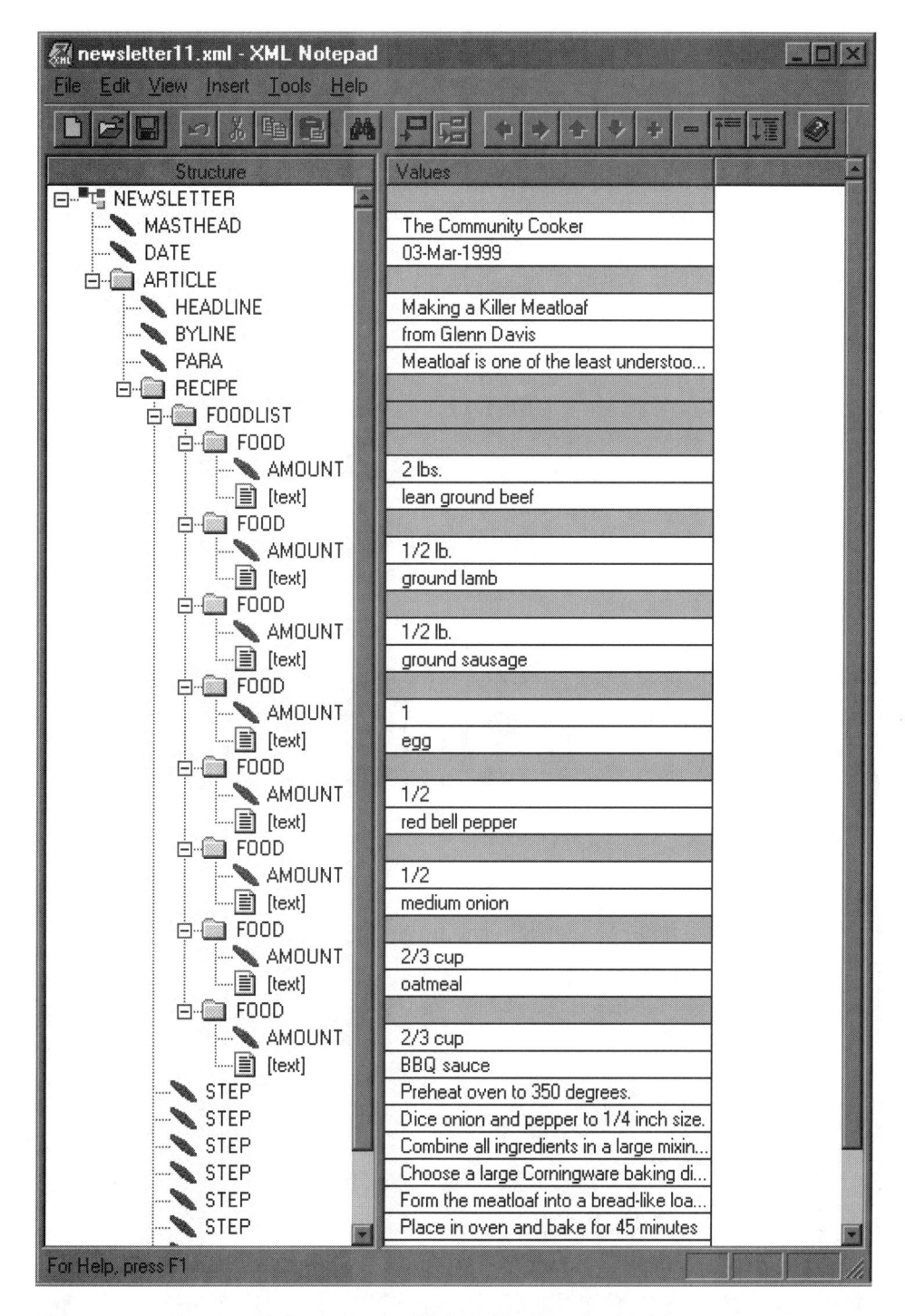

Figure 11.5 The parsed document as displayed in XML Notepad.

built-in non-validating parser) and presented visually based on the document structure.

Newly developed browsers may have non-validating parsers built in as well. For example, the 5X browsers will parse an XML document displaying it, and any errors will not be displayed in the document.

For now, however, you'll probably want to use an external parser to test your file after you've created it and before you display or publish it.

You can download a number of parsers. Most of these parsers run under Windows 95 or UNIX. Many are C programs, a few are Java applications, and one is even based in JavaScript.

In addition, both the W3C and Brown University's Scholarly Technology Group offer online parsers to which you can submit the URI and parse the file. Figure 11.6 shows Brown University's online parser, which is located at <http://www.stg.brown.edu/service/xmlvalid/>.

The companion website to this book at <http://www.projectcool.com/guide/xml> contains links to a number of both nonvalidating and validating parsers created in a variety of programming styles.

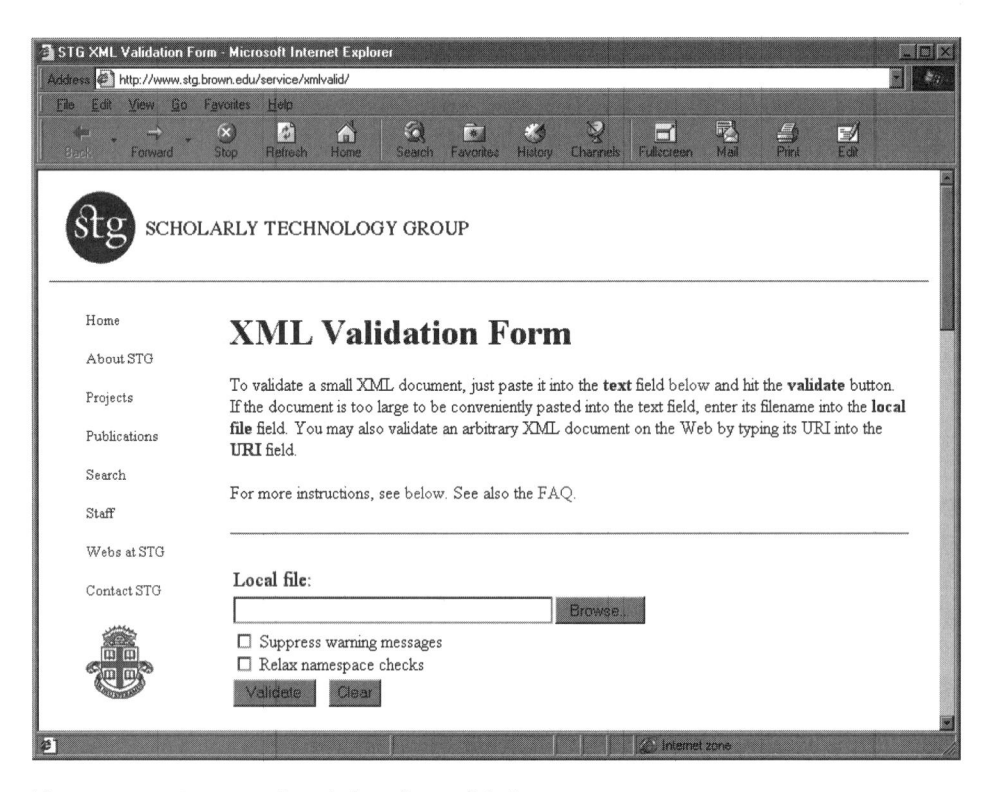

Figure 11.6 Brown University's online validating parser.

You'll need to try a few parsers and find the one that you like the best.

Whichever parser you select, the parsing process is similar. You specify which file or text to parse. The parser checks the material to be sure it conforms to XML syntax rules. Then, if it is a validating parser, it checks to be sure the document also conforms to the DTD rules. If there are any errors, the program will flag them and display cryptic error messages. If the document is correctly structured, the program will tell you that the file is OK.

Don't be surprised or dismayed if you receive error messages when you parse your DTD or document. XML syntax is very specific; one missing quotation mark or one missed delimiter can set off a cascade of errors. Almost everyone makes errors and the process of debugging a DTD can take days. The process of debugging an XML document can take minutes—or hours. Don't be discouraged, especially at first.

Use the error flags and messages as a clue to where the problem may lie. Look at your files line by line. When you find an error, fix it, save your file, and parse the file again. Many errors may be fixed with one correction.

In the future, there will be better tools for both creating and parsing XML documents and DTDs. These tools will help you make fewer errors while creating the document and also provide better feedback during the parsing process. Once the technology has matured a little and the tools catch up, the entire error checking and correction process will become faster and easier.

Displaying the Document

You've tested your document, and it conforms to XML syntax and/or your DTD. The next step is to prepare the style sheet.

Of course, because display and data creation are independent functions, you or your designers would have been creating style sheets for one or more displays while the XML file was being written. You could, that is, if you remembered to document the element tags and what they are used for! There's another good argument for recording your work.

In the future, XSL may well be your style tool of choice. As of this writing, however, CSS is your best bet.

You'll create a style sheet that tells a web browser how to display the elements in the document. We created a style sheet using the following code.

```
NEWSLETTER {font-family: Times New Roman;
     font-size: 14pt;
     color: black;
     margin: 1em;
     display: block;
}
```

```
MASTHEAD {
  display: block;
  font-family: arial;
  font-size: 36pt;
  text-align: center;
}

DATE {
  display: block;
  font-family: arial;
  font-size: 12pt;
  text-align: right;
}

HEADLINE {
  display: block;
  font-family: arial;
  font-size: 18pt;
  text-align: left;
}

BYLINE {
  display: block;
  font-family: arial;
  font-size: 12pt;
  text-align: left;
}

PARA {
  display: block;
  text-align: justify;
  margin-top: 1em;
  text-indent: 2em;
}

RECIPE {
  display: block;
  margin-left: 4em;
  margin-right: 4em;
  margin-top: 1em;
  font-size: 12pt;
  font-family: arial;
}

FOODLIST {
  display: block;
  margin-bottom: 1em;
}
```

```
FOOD {
    display: block;
    font-weight: bold;
}

AMOUNT {
    display: inline;
    margin-right: 1ex:
}

STEP {
    display: inline;
    margin-right: 1ex:
}

COMMENT {
    display: block;
    font-family: times new roman;
    font-size: 14pt;
    margin-top: 1em;
}
```

This is what the style code does. You can see the result in Figure 11.7.

NEWSLETTER is the root element. The style assigns the root element display font values of 14 point, Times New Roman. It makes the text black and it places it 1 em from the margin of the containing block, the web browser page. It sets the element as a display type block, which means it stands on its own rather than being displayed inline, within the contents of a block. All the branch and leaf elements will inherit the display values, unless they are overridden in the specific element display definition in the style sheet. For example, all the text will be black unless the color property receives a different value.

The style sheet assigns the MASTHEAD element font display values of 36 point Arial, centered. The text will be black because it inherits that value from the root element, NEWSLETTER. MASTHEAD is also a block element.

The style sheet assigns the DATE element font values of 12 point Arial, flush right. DATE is a block element.

The ARTICLE element does not need display information as it contains other elements and is itself displayed.

The style sheet assigns the HEADLINE element font values of 18 point Arial, flush left. HEADLINE is a block element.

The style sheet assigns the BYLINE element font values of 12 point Arial, flush left. BYLINE is a block element.

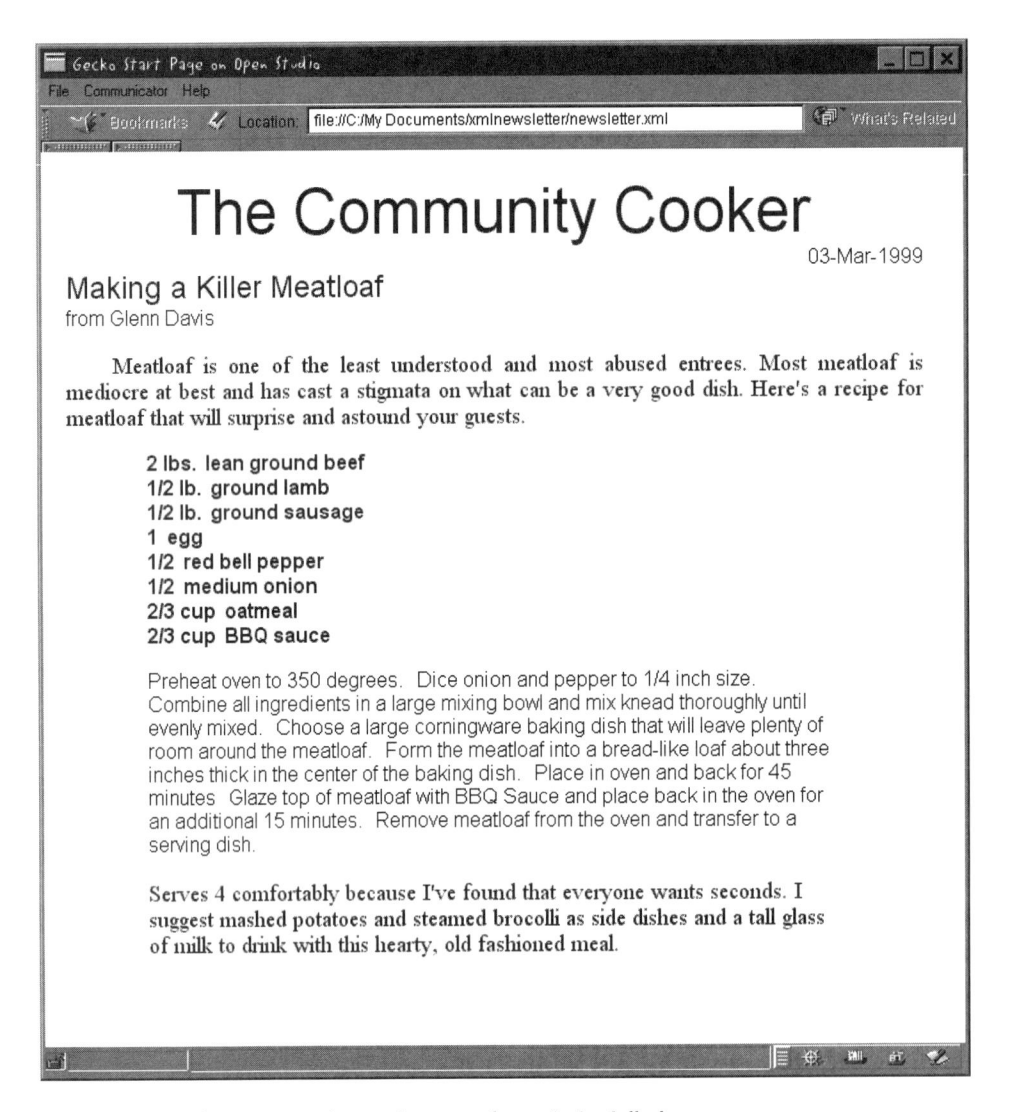

Figure 11.7 *The Community Cooker* newsletter in its full glory.

The style sheet lets the PARA element inherit font values from the root element NEWSLETTER—14 point Times New Roman. (TITLE is PARA's parent, but it contains no font display information, so the style sheet looks up one more level, to NEWSLETTER.) PARA is a block element. The PARA block will be placed 1 em down from its containing block. Text within the PARA block will be indented 2 em spaces. The text will be justified.

- **The style sheet assigns the RECIPE element font values of 12 point Arial.** RECIPE is a block element. The recipe block will display 4 em spaces in from both the right and left of the containing block, and 1 em space down from the top of the containing block.

- **The style sheet lets the FOODLIST element inherit its font values from its parent, RECIPE—12 point Arial.** FOODLIST is a block element. The block displays with a 1 em margin between its bottom and the containing block.

- **The style sheet lets the FOOD element inherit its font values from its parent, FOODLIST, but adds a display value of bold. FOOD is a block element.**

- **The style sheet lets the AMOUNT element inherit its font values from its parent, FOOD—12 point Arial bold.** AMOUNT is an inline element and is displayed inline as part of its containing block.

- **The style sheet lets the STEP element inherit its font values from its parent, RECIPE—12 point Arial.** It is not bold because the *font-weight: bold* property and value is part of FOOD, not RECIPE. STEP is an inline element. Each STEP element is displayed inline as part of its containing block, not as a separate visual unit.

- **The style sheet assigns the COMMENT element font values of 14 point Times New Roman.** COMMENT is a block element, with a 1 em margin at its top, relative to its containing block.

Summary

Although this example was quite simple, you can get a sense of the time and effort involved in creating a useful and meaningful document structure and DTD and/or element and attribute set.

Up-front planning is important. Even for a well-formed document, you should spend some time looking at the document structure and thinking about the elements and element attributes that make sense. If you're using entities, plan them well and use them in a way that makes your work easier.

Remember, it is more important to be intuitive and consistent in naming your elements than it is to worry about counting how many you're defining. The name of the game here is to make it easy for people to create documents.

Take the time to think about your data. Take the time to understand the needs of the system's users. If you remember common sense and keep the process of building an XML file in mind in both cases, you'll end up with a tag set that is useful, usable, and powerful. And you'll begin to tap the benefits of the XML document.

Chapter 12

Displaying an XML Document

If you're a designer, you not only want to structure a document but you also want to display it in an attractive and effective way. XML alone will not let you do this.

XML is about separating structure from format. An XML file doesn't inherently know anything about how to display itself. At first glance, this might seem like a gaping hole, but in practice, it is a great strength.

XML doesn't deal with style, but it does contain a great deal of information about the document and its elements. This combination, when used in conjunction with outside style rules, gives you enormous flexibility in how you visually present the document.

XML's approach lets you use appropriate style tools to focus on display without worrying about having to edit or change the actual content of the document. You can easily change, update, test, and deliver multiple display versions—all based on the same underlying content file. You can display the data in different ways, and you can display different portions of the document.

Even better, you can make the presentation contingent on what a user does. You can sort things on the fly, without drawing on server resources. For example, you could let readers see the recipes for all entrees that are vegetarian and display them in alphabetical order.

A Tiny Taste

To get a flavor of how style rules, combined with XML documents, can give you a great deal of power, let's look at a sample demo document that Netscape created.

This demo works with the under-development version of the Mozilla 5X browser. (You can find pointers to the browser and this demo from the companion website to this book, <http://www.projectcool.com/guides/xml>).

Figure 12.1 shows a page of books that match the search term "road." This looks pretty typical, right?

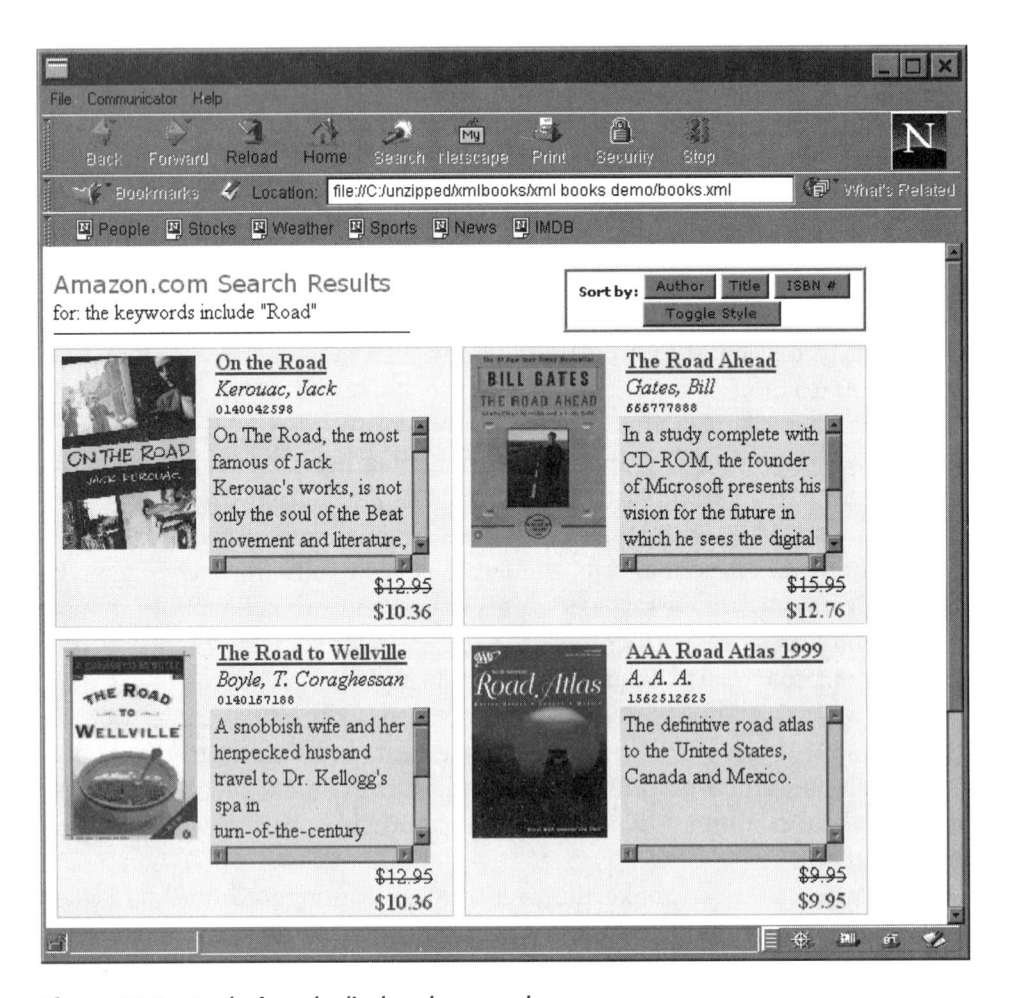

Figure 12.1 Books for sale displayed on a web page.

You could use plain old HTML to create the look of this page. There's nothing wrong with approaching the content this way. When you use HTML, though, you tie the display of this page into the content file.

What happens if you want your readers to be able to display the found set of books in alphabetical order by author? In this document, they click on the little check box and instantly the page is redisplayed, as you see in Figure 12.2.

No new pages were loaded from the server. No database was called. All of this was done by assigning a different set of styles and a little script to the same XML file.

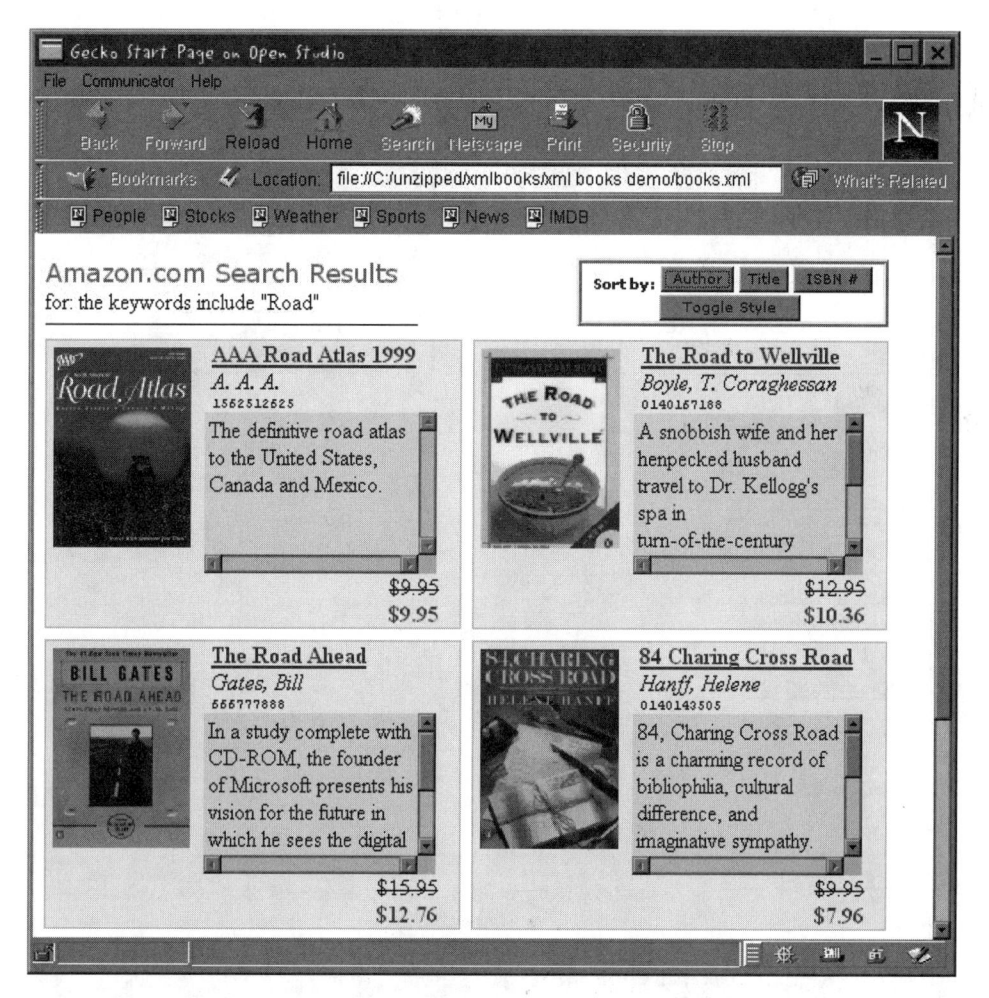

Figure 12.2 Books for sale are now displayed by author.

Still not convinced? OK, click on the box that displays books as a list. The entire structure of the visual presentation changes to what you see in Figure 12.3.

Once again, this display happened immediately. No new pages were loaded; no database was accessed. It was all done with the same XML file and a different set of style rules.

Style Options

You can apply display data to an XML file in several ways.

The most important work under way revolves around Extensible Style Language (XSL). We'll talk about XSL a little in this chapter, but the recom-

Figure 12.3 Books are now displayed as a list.

mendation is still under development as of this writing. XSL works specifically with XML data.

One method of applying style data currently in use is Cascading Style Sheets, or CSS. CSS works with both HTML and XML files.

HTML components (HTC) are another way of bringing display data to XML. One version of this technology was created by Microsoft, implemented in IE 5.0, and then submitted to the W3C in October 1998. Netscape has a similar submission, called "action sheets." We'll address HTC and behaviors in Chapter 13, "HTC Behaviors."

XSL

XSL is a language for expressing style sheets. It consists of two parts: a language for transforming XML and a language for specifying formatting information.

The transformation component of XSL turns XML elements into objects. The objects can then be manipulated and transformed in various ways, including being turned into HTML for display by older, non-XML-compliant browsers.

The formatting vocabulary of XSL builds on CSS to create a sort of style sheet with contextual programming.

CSS1 and CSS2

Cascading Style Sheets—CSS1 and CSS2—work with both HTML and XML files. They are a way of assigning various kinds of display values to page elements.

CSS1 became a standard in December 1996. The 4.X browsers offer mixed support for CSS, but with the 5.X releases, we are moving toward a fuller support.

CSS2 became a standard on May 12, 1998. CSS2 is a superset of CSS1 with CSS Positioning incorporated, along with support for different media types and many more enhancements. CSS Positioning allows you to explicitly position document elements, either absolutely on the display page or relatively to each other, using X,Y coordinates.

Because CSS is the best real tool we have right now, we'll spend much of this chapter talking about it and showing how you can implement it today.

HTC

HTCs provide a way to script a style. They can be used to create special effects, like a shaking browser window, or for functional tasks, such as automatically generating pullquote or footnote pop-up boxes. With HTC, you create an action and tie that action to an object in the web page.

XSL versus CSS

XSL and CSS are both style sheet languages. Both can work with XML files. And both will likely be part of your design arsenal in the next several years. But there are some important differences between the two.

XSL and CSS are complementary technologies, with XSL building on CSS. It is quite possible that you will use CSS and XSL in tandem, depending on what you are doing with your data.

We'll all be hearing a lot more about XSL over the next several years, and as we migrate to XML documents we will begin using XSL to express the display of these document on web browsers and on other types of display devices.

Table 12.1 compares CSS and XSL.

CSS Is in Use Today; XSL Will Be Used Tomorrow

Right now, a major difference between the two style options is that CSS is a W3C recommendation and a technology currently in use. Both 4.X and 5.X browsers support CSS to varying degrees. You can start using CSS right now with both HTML and XML files.

Take the words "supported" and "implementation" with a grain of salt, though. The exact support implemented varies from release to release of the major browsers, and it even varies from platform to platform of the same release. The Web Standards Project <http://www.webstandards.org/> has a CSS effort under way that is asking for full CSS support from browser vendors.

Table 12.1 Differences between CSS and XSL

ACTION	SUPPORTED BY CSS	SUPPORTED BY XSL
Works with HTML	Yes	No
Works with XML	Yes	Yes
Transforms objects	No	Yes

Source: WC3

If you are planning to do a lot of work with XML (and if you're reading this book, chances are good that you are), start using CSS today. Get in the practice of separating display information from content information. Using CSS with HTML provides a very natural bridge to the complete style/content separation that XML requires.

XSL Goes Further than CSS

CSS is a language for expressing style data. In a straightforward way, you use CSS to match display characteristics with an element.

XSL is a language for expressing style sheets. It consists of two parts: a language for specifying formatting information and a language for transforming XML. It allows for very flexible, contextual presentations of style, based on variables in the user environment. It also allows you to convert XML files into HTML files so that older browsers can display them.

CSS Defines Style; XSL Adds Transformation Powers

CSS maps styles directly to HTML and XML elements. This means that in a style declaration, you specify display properties, and those are connected directly to each use of the element in the web page. Basically, you are saying something like this: "Hey, browser, every time you see a <P> element, display it in a 10-point Arial font and make it bold, too." It is a fairly direct relationship.

XSL takes this mapping process one step further. It lets you specify objects and then map elements in a document to those objects. The objects, in turn, provide formatting and style information to the elements. The benefit of this approach is that you can use XSL both to view XML documents in a browser and to transform XML documents to HTML documents or other XML documents.

For example, if you have an XML document that you want readers using 4.X browsers to read, you can't do so with style sheets alone. You'll need to do a style transformation that turns your XML tags into some sort of HTML that the 4.X browser understands.

CSS Works with HTML and XML; XSL Focuses on XML

CSS is nice technology to apply right now because it works with both HTML and XML documents. It offers a more limited range of options than XSL does, however.

XSL will not work with HTML. It is being created to take advantage of XML and the potential for displaying XML documents to meet specific needs.

CSS Isn't Contextual; XSL Is

XSL also differs from CSS in that XSL is contextual. That is, you can program the way it displays data based on certain variables that you specify. It is more complex, but XSL adds a bit of programming power to the application of style.

For example, with XSL you could set a style for displaying elements in a web browser and a style for displaying elements on a PDA. The style would test to see what sort of display device is requesting the style data and would deliver the appropriate version of the XML document.

Cascading Style Sheet Concepts

CSS is a relatively straightforward idea. Much of the confusion that some people feel with it has more to do with uneven browser support for the CSS recommendation than with what the technology actually enables you to do.

CSS is a way of assigning style rules, called *properties*, to document elements. It is that simple.

You put a pointer to the style data into your XML file. When a web browser processes the XML file, it goes and gets the style information and uses it to display the XML document in the web browser window.

What Is a Style?

The very first thing you need to understand about CSS is the idea of style. The word *style* plays a big role in CSS. CSS defines style as being everything that describes how to display the document. This includes obvious features such as font and color, plus information about how an element is placed related to other elements and whether it is visible or hidden.

What Is Cascading?

The notion of *cascading* is also important in CSS. Cascading means that style information spills down from one level to the next.

Unfortunately, cascading and inheritance implementations in CSS are two of the weakest areas of current browsers. We hope this will change with the 5.X browsers.

The idea of cascading applies in two ways. First, it describes the way styles cascade from one element to the next—from parent to child, from branch to leaf. Second, it describes the way styles cascade from one level of declaration to the next—from external to internal to inline.

Part of the notion of cascading is inheritance. That means a child element inherits the style assigned to its parent, unless that style is overruled with additional style data.

For example, suppose the root element of your document is called <BOOK>. <BOOK> contains an element called <CHAPTER>. <CHAPTER> contains individual paragraphs (<PARA> and song titles <SONG>). You can use a style declaration to set style rules for the <BOOK> element. Any displayed content within <CHAPTER>, <PARA>, or <SONG> will use these values. You don't need to declare them for each element down the hierarchy.

For example, you might set a style rule for <BOOK> that says to display fonts in 12-point Helvetica:

```
BOOK {font-size: 12pt;
     font-family: helvetica;}
```

That style data cascades down into the child elements <PARA> and <SONG>. You would not have to give <PARA> and <SONG> the same display data again.

If you wanted to change the display data for a child element, you would need to change only those properties which have different values. For example, if you wanted song titles to appear in bold, you could add a weight property to the style rule for the SONG element, like this:

```
SONG {font-weight: bold;}
```

The other part of cascading involves the way you can apply styles at external, internal, and inline levels. The style data will flow from one level of declaration to the next. All style data is inherited down the levels, but more specific style data overrides more general rules. This is an important consideration with HTML documents, where styles are added at all levels. However, you won't be using inline styles with XML documents. Inline is a way of inserting style data into the content file, at the place where the element appears. Inline styles are something you might want to do with HTML, but using them with XML completely defeats XML's purpose and adds data that will create XML errors.

What Are Style Sheets?

A style sheet is a collection of style rules. The style sheet describes the display properties for a set of document elements. Typically, a style sheet is saved in an external ASCII file, with a .css extension.

A Style Sheet Example

Remember that Mozilla example at the beginning of the chapter? The following code is part of one of the style sheets that goes with it. This style sheet describes the display characteristics of the list. Netscape used CSS as the display tool to work with the XML document:

```
Title {
        display: block;
        font-weight: bold;
        color: blue;
      text-decoration: underline;
        cursor: pointer;}

Author {
        display: block;
        font-style: italic;}

Synopsis {
        display: none;}

Price {
        display: block;
        color: rgb(20,100,0);
        font-weight: bold;}
```

You'll see a pattern emerging here. The basic structure for a style rule is that you enter the name of the element (remember to enter it the way it is defined in the DTD and used in the XML document!). Then you type an open brace. Inside the open brace will be one or more style rules. The rules are a listing of a style property and the value you are assigning to it for this element. Each rule ends with a semi-colon. The entire rule set ends with a closing brace.

For example, this code tells you that:

1. The <Title> element is a block that displays in bold, blue, underlined text.

2. The <Author> element is a block displayed in italic text.

3. The <Synopsis> element is hidden (it has a display value of "none").
4. The <Price> element is a block displayed in a particular color as defined by RGB values and is bold.

If we look at the XML file for this example, we can see that there are <Title>, <Author>, <Synopsis>, and <Price> elements, but no information about RGB values or fonts. The following is a snippet from that example file:

```
<Book>

<Title xml:link="simple" show="replace"
href="http://www.amazon.com/exec/obidos/ASIN/0140042598/002-5969498-
2733628">On the Road</Title>

<Author>Kerouac, Jack</Author>

<ISBN>0140042598</ISBN>

<Synopsis>

On The Road, the most famous of Jack Kerouac's works, is not only the
soul of the Beat movement and literature, but one of the most important
novels of the century. Like nearly all of Kerouac's writing, On The Road
is thinly fictionalized autobiography, filled with a cast made of
Kerouac's real life friends, lovers, and fellow travelers. Narrated by
Sal Paradise, one of Kerouac's alter-egos, On the Road is a cross-
country bohemian odyssey that not only influenced writing in the years
since its 1957 publication but penetrated into the deepest levels of
American thought and culture.

</Synopsis>

<ListPrice>$12.95</ListPrice>

<Price>$10.36</Price>

</Book>
```

When Mozilla 5.X processes this XML file, one of the things it does is look at the style sheet files that are specified in the beginning of the XML document. When Mozilla 5.X encounters an element in the document, it refers to that style sheet for information about how to display it in the browser window. Figures 12.4, 12.5, and 12.6 show the CSS style sheet, the XML document, and the displayed page in a web browser. Note that the XML file contains no style information; the web browser draws on the XML data, and the CSS style properties to produce the page a reader sees.

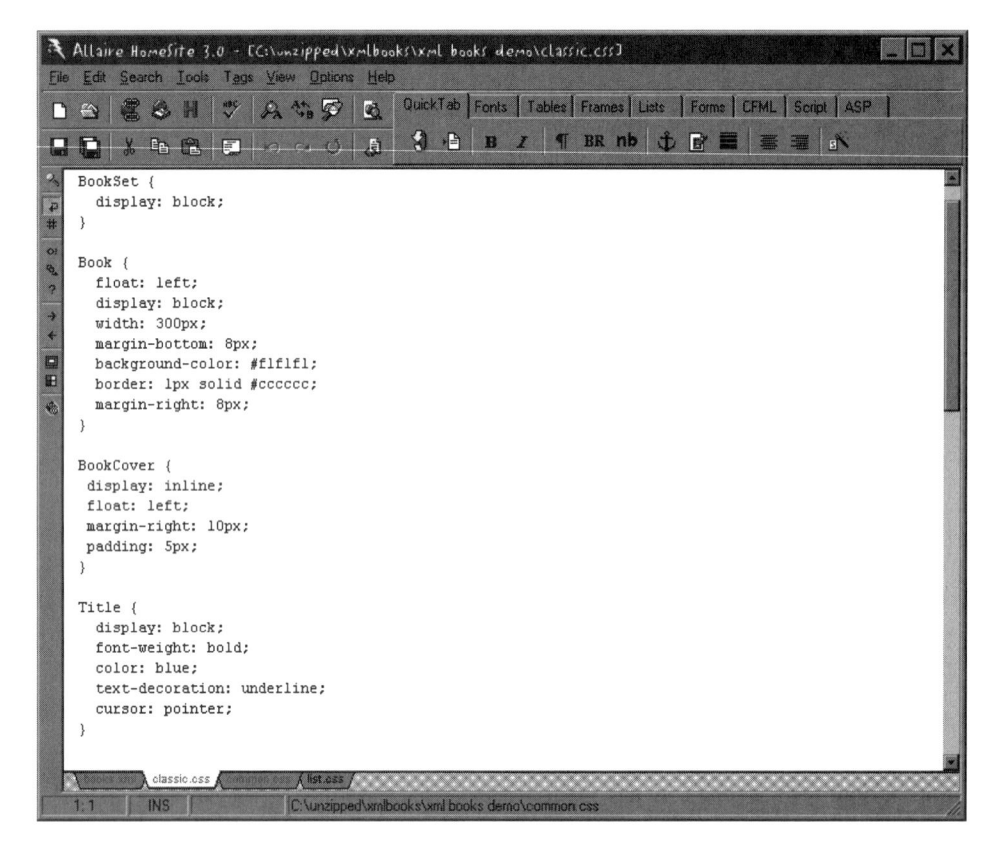

Figure 12.4 The CSS file.

Creating a CSS Style Sheet

A style sheet is a collection of style rules. Each rule defines the value of a display property. Rules for the same element may be grouped together in a style declaration for that element.

For example, this code sets the display properties of *font-size*, *font-family*, and *color* for the <SCI-NAME> element.

```
SCI-NAME {
display: inline;
font-size: 12pt;
font-family:  "Arial, Helvetica, Geneva";
color: 9966cc}
```

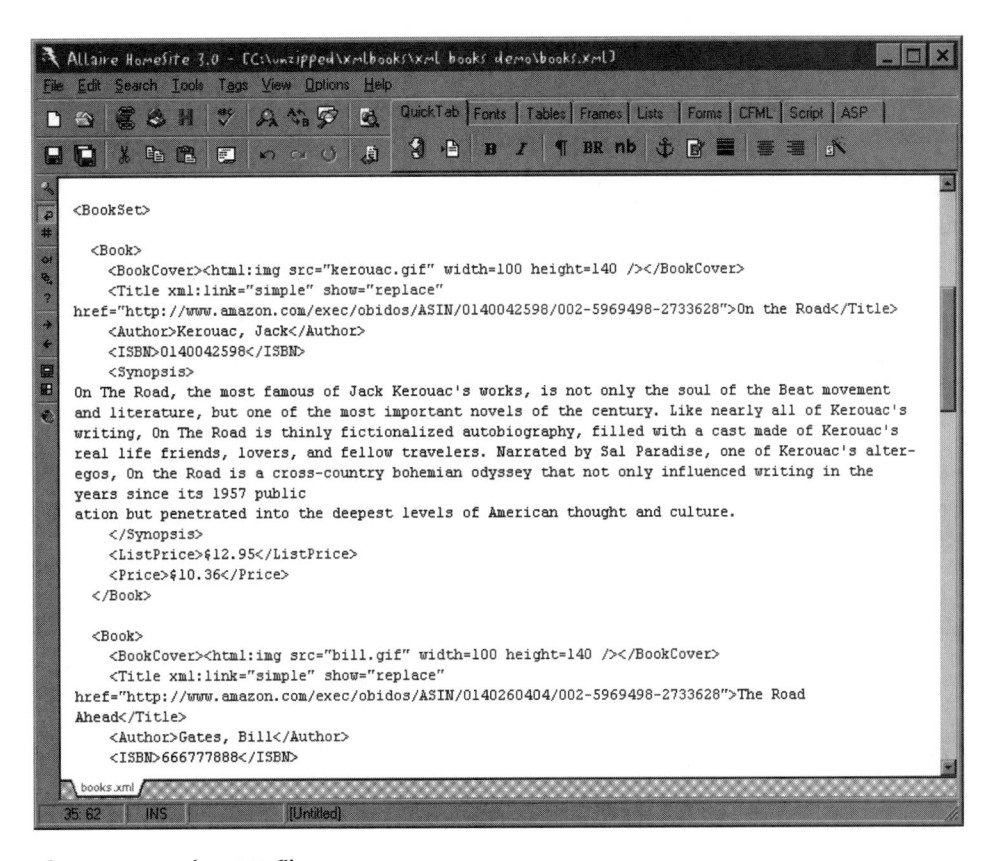

Figure 12.5 The XML file.

ASCII Text File

The style sheet file is simply an ASCII text file. It is saved with the extension .css; for example, mypage.css.

Inside the file is a list of style declarations, each containing one or more rules.

Style Properties

A style property is the way an element is displayed in a web browser. Each element is likely to have many different style properties, such as *font-family* and *text-indent*.

In HTML, elements use default properties when they are displayed in a web browser. This is why you can create and display an HTML page in one

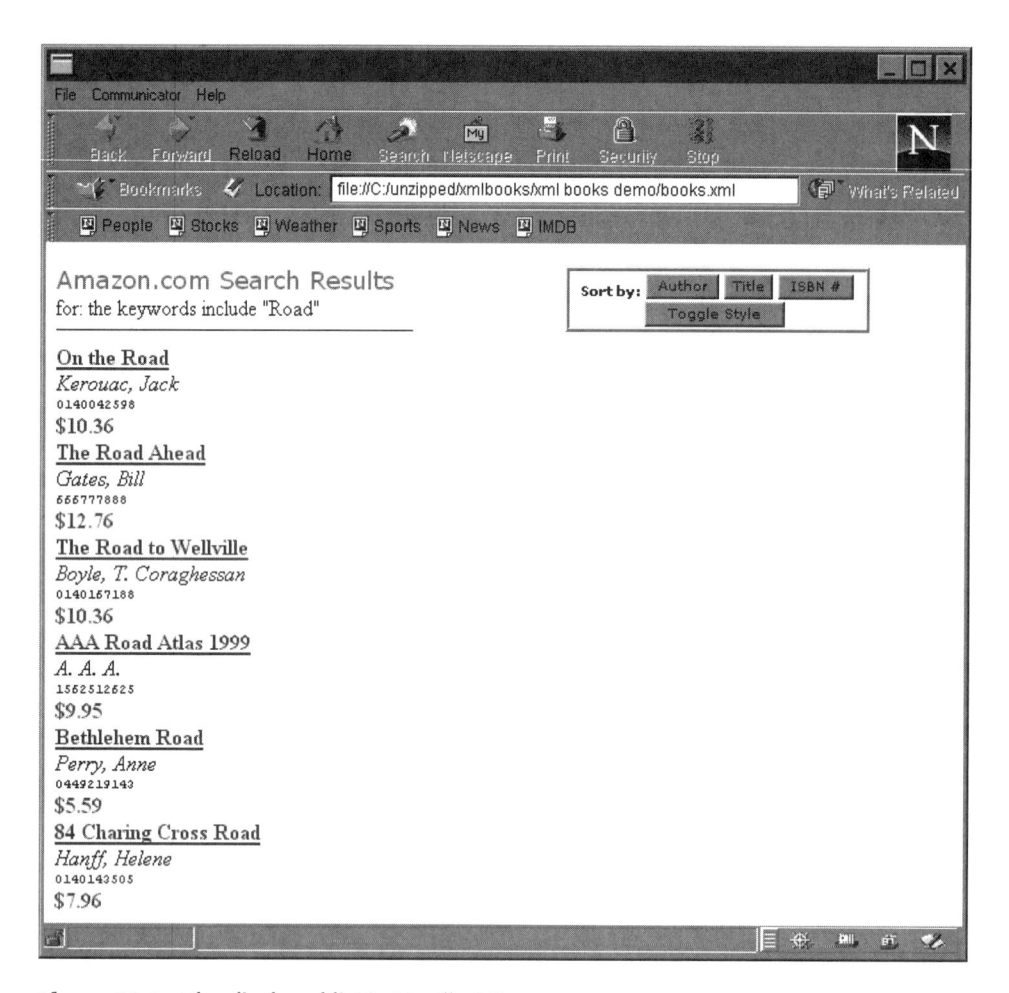

Figure 12.6 The displayed list in Mozilla 5.X.

step. The fixed set of HTML tags also has a fixed set of default display property values.

XML has neither a fixed set of elements nor a fixed set of default style values. That's why you must use a style sheet to specify the display properties for any element that you want to display in your web browser.

There are four basic categories of properties: color and background, fonts and text, position and classification, and spacing and areas. These are outlined in more detail in the Appendix of this book.

Color and background properties. Control an element's display color, background color, and use of background images.

Fonts and text properties. Control a textual element's typographic display characteristics.

Position and classification properties. Describe the display category to which an element belongs, and control an element's position within the containing element, the element's z-position, and whether the element is visible. You will need to assign a display property to any element you want to display in a web page; this is an important property that is not often used in HTML and we'll discuss it in more detail later in this chapter.

Spacing and areas properties. Control an element's borders, margins, and padding.

Style Rules

A style rule names a style property and assigns a value to it for a specific element. The Appendix of this book contains a guide to the CSS1 properties.

A style rule looks like this:

```
property: value;
```

- The property is the name of the property whose values you are setting.
- The value is the value you are giving to the property for this element.

For example:

```
font-family: arial, geneva, helvetica;
```

makes a rule that sets the *font-family* display property to be "arial, geneva, helvetica."

Style rules are placed into style declarations, which assign one or more rules to a specific element. Style sheets are comprised of a set of style declarations.

Style Declarations

A style declaration is a collection of one or more rules assigned to a particular element. A style declaration looks like this:

```
Element {
property: value;}
```

- The element name is the element for which you are creating the rule.
- The property is the name of the property whose values you are setting.
- The value is the value you are giving to the property for this element.

For example:

```
TITLE {
font-family: arial, geneva, helvetica;}
```

sets the *font-family* display property for the TITLE element to be "arial, geneva, helvetica."

For example:

```
TITLE {
font-family: arial, geneva, helvetica;
font-size: 18pt;
text-align: center;
display: block;}
```

sets a series of rules for the TITLE element. It assigns the *font-family* property a value of "arial, geneva, helvetica." It assigns the *font-size* property a value of 18 points. It assigns the *text-align* property a value of "center." And, most importantly, it assigns the *display* property a value of "block."

Every element that you are going to display must have a display property explicitly set. The display property is neither inherited nor assumed.

To create a style declaration, follow these steps:

1. Specify the element for which you are setting the rule. Make sure you type the element with the exact capitalization you use in the XML document (remember, XML is case sensitive, and if you set a display rule for the element <TITLE > it won't work for the element <Title>):
   ```
   TITLE
   ```

2. Next, type a space and then the open brace, {. Or, if you prefer, type a return and the open brace. Either one is fine. Use whichever approach makes it easier for you to read your style file.
   ```
   TITLE {
   ```

3. Now, type the name of the first property for which you want to set a value. (Some people like to start the actual properties on their own line, with each slightly indented; others don't. If you start on a new line it can make your rule easier for other people to read later on when they want to edit your style sheet.)

```
TITLE {
    font-size
```

4. Type a colon and then the value you are setting for the property:
```
TITLE {
    font-size: 18pt
```

5. Type a semi-colon to separate this property rule from the next:
```
TITLE {
    font-size: 18pt;
```

6. Continue entering property rules. When you are done, close the declaration with a closing brace, }. (Some people put the brace on its own line for ease of human reading.)
```
TITLE {
    display: block;
    font-size: 18pt;
    font-weight: bold;
    color: ffffff;
    background color: 9966cc;}
```

Property Values

You can measure CSS property values in one of two ways: as absolute values or as relative values.

Absolute values have a fixed, specific value. For example, the *font-size* property might have a value of 14 points. When you are using absolute values always remember that the reader might be viewing your page in an environment different from what you expect.

Table 12.2 shows a chart with the CSS absolute measurement values.

Relative values have no fixed, specific value. Rather, they are calculated in comparison to a current value. For example, the *font-size* property has a

Table 12.2 Absolute Values

UNIT	ABBREVIATION	EXAMPLE
Points There are 72 points to an inch, 12 points to a pica.	pt	`font-size: 12pt;`
Picas There are 6 picas to an inch.	pc	`text-indent: 2pc;`
Centimeters	cm	`text-indent: 4cm;`
Inches	in	`text-indent: 1in;`
Millimeters	mm	`text-indent: 8cm;`

Table 12.3 CSS Relative Values

UNIT	ABBREVIATION	EXAMPLE
Pixels A pixel is one picture element on the display monitor; there are typically between 72 and 90 pixels/inch.	px	`text-indent: 30px;`
em space An em space is the width and height of the capital letter M in the current font size and design.	em	`text-indent: 4em;`
X space.	ex	`line-height: 3ex;`
Percentage of containing element (parent) value.	XX%	`Text-indent: 5%;`

value of larger or smaller. *Text-indent* might be specified in em spaces, which vary with the display size of the text.

Because web pages are viewed in so many different ways, it is often a good idea to use relative values. They give you less absolute control, but they often create a better experience for your readers and let your page flow dynamically. The types of values you select will vary based on your and your readers' needs.

Table 12.3 shows CSS relative values.

The Display Property

The display property is very important in a style sheet for an XML document. You use the display property to define the type of display this element uses. Elements can be block elements, inline elements, or list-item elements. Most elements will have a display property value of either block or inline.

Block elements are elements that are displayed as boxes on the page. CSS uses a simple formatting model in which every block element generates a rectangular box. All boxes contain a content area within and may be surrounded by optional padding, border, and margin areas. Headlines and paragraphs are block elements. In Figure 12.7, the paragraph is a block element, with padding and border set.

Blocks either butt up to other blocks or are contained within parent blocks. You can define both the positional relationship of one block to

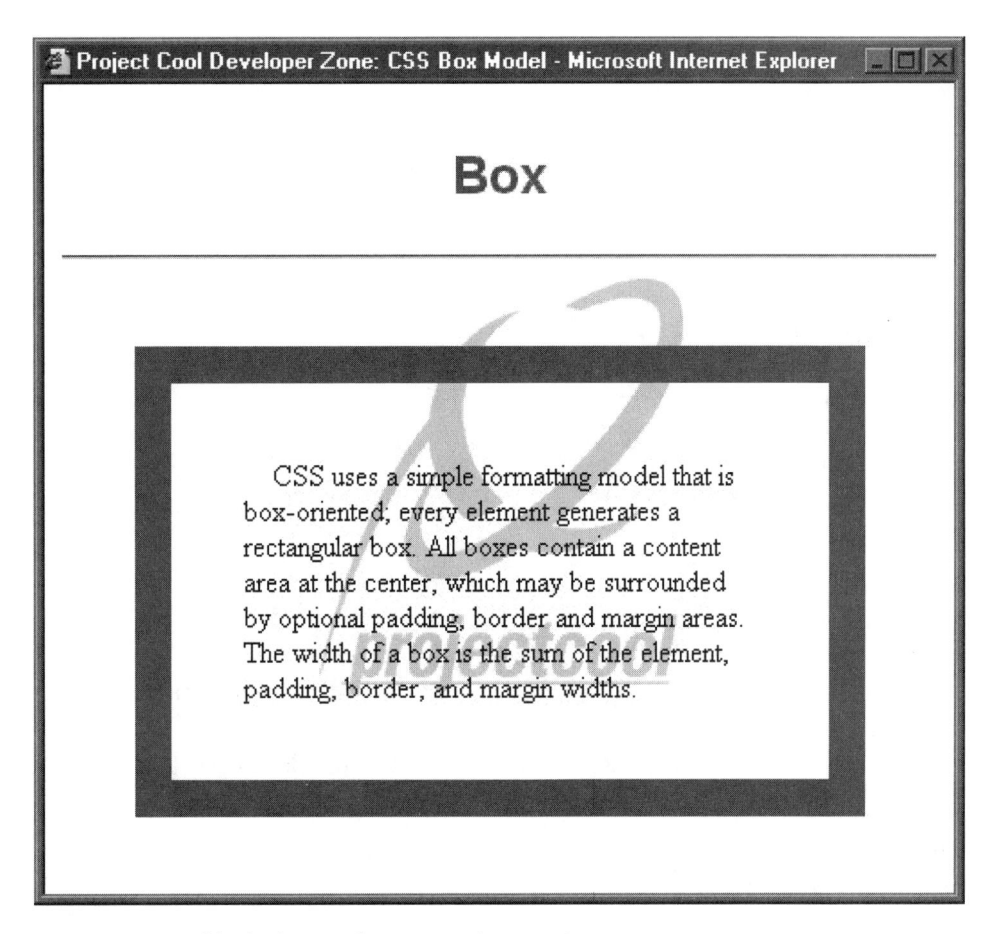

Figure 12.7 A block element becomes a box on the page.

another and the positional relationship of content within the block. For example, you can tell a paragraph block to have a top margin of 1 em, so that there will always be 1 em of space between the top of this block and a block above it.

For an interactive, visual presentation of this container concept, visit the *Examples* section of the companion website to this book, <http://www.projectcool.com/guide/xml>.

Inline elements are not blocks. They are elements that flow within their containing element. For example, in *The Community Cooker* example in Chapter 11, the STEP element was set to have a display property value of inline. Instead of breaking each step into a separate box in the display, all of the steps ran together, inline, within the same block.

Elements can also be hidden using the display property. A hidden element is not visible on the page, and its block does not take up any space. Scripts will often hide and display elements to create certain use interface effects.

Connecting an XML File to a Style Sheet

You connect an XML file to one or more style sheets through a simple declaration. The declaration goes at the beginning of the file, just after the XML declaration and before the DOCTYPE declaration:

```
<?xml version="1.0?">
<?xml-stylesheet href="mypage.css" type="text/css"?>
<!DOCTYPE personalpage>
```

The declaration begins with the keyword <?xml-style sheet.
The href value points to the location of the style sheet.
The type is text/css, indicating that this is a CSS style sheet.
The declaration ends as it began, with the question mark and a closing delimiter, ?>.
You can point to several style sheets. You can use JavaScript to display the page with one or the other, based on user actions.

A Few Practical Pointers

With HTML, you can make a number of assumptions. For example, there is a known universe of tags. Most of these tags have default values for key display properties, including the display type property. None of this is a given in XML.

Start with a Checklist

You'll need to provide display data for every element in your document that you want to display in the web browser window. It is a good idea to have a list of each element and what it does. Treat it as a checklist and make sure all elements are covered in the style sheet.

Start at the Top

Start by creating display rules for the uppermost elements in the hierarchy. In theory, the children of these elements should inherit the property values from the parents; consequently, you should need to define less and less as you work out the tree.

Remember the Display Property

XML elements have no default values for the display property, so you must explicitly provide elements with a display property value. The display property is not inherited. Without a display property value, the web browser won't display the element on the page, no matter how many other style rules you set. In most cases, the display property will either have a value of block or inline, like this:

```
PARA
{display: block;}

SONG-NAME
{display: inline;}
```

Test, Test, Test

Never assume any level of support. Make sure you test your style sheet on different browsers and platforms.

Although CSS has been a W3C Recommendation since December 1996, the browser vendors have been very slow to fully support the standard. Each browser supports a slightly different sub-set of the Recommendation, so it is important to look at your page using the browsers your readers are most likely to be using.

Summary

To display an XML file, you'll need to create a style component for the file. In the future this might be an XSL file, but for the near future it will most likely be a CSS style sheet.

Cascading Style Sheets are a great way to add display data to an XML document. CSS works with both HTML and XML, making it an ideal bridge technology.

With CSS, you define stylistic characteristics for each element. If you are a designer working with XML, learn CSS. This chapter provides an overview of what it can do. Take the time to play with and explore the power of style sheets.

CHAPTER 13

HTC Behaviors

HTC behaviors are a way to create dynamic HTML effects in a reusable script tied to an XML tag. They combine a CSS property with an HTML component model. The end result is that you create a custom tag that performs a scripted display action. For example, you can use a behavior to make a pullquote appear in a page or create a pop-up footnote box when a reader clicks on the footnote number.

There are two portions of HTC behaviors. The HTML component (HTC) portion describes a way of creating and using small scripted actions. The behavior portion describes a CSS property you can assign to an element.

What a Behavior Does

The best way to understand HTC behaviors is to see one in action. You can see several working examples in the companion website to this book, <http://www.projectcool.com/guides/xml>. Figures 13.1 through 13.6 also show the working of a behavior, although they don't begin to do it justice.

Figure 13.1 shows a page displayed in IE 5.0. You'll see that it contains some large pullquotes. These pullquotes were created dynamically with an

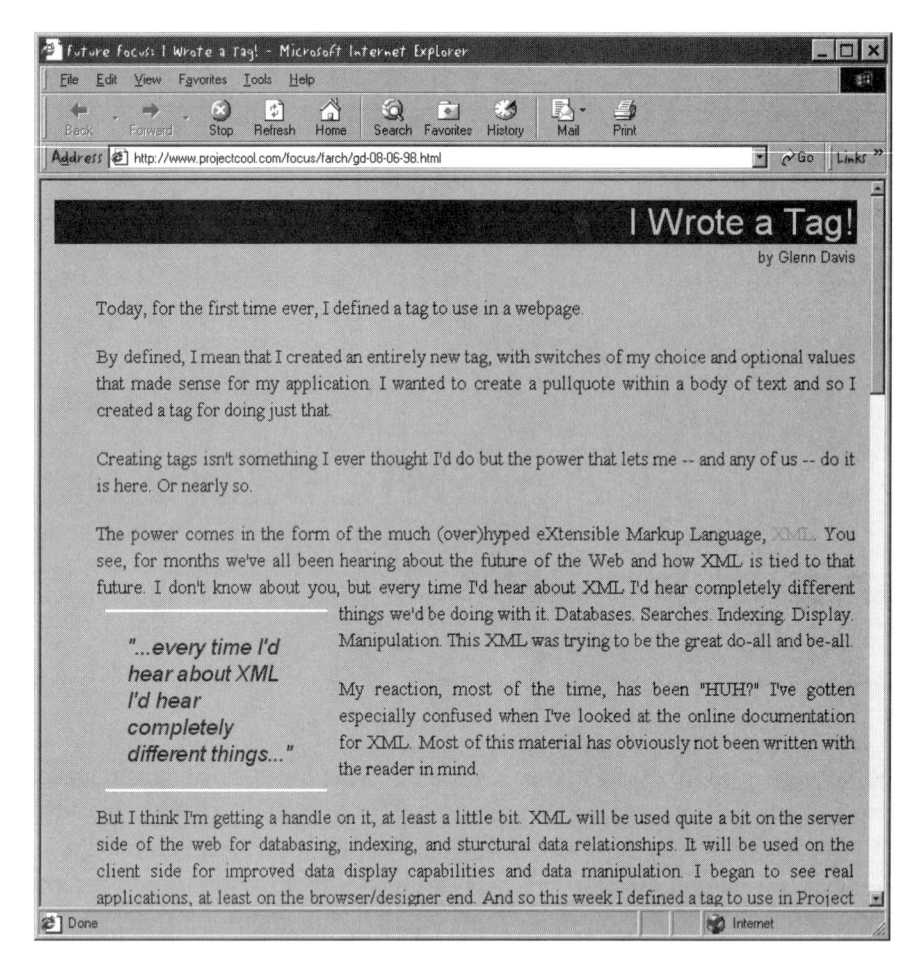

Figure 13.1 The pullquote as it is displayed in IE 5.0.

HTC that we created (you can read designer and scripter Glenn Davis's view of the process in the sidebar later in this chapter, *I Wrote a Tag!*).

The hard work in creating this display effect is contained in the .htc file, the HTML component file. Once that file is created, the author of the article doesn't need to worry about scripting, CSS, or any fancy code work. He or she just enters the XML tag <FF:PULLQUOTE> to identify the pullquote text, as you see in Figure 13.2.

Figures 13.3 and 13.4 show a pop-up footnote. This, too, is created using HTC technology. The little footnote number appears in the body of the text. When a reader clicks on it, a footnote pops up. In browsers other than IE 5.0, the footnote appears at the bottom of the page.

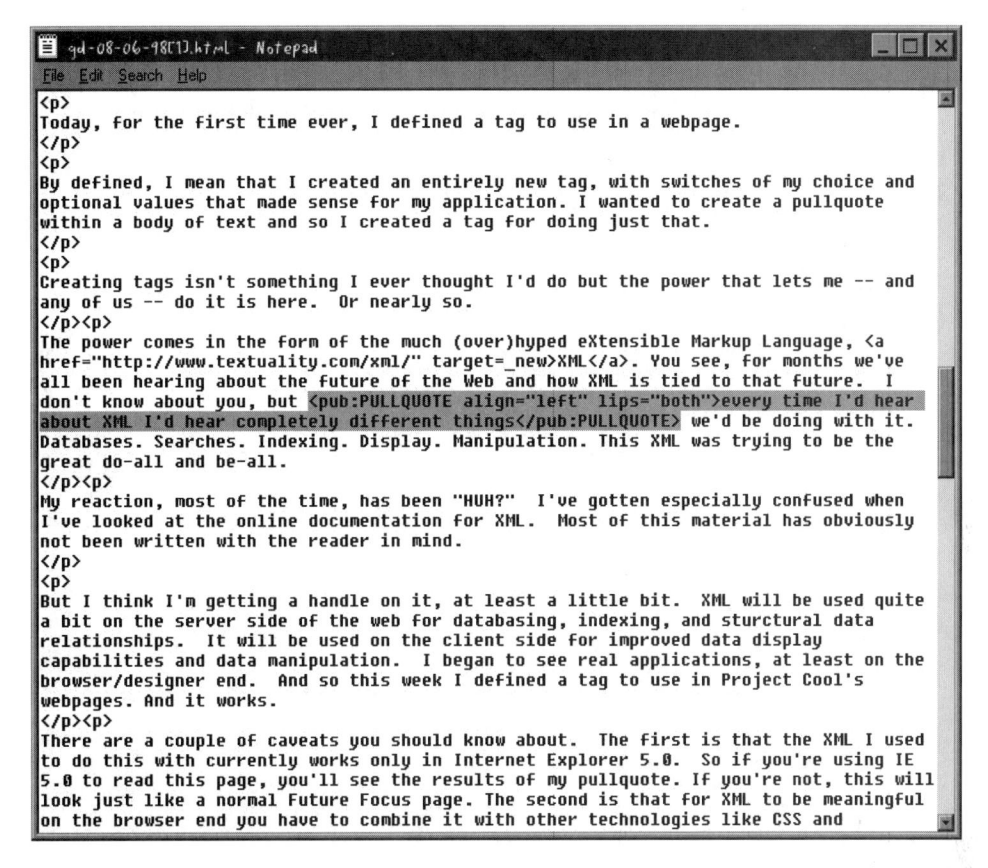

Figure 13.2 The creator of the page doesn't need to know any scripting, just one simple tag.

Again, as with pullquotes, this approach required the author of the page to learn only one XML tag, as shown in Figure 13.5. Figure 13.6 shows the programming code behind the footnote behavior.

By separating structure from display, the designer gets control over visual presentation while the author is able to note that a footnote is a footnote and not get pulled into scripting or design issues. And if the designer and author are the same person, the process gets separated into discrete—and easy-to-manage—portions.

Support for Behaviors

The biggest catch in HTC behaviors is that they are a non-standard feature. That is, Microsoft went ahead and implemented the feature in its IE 5.0

Figure 13.3 Footnotes are marked with numbers in the body of the text.

release, although it is not a W3C Recommendation. If you are using an IE5X browser, you'll see the results of this function; if you are using another browser, it will be as if the behavior doesn't exist at all.

Microsoft has submitted the component portion, HTC, to the W3C as a stand-alone submission. It has also submitted the behavior portion to the W3C CSS Working Group.

We think it is worth talking about HTC behaviors, however, for several reasons. First, if your readers are using IE 5.X, it is a nice way to begin

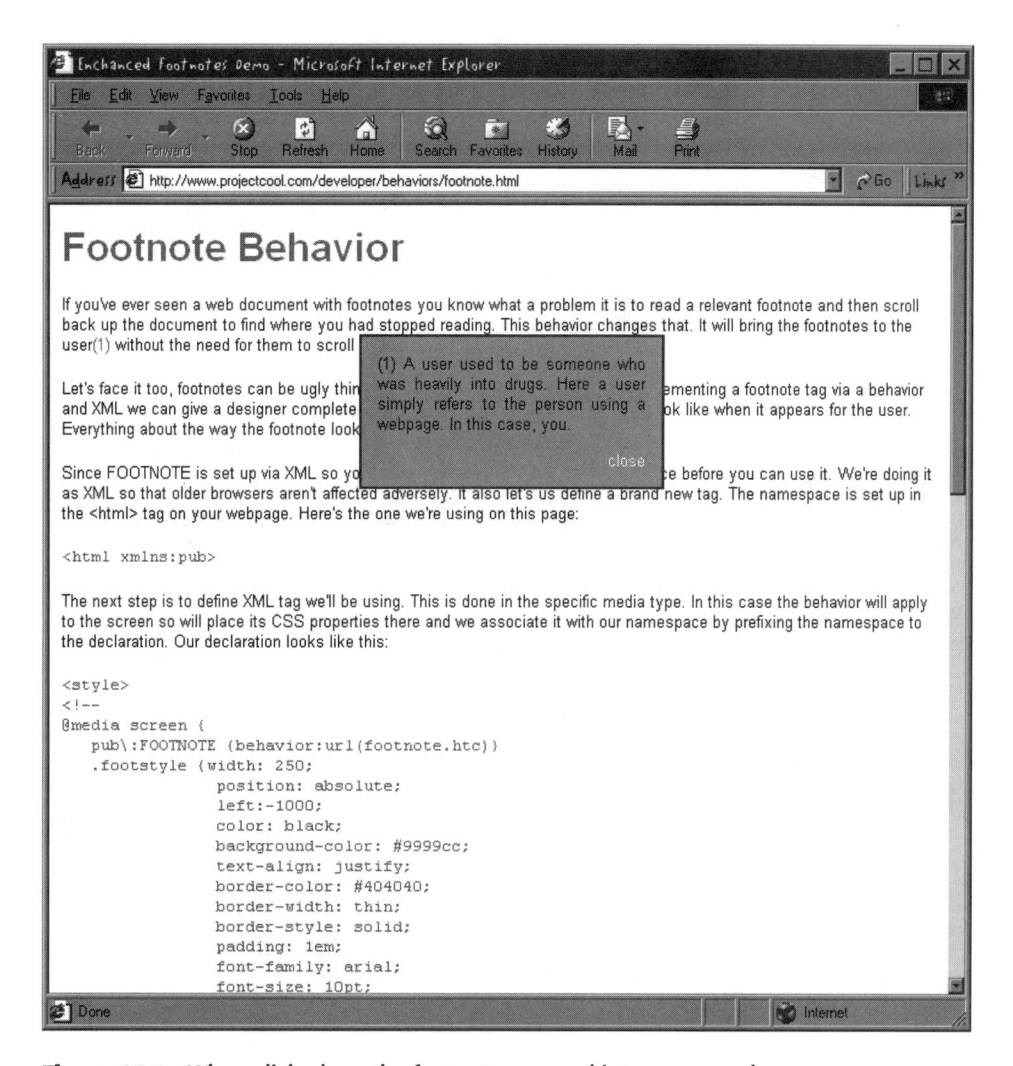

Figure 13.4 When clicked on, the footnotes expand into a pop-up box.

using pockets of XML within your HTML files and a way to begin to understand the value of separating content from format.

Second, it shows the design potential of the component approach to online publishing. While it is unlikely that this exact implementation of behaviors will become a standard, it *is* likely that many of the concepts will be included in a future Recommendation.

Third, some of the things you can do with behavior are just downright cool. And if you have some time to explore, behaviors can give you some new ways of thinking about the presentation of your content.

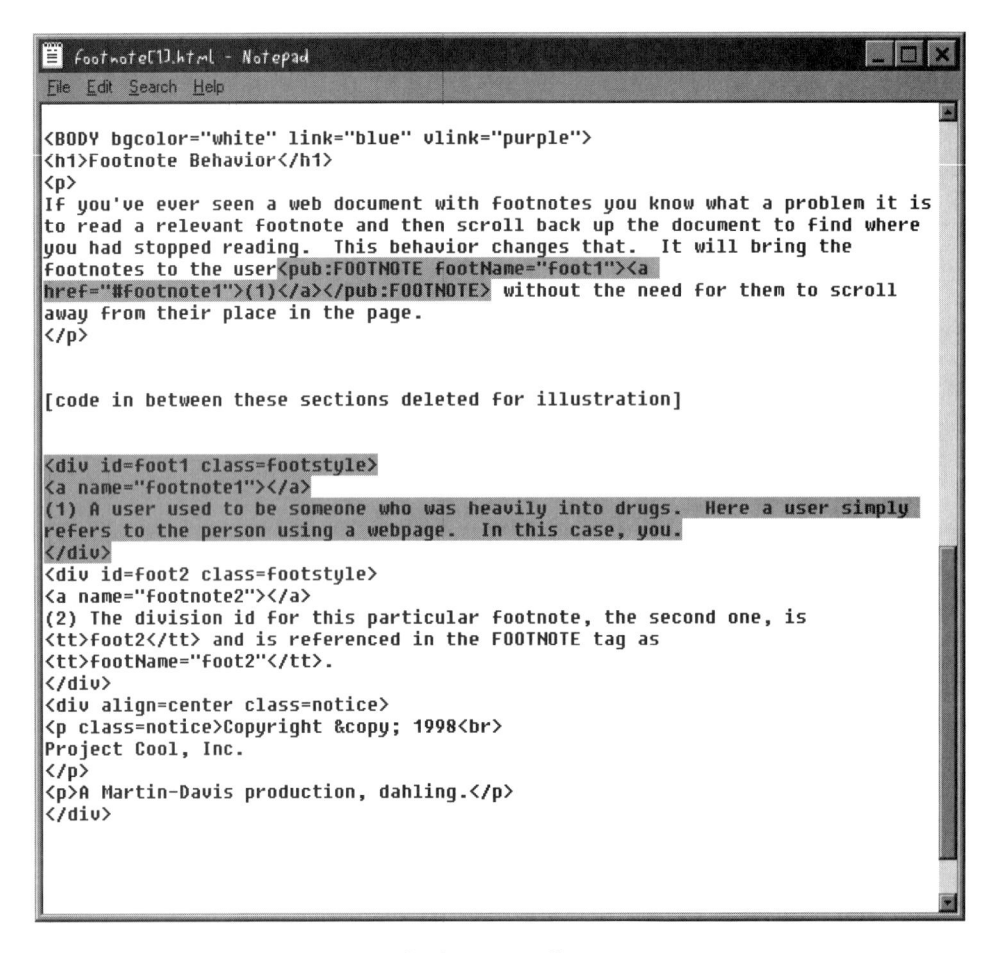

```
<BODY bgcolor="white" link="blue" vlink="purple">
<h1>Footnote Behavior</h1>
<p>
If you've ever seen a web document with footnotes you know what a problem it is
to read a relevant footnote and then scroll back up the document to find where
you had stopped reading.  This behavior changes that.  It will bring the
footnotes to the user<pub:FOOTNOTE footName="foot1"><a
href="#footnote1">(1)</a></pub:FOOTNOTE> without the need for them to scroll
away from their place in the page.
</p>


[code in between these sections deleted for illustration]


<div id=foot1 class=footstyle>
<a name="footnote1"></a>
(1) A user used to be someone who was heavily into drugs.  Here a user simply
refers to the person using a webpage.  In this case, you.
</div>
<div id=foot2 class=footstyle>
<a name="footnote2"></a>
(2) The division id for this particular footnote, the second one, is
<tt>foot2</tt> and is referenced in the FOOTNOTE tag as
<tt>footName="foot2"</tt>.
</div>
<div align=center class=notice>
<p class=notice>Copyright &copy; 1998<br>
Project Cool, Inc.
</p>
<p>A Martin-Davis production, dahling.</p>
</div>
```

Figure 13.5   One XML tag creates the footnote effect.

HTC Behavior Concepts

There are several basic concepts behind HTC behaviors. These concepts, which could take on other forms of implementation in addition to HTC behaviors, point to some future directions of web presentation.

Separate Content from Display

XML is all about separating content from display data. So are HTC behaviors.

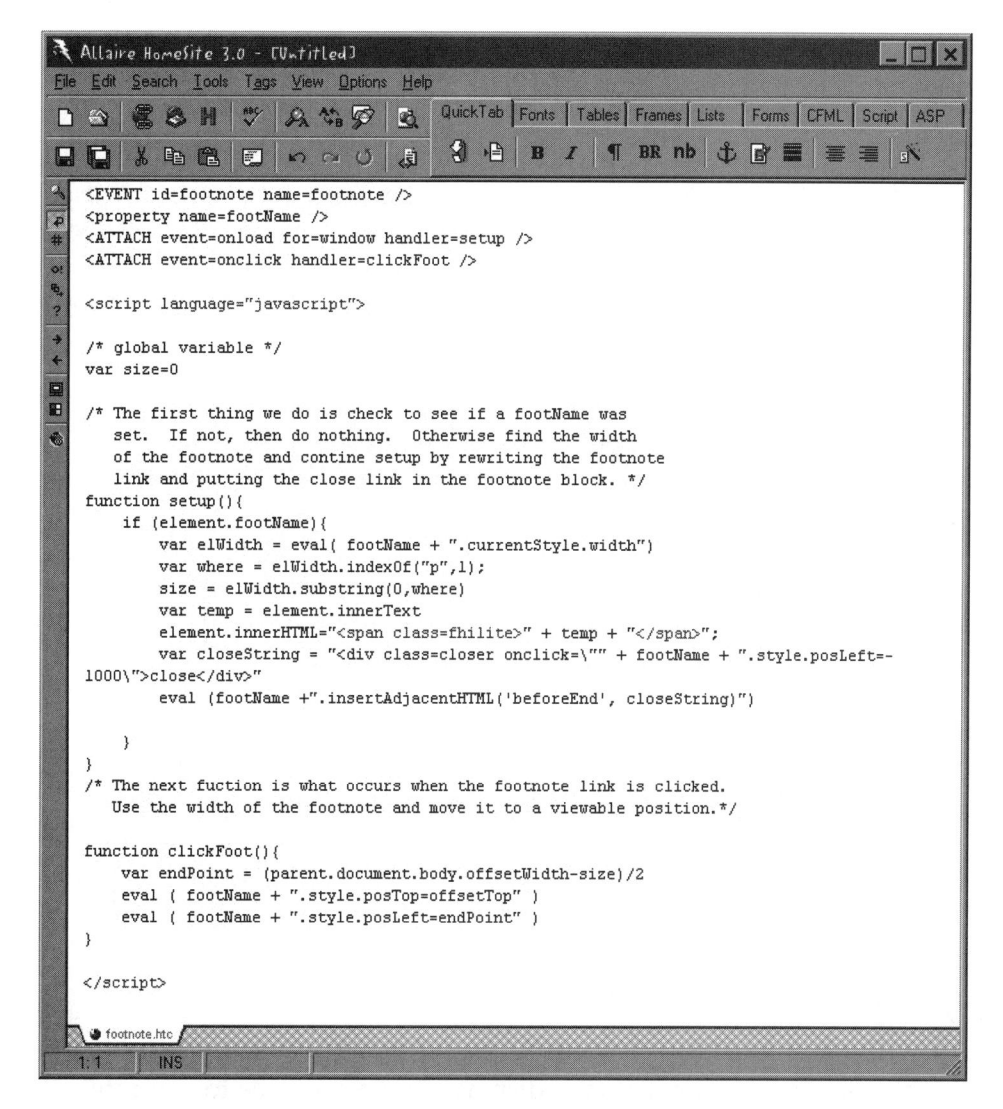

```
<EVENT id=footnote name=footnote />
<property name=footName />
<ATTACH event=onload for=window handler=setup />
<ATTACH event=onclick handler=clickFoot />

<script language="javascript">

/* global variable */
var size=0

/* The first thing we do is check to see if a footName was
   set.  If not, then do nothing.  Otherwise find the width
   of the footnote and contine setup by rewriting the footnote
   link and putting the close link in the footnote block. */
function setup(){
    if (element.footName){
        var elWidth = eval( footName + ".currentStyle.width")
        var where = elWidth.indexOf("p",1);
        size = elWidth.substring(0,where)
        var temp = element.innerText
        element.innerHTML="<span class=fhilite>" + temp + "</span>";
        var closeString = "<div class=closer onclick=\"" + footName + ".style.posLeft=-1000\">close</div>"
        eval (footName +".insertAdjacentHTML('beforeEnd', closeString)")

    }
}
/* The next fuction is what occurs when the footnote link is clicked.
   Use the width of the footnote and move it to a viewable position.*/

function clickFoot(){
    var endPoint = (parent.document.body.offsetWidth-size)/2
    eval ( footName + ".style.posTop=offsetTop" )
    eval ( footName + ".style.posLeft=endPoint" )
}

</script>
```

Figure 13.6 One script lies behind the behavior.

A behavior is almost like Dynamic HTML for the new age. DHTML lets you change the way something displays in response to reader action, without downloading a new page from the server. It does this by using CSS and scripting. Unfortunately, all the code for the DHTML display effect—all the script and CSS code—lies within the HTML page. This means it can't easily be reused in other files short of a copy-and-paste routine. And, if you want to change any portion of the display effect, you need to go into the content file to make your changes.

There has to be a better way!

There is. HTC behaviors provide a way of separating the DHTML effect from the HTML or XML file content. It turns the effect into a *behavior*, which is an HTML component that can reused in many different documents.

Separate Skill Sets

Remember, early on in this book you promised to chant "I can't do it all myself, I can't do it all myself!" HTC behaviors are a perfect example of how different skill sets can work in a complementary way to create an effective display effect.

A behavior requires three types of skills: content skills to create the actual material in the document, design skills to display the document attractively and effectively, and engineering or programming skills to create a script that makes the dynamic changes happen.

Maybe you have all three skill sets, but more likely you focus on one or another. By separating content from format, your content staff can create documents, your design staff can make visual decisions, and your programming staff can code the scripts that make the document dynamic.

With the component approach, the content staff can use the work of the designers and programmers without having to be a designer or programmer themselves. The designers can focus on design and display style while the programmers create the underlying functionality.

Custom Tags

It makes sense to create dynamic displays. It makes sense to separate out the script and CSS from the document. But what does this have to do with XML? Well, a simple application of XML within an HTML file lets you make the behaviors easy to apply.

Because XML is extensible, you can create any element along with any attributes your application needs. Because the element defines content and structure—not display—you can easily apply a behavior to an XML tag. Suddenly you have created the ability for an author to type the tag <pullquote> around the text he or she wants in a pullquote—and have the browser create a pullquote when the page displays.

XML tags provide the step that enables anyone to use an HTC behavior in a document by learning only that one tag and its attributes. Of course, the danger is making sure the XML tags remain focused on content and don't start down the slippery slope to becoming display tags. Remember, the HTC behavior is scripted information about displaying a certain element—and not an element itself!

For example, footnotes are an element that can be displayed in many different ways. One way is to have the style sheet associate the footnote element with a scripted HTC behavior. But another style sheet can choose an entirely different display style for the footnote element.

Creating an HTC

If you are a programmer *and* a designer, this overview may provide you with all that you need to start creating an HTC behavior of your own.

If you are not a programmer, you'll need to work with a programmer for the scripting portion of the HTC.

If you are not a designer, you'll want to work with a designer for the visual display and CSS portion of the HTC.

(See what we mean about complementary skills working together?)

Three Files, Three Skills

You'll actually have three files involved in using an HTC behavior.

First, you'll have your content file—your .html or .xml file. This will be the page your reader views in a web browser.

The content file will reference a .css file, which contains style data about the document elements.

The .css file will reference one or more .htc files, which contain scripting data about the behavior.

The Content File

The content file is stored in an ASCII file with the extension .xml.

The content file contains your document and element tags. It includes a namespace reference and a style sheet link.

For example, this .html file uses a namespace reference called MAG and links to a style sheet named "magazine.css." In the body it uses an XML tag called <quote>.

```
<html xmlns:MAG>
<head>
<link rel="stylesheet" type="test/css" href="styles/magazine.css">
```

```
</head>
<body>
<p>In the beginning there was nothing but fire, the fire that burns from
the inside out, melting gaseous auras into something that we might
someday call a planet. <MAG:quote>It's a tough beginning</MAG:quote>
says researcher Janet Sparks.
</p>
```

The .css File

The style data is stored in an ASCII text file with the extension .css.

Style data about the elements is contained in the .css file. In the .css file, elements are assigned display properties that the web browser uses to render the .xml file in the browser window.

For example, in this file, the code sets a value for a CSS2 property, @media screen, for the QUOTE element. The @media screen property identifies the QUOTE element as belonging to a screen display.

The element's style is linked to a specific .htc file.

```
@media screen {
MAG:\QUOTE {behavior:url(http://www.mysite.com/behaviors/quote.htc)}
}
```

The .htc File

The HTC is stored in an ASCII text file with the extension .htc. For example:

```
article.htc
```

Each .htc file contains a script that describes one behavior. For example, the script might turn the element's *style.color* property shocking fuchsia on mouseover and return the element's *style.color* property to its original value on mouseout.

Chain Reaction

When your browser encounters an XML tag it goes to the linked style sheet for information on how to display it. For display data, it is sent to an .htc file. The browser then runs the script as defined in the .htc file.

Steps in the Process

To incorporate an HTC behavior into your page, you'll need to do three things:

1. Specify what you want the behavior to do.
2. Connect the HTC script with the particular element that will be displayed in this style in the style sheet.
3. Create the .htc file that contains the HTC script.

You, personally, might not be the one to do all these steps. You may assign the programming portion to a programmer, for example.

Specify the Behavior

You first need to decide what sort of stylistic action is going to add value to your presentation. Do you want to make a little box that pops up with information when a reader clicks the footnote marker? Do you want to make the page shake when the reader mouses on the border? Do you want parts of the text to be duplicated and appear as captions or as pullquotes?

A behavior isn't something you add just because you can. A behavior is a way of filling a need for presenting your content in a better or more powerful way to your readers. Think about what your content presentation needs and then explore whether a behavior is a tool you might want to use.

You'll also define how a behavior is going to act and what variables it will have. Will the behavior be something that happens when the page is displayed, or will it be a response to a reader action? With each use of the behavior, will the page creator be able to define attributes, such as the flushing text left or right, setting a speed for movement of an object, or controlling the size of a new window? Specify the details of your planned behavior.

Your behavior is interactive stylistic data that is, in the style sheet, assigned to an element on the page. You could (although this goes against the grain of XML!) create an element specifically to include a behavior in your page. The behavior then becomes an element that you'd enter with a tag like any other element. This is a way of using behaviors in an HTML environment, but don't get in the habit of thinking of behaviors this way in an XML world.

Use the .css File to Match Element to Behavior

In your .css file, you'll need to assign the element that will carry this behavior a style. The style will be a pointer to a specific .htc file. For example, the style for footnote, instead of a set of .css properties, becomes a pointer to an .htc file.

Create the HTC Script

Of course, before the behavior will actually do anything you'll need to create the HTC script. Once the script is complete, it can be assigned to different elements in a style sheet and used in many different pages. That's the beauty of the component approach—once created, the components can be used in many different ways.

The next section of this chapter outlines the HTC specification and how HTCs are created.

HTC Elements

The HTC model has its own set of elements that you use in creating an HTC. The following is a summary of these elements.

Element: <COMPONENT>

What It Is

It is a container that identifies an HTC. It is optional.

Parents and Children

Parent: none

Children: PROPERTY, METHOD, EVENT, ATTACH

Attributes

URN. Uniform Resource Name that identifies the component (required).

Element: <PROPERTY>

What It Is

It is a property of the HTC.

Parents and Children

Parent: COMPONENT

Children: none

Attributes

Name. Name of the property (required).

ID. A value that identifies the property within the component (optional).

Get. Specifies a function that is called when the property is retrieved (optional).

Put. Specifies a function that is called when the property is set (optional).

Persist. Specifies whether the property persists as part of the page (optional).

Element: <METHOD>

What It Is

It is a method of the HTC.

Parents and Children

Parent: COMPONENT
Children: None

Attributes

Name. Name of the method (required).

Element: <EVENT>

What It Is

It is an event used by the HTC to communicate with the document. It lets you go beyond predefined HTML events such as onmouseover.

Parents and Children

Parent: COMPONENT
Children: None

Attributes

Name. Name of the event (required).

ID. Identification value that identifies the event within the component (optional).

Methods

this.fire. Fires the event to the document.

Element: <ATTACH>

What It Is

This element attaches a function to an event, causing the function to be called every time the event occurs.

Parents and Children

Parent: COMPONENT

Children: None

Attributes

Event. Name of the event to which the function is tied (required).

Handler. The name of the function that handles the event.

For. Identifies the document object to which events are attached. Values are document, element, or window (optional).

URN. URN of a source of the event (optional).

HTC-Specific Elements

These elements are event calls that work specifically with HTC elements.

ondocumentready

This event fires when the content document that calls it has been parsed.

oncontentready

This event fires when the element has been parsed.

I WROTE A TAG!

by Glenn Davis

This column by web designer Glenn Davis, CTO of Project Cool, was first published in Future Focus. In it, he talks about discovering how XML via an IE 5 behavior gave him a hint of why XML can be exciting for designers.

To show how easy it is to use a behavior once it has been created, we've left the PULLQUOTE tags in the text.

Today, for the first time ever, I defined a tag to use in a web page.

By defined, I mean that I created an entirely new tag, with switches of my choice and optional values that made sense for my application. I wanted to create a pull quote within a body of text and so I created a tag for doing just that.

Creating tags isn't something I ever thought I'd do, but the power that lets me—and any of us—do it is here. Or nearly so.

The power comes in the form of the much (over)hyped eXtensible Markup Language, XML. You see, for months we've all been hearing about the future of the web and how XML is tied to that future. I don't know about you, but <pub:PULLQUOTE align="left" lips="both">every time I'd hear about XML I'd hear completely different things</pub:PULLQUOTE> we'd be doing with it. Databases. Searches. Indexing. Display. Manipulation. This XML was trying to be the great do-all and be-all.

My reaction, most of the time, has been "HUH?" I've gotten especially confused when I've looked at the online documentation for XML. Most of this material has obviously not been written with the reader in mind.

But I think I'm getting a handle on it, at least a little bit. XML will be used quite a bit on the server side of the web for databases, indexing, and structural data relationships. It will be used on the client side for improved data display capabilities and data manipulation. I began to see real applications, at least on the browser/designer end. And so this week I defined a tag to use in Project Cool's web pages. And it works.

There are a couple of caveats you should know about. The first is that the XML I used to do this with currently works only in Internet Explorer 5.0. So if you're using IE 5.0 to read this page, you'll see the results of my pull quote. If you're not, this will look just like a normal Future Focus page. The second is that for XML to be meaningful on the browser end you have to combine it with other technologies like CSS and scripting. With my tag I used a bit of both.

I live at the bleeding edge of the web most of the time. I'm never happy with the past and am always looking to try out new things. When a new browser comes out I'm always in line for it. That's how I came to be using IE 5 even though it's out only in a developer beta that isn't recommended for the average user. Perfect! I can play.

continues

I WROTE A TAG! *(Continued)*

And play I did. I started out by going through the online demos that Microsoft released when it announced that the developer beta was available. There was some interesting stuff there, but I've never been particularly amazed with the demos that Microsoft makes, Asteroids being the exception. One demo really caught my attention, though. It was a demo of using XML and these elements called behaviors to create footnotes. Sounds pretty lame, doesn't it? But it wasn't. It got my head spinning with some of the possibilities.

One of the problems with web publishing is all the work that has to go into it before the pages get to your browser. There are writers, editors, designers, coders, etc. Some of us wear all of those hats, others only one. Anything that can make web publishing easier is always a plus.

Picture this process: Someone writes an article, the editor reviews it and decides on a couple of pull quotes that should go on the page. (I'm sure you've all seen pull quotes in magazines. They are the bits of text from the articles that are set off by themselves in hopes they'll lure you into reading the article.) Then the designer/coder looks at it and comes up with the design guidelines and either codes it or turns it over to a coder who puts it all together, doing some fancy table or image work to make the pull quotes happen. End result, a nice web page.

But <pub:PULLQUOTE align="right" lips="pre">XML can change that process.</pub:PULLQUOTE>

Today I created the pull quote tag using XML and now to do a pull quote here in Future Focus all anyone has to do is to use the *pullquote* tag. All of the coding to make it work needed to be done just once and the tag itself can be used by designers who never have to look at a snippet of script. Whole libraries of custom tags and functions can be created using XML and then applied to content with little effort.

Let me quickly summarize how my *pullquote* tag works. It's really quite simple.

First, there's a bit of JavaScript code that is on our server in the form of an HTML Component. An HTC is a self-contained script that can be applied to different parts of a web page and used over and over again as often as needed and on as many pages as needed. That component holds most of the power of the tag.

In the CSS definitions for my page I defined the style for *pullquote* as one that uses the *pullquote* component. Whenever the *pullquote* tag shows up in an HTML page, the browser applies that script to the contents of it and transforms it into a pull quote block that appears in the display window of the browser.

The *pullquote* component itself is quite straightforward. It copies the text within the *pullquote* tag and creates some HTML code that floats the pull quote text in the document using a predefined CSS style.

One of the other wonderful things about this is that it degrades gracefully down the full browser food chain. Those of you reading this column without IE 5 don't notice

> anything at all unusual, but the XML parser in IE5 shows those viewers the full text of the column, with pull quotes added.
>
> So imagine a future in which you have a library of new tags at your disposal. Tags that degrade for older browsers yet offer your users new and wondrous possibilities. Imagine those possibilities and then picture three letters: XML.

Summary

HTCs, or behaviors, are a good way to begin to use XML pockets within HTML documents. The behaviors can add a layer of interactivity to your presentation. Because they are components, the same functionality can be reused in many different locations without programming overhead. Once built, they are also easy for the document creator to use.

HTCs are created by a programmer, or a designer comfortable with scripting. And they are, as of this writing, a non-standard IE5-only feature. Despite this, they are worth taking some time to play with because they can provide useful display effects and show the direction of the future of web content display.

APPENDIX A

CSS Reference

This Appendix lists the CSS properties, along with an example of each in use. They are grouped by category.

The color and background properties control an element's display color, its background color, and its use of background images.

The fonts and text properties control a textual element's typographic display characteristics.

The position and visibility properties control an element's position within the containing element, the element's z-position, and whether the element is visible.

The spacing and areas properties control an element's borders, margins, and padding.

You can see full examples and a more detailed explanation at the companion website to this book, <http://www.projectcool.com/guide/xml>.

Color and Background Properties

This set of properties controls the color in which an element is displayed or the background which is displayed behind the element.

273

Color

```
{color: name/#hex/rgb(R%, G%, B%)/rgb(R, G, B)}
```

Description

The *color* property selects a foreground color. Typically, the foreground color is the color of the text in the HTML element.

Example

This creates colored text for the paragraph element.

```
P {color: red;}
```

bgcolor

```
{background-color: colorname/hexvalue/rgb(R%,
G%, B%)}
```

Description

The *background-color* property specifies a background color. The background of an element is the space around the element.

Example

This sets a style rule for the background color of a first-level head:

```
h1 {background-color: #99cc77;}
```

background-image

```
{background-image: url(urlname)}
```

Description

The *background-image* property specifies what image to display in the HTML element's background area.

Example

This sets a style rule that calls an image named logo.gif as the background for the table element:

```
table {background-image: url(../images/logo.gif)}
```

background-repeat

```
{background-repeat: repeat/repeat-x/repeat-y/no-repeat}
```

Description

The *background-repeat* property specifies how and if a background image gets repeated.

Example

This sets a style rule that calls an image named logo.gif as the background for the body element and repeats it in both the X and Y directions:

```
body {background-image: url(../images/logo.gif);
      background-repeat: repeat;}
```

background-attachment

```
{background-attachment: scroll/fixed}
```

Description

The *background-attachment* property specifies whether the background image scrolls or remains fixed in the same location on the page.

Example

This sets a style rule that calls an image named logo.gif as the background for the body element and prevents the background image from scrolling with the page:

```
body {background-image: url(../images/logo.gif);
      background-attachment: fixed;}
```

background-position

```
{background-position: %vertical % horizontal}
```

- or -

```
{background-position: top/center/bottom left/center/right}
```

Description

The *background-position* property lets you place a background image in a specific location within the element's background.

Example

This places an image named logo.gif 20 percent from the top of the page and 30 percent from the left of the page:

```
body {background-image: url(../images/logo.gif);
      background-position: 20% 30%;}
```

This places an image named logo.gif on the page at the top vertically and centered horizontally:

```
body {background-image: url(../images/logo.gif);
      background-position: top center;}
```

Fonts and Text Properties

This group of style properties sets the display font values and the text alignment values for the element.

font-size

```
{font-size: XXunits/%/sizevalue}
```

Description

The *font-size* property lets you specify the size of the element's text.

Example

This sets a style rule that makes paragraphs 12-point text:

```
p {font-size: 12pt;}
```

font-family

```
{font-family: name,name generic name}
```

Description

The *font-family* property lets you specify a font for the element's text.

Example

This sets a style rule making paragraphs appear in Helvetica. If Helvetica is not available, they will appear in Arial.

```
p {font-family: helvetica, arial;}
```

font-style

```
{font-style: normal/italic/oblique}
```

Description

The *font-style* property lets you select an italic or oblique style.

Example

This sets a style rule that makes paragraphs Helvetica italic:

```
p {font-family: helvetica;
    font-style: italic;}
```

font-variant

```
{font-variant: normal/small-caps}
```

Description

The *font-variant* property lets you select a small caps style.

Example

This sets a style rule that makes paragraphs Century small caps:

```
p {font-family:century serif;
    font-variant: small-caps;}
```

font-weight

```
{font-weight: normal/bold/bolder/lighter/XXX}
```

Description

The *font-weight* property lets you select the darkness or lightness of the element's font.

Example

This sets a style rule that makes paragraphs Helvetica bold:

```
p {font-family:helvetica;
     font-weight: bold;}
```

line-height

```
{line-height: normal/XXunits/%}
```

Description

The *line-height* property specifies the space from the baseline of one line of text to the baseline of the next.

Example

This sets a style rule that makes the line height 12 points:

```
P {font-size: 10pt;
   line-height: 12pt;}
```

text-indent

```
{text-indent: XXunits/%}
```

Description

The *text-indent* property controls the amount of indent for the first line of the text element.

Example

This sets a style rule that makes the first line indent two em spaces:

```
P {text-indent: 2em;}
```

text-align

```
{text-align: left/right/center/justify}
```

Description

The *text-align* property aligns the element horizontally across the page or within the division.

Example

This sets a style rule that makes the P element align right:

```
P {text-align: right;}
```

text-decoration

```
{text-decoration: underline/overline/line-through/blink}
```

Description

The *text-decoration* property lets you make the text appear underlined or with a line through it.

Example

This sets a style rule that makes the P element underlined:

```
P {text-decoration: underline;}
```

text-transform

```
{text-transform: uppercase/lowercase/capitalize/none}
```

Description

The text transformation (*text-transform*) property controls the element's capitalization.

Example

This sets a style rule that makes the P element all caps:

```
P {text-transform: uppercase;}
```

letter-spacing

```
{letter-spacing: normal/XXunit/%}
```

Description

The *letter-spacing* property lets you control the amount of space between each letter in a text block.

Example

This gives the P element a letter-spacing value of -2:

```
P {font-size: 18pt; letter-spacing: -2pt;}
```

word-spacing

```
{word-spacing: normal/XXunits/%}
```

Description

The *word-spacing* property lets you control the amount of space between words.

Example

This gives the P element a word-spacing value of 10 pixels. That means 10 extra pixels are inserted between each word in the text block:

```
P {word-spacing: 10px;}
```

Position and Visibility Properties

These style properties set the display value type and position the element within its containing element.

position

```
{position: normal/relative/absolute}
```

Description

The *position* property lets you set a box's position in the layout of a page.

Example

This assigns the list element a relative box position:

```
LIST {position: relative;}
```

left

```
{left: XXunits/%}
```

Description

The *left* property lets you set the distance between the element box and the left edge of the containing block.

Example

This tells the list element to display 1 em in from the left side of the containing element:

```
LIST {position: relative;
      left: 1em;}
```

top

```
{top: XXunits/%}
```

Description

The *top* property lets you set the distance between the element box and the top edge of the containing block.

Example

This tells the LIST element to display with its left edge 3 ems in from the left side of the containing element and 2 ems down from the top of the containing element:

```
LIST {position: relative;
      left: 3em;
      top: 2em;}
```

display

```
{display: none/""/block/inline/list-item}
```

Description

The *display* property hides or shows the element. This element is often used with scripting to hide or show an element based on certain user actions.

Example

This creates a title whose display property is hidden:

```
TITLE {display: none;}
```

z-index

```
{top: XXunits/%}
```

Description

The *z-index* property lets you set the stacking order of elements.

Example

This orders the layers of three elements:

```
TITLE {z-index:1;}
BYLINE {z-index: 2;}
ABSTRACT {z-index: 3;}
```

Spacing and Area Properties

These style properties set display borders that display relationship values for the element.

clear

```
{clear: none/left/right/both}
```

Description

The *clear* property lets you specify whether to float the element or to have it clear to below other elements when it is displayed.

Example

This places the PHOTO element below all elements above it:

    PHOTO {clear: both;}

float

    {float: none/left/right}

Description

The *float* property lets you place an element, such as an image, to the left or right of its containing block and allows other elements, like text, to flow around it.

Example

This places the PHOTO element to the left of its containing element:

    PHOTO {float: left;}

height

    {height: XXunits/%}

Description

The *height* property lets you set the height of an element.

Example

This tells the LOGO element to display at 150 pixels high:

    LOGO {height: 150px;}

width

    {width: XXunits/%}

Description

The *width* property lets you set the width of an element.

Example

This tells the LOGO element to display at 200 pixels wide:

```
LOGO {qidth: 200px;}
```

border-color, border-style, border-width

```
{border-color: colorname/hexvalue/RGB(R%,G%,B%)}
{border-style:
none/solid/double/dashed/dotted/groove/ridge/inset/outset}
{border-width: XXunits/thin/medium/thick}
```

Description

The *border* properties set the display value for the element's color, or style, or width. The properties apply to all four sides.

Example

This tells the CHAPTERNUM element to be displayed surrounded by a solid border:

```
CHAPTERNUM {border-style: solid;}
```

border-top-width, border-bottom-width, border-right-width, border-left-width

```
{border-top/bottom/right/left-width: XXunits/thin/medium/thick}
```

Description

The various *border-x-width* properties let you set the width of an element's border one side at a time.

Example

This tells the CHAPTERNUM element to be displayed surrounded by a solid border on top:

```
CHAPTERNUM {border-top-width: solid;}
```

border, border-top, border-bottom, border-right, border-left

```
{border: width style color}
{border-top: width style color}
{border-bottom: width style color}
{border-right: width style color}
{border-left: width style color}
```

Description

The various all-inclusive border properties let you set the width, style, and color of all four of an element's borders simultaneously (*border*), or the top border only (*border-top*), or the bottom border only (*border-bottom*), or the right border only (*border-right*), or the left border only (*border-left*).

Example

This tells the CHAPTERNUM element to be displayed surrounded by a thin, solid, blue border:

```
CHAPTERNUM {border: thin solid blue;}
```

margin, margin-top, margin-bottom, margin-right, margin-left

```
{margin: XXunits/%}
{margin-top: XXunits/%}
{margin-bottom: XXunits/%}
{margin-right: XXunits/%}
{margin-left: XXunits/%}
```

Description

The *margin* properties let you set the displayed margin width of the element.

Example

This tells the CHAPTERNUM element to be displayed with a 12-pixel margin on all four sides:

```
CHAPTERNUM {margin: 12px;}
```

padding, padding-top, padding-bottom, padding-right, padding-left

```
{padding: XXunits/%}
{padding-top: XXunits/%}
{padding-bottom: XXunits/%}
{padding-right: XXunits/%}
{padding-left: XXunits/%}
```

Description

The *padding* properties let you set the displayed padding width of the element.

Example

This tells the CHAPTERNUM element to be displayed with a 5 percent padding on the right and left sides:

```
CHAPTERNUM {padding-right: 5%;
            padding-left: 5%;}
```

APPENDIX B

The Companion Website

This book has a companion website that contains additional reference material. We could print the URLs here, but they will likely be superceded by new data by the time this book makes it from the press to the store to your hands, and isn't it a heck of a lot easier to just click on a link?

The website is located at http://www.projectcool.com/guide/xml>.

XML Resources. The site points to current specifications of XML and XML technologies, as well as emerging resources about these technologies.

XML Vendors. The site provides links to some of the vendors who are offering XML authoring capabilities.

Parsers. The site identifies some of the current validating and non-validating parsers and where to use or download them.

Live Examples. The site contains "live" versions of many of th examples in this book. You can see CSS and DHTML in action, for example. And you can look at the XML document, DTD, and style sheet shown in Chapter 11, "Under the Hood: A Simple XML Example."

Glossary

Attribute. Information that further defines an element.
Attribute lists. A means of defining an element's attributes. Part of a DTD.
Behavior. A technique that combines scripting and style to create a component and ties the component display data to an XML element.
Branch. An element within a document tree. A branch element contains other elements.
CDATA (Character Data). Unparsed characters.
Child element. An element that is contained inside of another. A list item is a child element of a list.
CSS1 (Cascading Style Sheets [version 1]). A way of assigning style data to HTML and XML tags.
CSS2 (Cascading Style Sheets [version 2]). An expansion of CSS1.
DCD (Document Content Description). A "structural schema facility" for XML, based on the Resource Description Framework (RDF).
DDML (Document Definition Markup Language). A schema language for XML documents. Until January 1999 it was referred to as Xschema.
DHTML (Dynamic HTML). A blanket term that describes the ability to access and manipulate individual elements in a web page.
DOCTYPE. Document Type Declaration.
Document. A set of data in a file.
Document element. A component of a document that can contain data and can be addressed individually.

Document tree. The structure of a document, in which one element serves as the root, with other elements branching out and forming a hierarchical relationship.

Document Type Declaration. A statement about the type of document the file contains.

DOM (Document Object Model). A means of addressing individual elements in a web page.

DSSSL (Document Style Semantics and Specification Language). DSSSL is SGML's style language.

DTD (Document Type Definition). A set of rules that defines the structure of your document.

Element. A piece of data in a document.

Entity. A word that represents other data. An entity is somewhat like a macro.

External entity. An entity whose data lives in a file outside of the file in which it is used.

HTC (HTML Components). A way of tying action and style to XML elements. HTC started out life as something called "behaviors." It was created by Microsoft, implemented in IE 5.0, and then submitted to the W3C in October 1998. Netscape has a similar submission, called "action sheets."

HTML (Hypertext Markup Language). The basic building block of the web, a set of tags that allow a web browser to display a document.

ICE (Information Content and Exchange Protocol). A proposed XML-based solution for sharing data from site to site.

Inheritance. The passing down of information from a parent to a child element.

Instance. One particular occurrence of an element. Typically, there are multiple instances of the same element; for example, there may be three <SPECIES> in a document. Each <SPECIES> is an instance of the *species* element.

Internal entity. An entity that is both defined and used within a single document.

Leaf. The outermost element in a DTD.

Marked section. Part of a DTD that has been marked "ignore" or "include."

Math ML (Mathematical Markup Language). An application of XML that describe mathematical notation.

Metadata. Data about data.

Namespace. A means of using tags from multiple tag sets in the same document.

Parent element. An element that contains other elements.
Parse. The action of interpreting an XML document.
Parsed entity. An entity whose replacement string contains parsed, or textual, data.
Parser. A tool that interprets the contents of an XML file and passes the information along to an application.
PCDATA. Parsed character data.
Query. To ask the computer to find a specific piece of information.
RDF (Resource Description Framework). A means of expressing metadata in a way that makes the data machine-understandable, thus enabling automation of certain processes.
Schema. A description of the rules for data, including the elements that are part of the set and the type of data that can be contained within an element.
SGML (Standard Generalized Markup Language). An international standard from 1986 that solves the problem of data interchange by separating format from content.
SMIL (Synchronized Multimedia Integration Language [pronounced "smile"]). An application of XML that should make authoring audio and video within a web page easier.
Style property. A specific piece of display information, such as "color" or "font," that is assigned to an element in a style sheet.
Unparsed entity. An entity whose replacement data is nonparsed, or something other than textual data.
Valid. An XML document that both follows XML syntax rules and conforms to the rules of a DTD.
Validate. The process of comparing an XML document to the DTD rules.
Validating parser. A parser that not only checks syntax and builds an element tree, but also compares the contents of the XML file to a DTD rule set.
Well-formed. An XML document that conforms to XML syntax rules but does not validate against a DTD.
W3C (World Wide Web Consortium). Organization that coordinates development of possible standards for web-based information.
XFDL (Extensible Forms Description Language). An application of XML for digital forms.
Xlink. A way of describing a relationship between pieces of data.
XML (Extensible Markup Language). The language recommended by the W3C that enables you to create a structured document that you can use across many different types of publishing applications, ranging from the Web to databases.

XML data. An early submission to the W3C, addressing the structural rules of an XML document. It has since been superceded by the Document Content Description (DCD).

XML NS (XML Namespace). A means of using tags from multiple tag sets in the same document.

XML-QL (XML Query Language). A proposal for querying XML documents, drawing from SQL.

Xpointer. A way of identifying data inside a link in an XML document.

XQL (Extensible Query Language). A proposal for querying XML documents. Uses XSL.

Xschema. A schema language for XML documents. Now known as DDML (Document Definition Markup Language).

XSL (Extensible Style Language). A language for expressing style sheets.

Index

&amp, 155
&apos, 155
&gt, 155
&lt, 155
&quot, 155
#FIXED, 180, 206
#IMPLIED, 180, 206
#REQUIRED, 180, 205, 206

Ad Markup, 91, 112
analyze your document, 21–23
API (Application Programming Interface), 52–53
Application Programming Interface (API), 52–53
applications, 166
application-specific XML, 111–113
  Ad Markup, 91, 112
  ICE, 91, 112
  Math ML, 91, 112–113
  SMIL, 91, 112
  summary, 91
  XFDL, 91, 112
area and spacing properties, 247, 282–286
  border properties, 284–285
  clear, 282–283
  float, 283
  height, 283
  margin properties, 285
  padding properties, 286
  width, 283–284
attribute lists, 141–142
  CDATA, 150
  creating, 202–203
  identifying, 178
  reading a DTD, 178–181
attributes, 121–122. *See also* attribute lists
  #FIXED keyword, 180, 206
  #IMPLIED keyword, 180, 206
  #REQUIRED keyword, 180, 205, 206
  CDATA keyword, 179, 203–204
  default values, 180–181, 205–207
  defined by DTD, 167
  description, 38
  encoding attribute, 132, 135
  ENTITY keyword, 179, 203, 205
  ID keyword, 179, 203, 204
  IDREF keyword, 179, 203, 205
  name of attribute, 179
  NMTOKEN keyword, 179, 203, 204
  NOTATION keyword, 179, 203, 205
  quotation marks, 41, 122, 125–126
  reading a DTD, 177–178
  specifying an attribute, 122
  standalone attribute, 132, 135
  types, 179–180
  values, 203–205
  version attribute, 132, 135
  XML declaration attributes, 132, 135

background and color properties, 246, 273–276
  background-attachment, 275
  background-image, 274–275
  background-position, 275–276
  background-repeat, 275
  bgcolor, 274
  color, 274
behaviors. *See* HTC
bitmapped file, 10–11
browsers
  and display, 60
  DTD recognition, 25
  HTC behavior support, 257–258
  HTML support, 19
  and HTML tags, 34
  initial purpose of, 2
  XML support, 19, 25

CALS (Computer Aided Logistics and Support), 8, 9
cascading, 94, 240–241
Cascading Style Sheets. *See* CSS
case sensitive, 40, 125
CDATA (character data), 150–153
  create CDATA section, 151
  and DOM Core spec, 63
  value of CDATA attribute, 179
character data. *See* CDATA
color and background properties, 246, 273–276
  background-attachment, 275
  background-image, 274–275
  background-position, 275–276
  background-repeat, 275
  bgcolor, 274
  color, 274

293

294   Index

comments, 123, 149–150
　creating a DTD, 191
　reading a DTD, 170–171
Community Cooker example, 213
　apply DTD to documents, 223–224
　building DTD, 218–222
　displaying the document, 227–231
　newsletter illustration, 214
　parsing the document, 224–227
　summary, 231–232
　understanding your data, 213–217
Computer Aided Logistics and Support (CALS), 8, 9
CSS (Cascading Style Sheets), 26, 93–95, 237–238
　concepts, 240–242
　creating a style sheet, 244–252
　CSS1, 93
　CSS2, 93
　description/status/resources, 87
　and DHTML, 97–98
　display property, 250–252
　and DOM, 60
　extension, 245
　interaction, 61
　properties. See CSS properties
　property values, 249–250
　reference, 273–286
　and standards, 71
　style properties, 245–247
　style sheet example, 227–231
　and XSL, 96, 238–240
CSS properties, 245–247, 273–286
　color and background, 246, 273–276
　fonts and text, 247, 276–280
　position and visibility, 247, 280–282
　spacing and area, 247, 282–286
customized meaning, 20–21

data
　data about data (metadata), 29–30, 37
　know your data, 118–119

metadata, 29–30, 109–110. See also RDF
　understanding your data, 213–217
data schema, 103
DCD (Document Content Description), 88, 103
DDML (Document Definition Markup Language), 88, 101–103
declaration. See DOCTYPE definition; XML declarations
DHTML (Dynamic HTML), 97–98
　description/status/resources, 87
　and DOM, 53–56
display
　and benefits of structure, 19–20
　custom presentations, 20
　display demo document, 234–236
　flying Saturn, 53–56, 64
　interaction, 60–62
　style options, 236–238. See also CSS; HTC; XSL
　tying to structure, 25–26
　and XML, 117
DOCTYPE definition, 135–136
　create elements within, 138
　creating a DTD, 191
　defining entities, 156–157
　and internal entities, 155
　and namespaces, 159
　putting DTD data into, 136–139
　using, 211
　and well-formed document, 131
document. See also structure; XML documents
　general description of, 2–4
　hierarchy of elements, 164. See also document tree
　meaning of structure, 4–5
　objects, 51–52
　purpose of markup, 33–34, 85–88
　structure vs. format, 5–6
　structured model, 10–11
　turning document data into XML file. See XML example

documentation, 221
Document Content Description (DCD), 88, 103
Document Definition Markup Language (DDML), 88, 101–103
Document Object Model. See DOM
Document Style Semantics and Specification Language (DSSSL), 87, 97
document tree, 163–166
　branch element, 164–166
　child element, 164–165
　DTD example, 181–184
　examples, 13–14, 16, 17, 18
　leaf element, 165–166
　root element, 164, 166
document type definition. See DTD
DOM (Document Object Model), 49–50, 104
　API, 52–53
　Core, 63
　and CSS, 60
　description/status/resources, 89
　and DHTML, 53–56, 98
　flying Saturn, 53–56, 64
　goal, 104
　history of DOM, 43, 64–66
　and JavaScript, 56, 58
　objects, 51–52
　pizza analogy, 50–51
　specification, 62–63
　summary, 67
　using DOM, 66
　and XML, 58–60
　web site, 50
DTD (document type definition), 100–101
　and browser, 25
　creating a DTD. See DTD, creating a DTD
　and DCD, 103
　and DDML, 101–102
　defining entities, 156–157
　description/status/resources, 88
　and DOCTYPE definition, 136–139, 191, 211
　embedded in the file, 133
　example, 221–222
　external DTDs, 133, 136

Index

file extension, 190
finding a DTD, 169–170
and HTML, 99, 101
internal DTD, 170, 210–211
learning curve, 219–221
locally defined DTD data, 136
override external DTD, 170
overview, 163
parameter entity, 154, 207
and parser, 130, 132, 166
planning, 119–120
public DTDs, 133, 136
purpose of DTDs, 23–24
reading a DTD. *See* DTD, reading a DTD
and SGML, 9, 42, 101, 167
sharing existing DTDs, 169
and valid documents, 132
web site for existing DTDs, 120, 169
what a DTD defines, 166–167
when to use a DTD, 167–169
and XML, 23–24, 99–100
DTD, creating a DTD, 169–170, 189
 apply DTD to documents, 223–224
 attribute defaults, 205–207
 attribute list, 202–203
 attribute values, 203–205
 comments, 191
 create elements, 192
 DOCTYPE declaration, 191, 211
 element rules, 192–193, 194–201
 element within element rules, 194–201
 elements within elements, 194
 empty elements, 202
 entities, 207–209
 example, 218–222
 file extension, 190
 free-form elements, 193
 ignore sections, 209–210
 include sections, 209–210
 internal DTD, 210–211
 mixing elements, 201
 notations, 209
 planning, 190
 summary, 211–212
 textual elements, 193
 time it takes, 190

DTD, reading a DTD, 170–186
 attribute lists, 178–181
 basic elements, 171
 comments, 170–171
 element attributes, 177–178
 element declarations, 171
 element's data, 172–177
 entities, 185–186
 example, 181–185
 notations, 186
 parent/child relationships, 172
Dynamic HTML (DHTML), 87, 97–98
and DOM, 53–56

elements, 120–121
 #PCDATA data value, 193
 ANY keyword, 172, 193
 branch element, 164–166
 child elements, 120–121, 140, 164–165, 172, 177, 194
 and consistency, 24
 creating, 192
 description, 3–4, 38
 document tree, 13–14, 16, 17, 18, 163–166
 and DTD, 120–121, 166–167, 171–179
 element declaration, 171
 elements within element rules, 194–201
 elements within elements, 173–174, 194
 empty element, 139, 177, 202
 free-form elements, 193
 grouped elements, 175–177, 199–200
 hide and show example, 54–55, 57
 hierarchy of elements, 163–166
 HTC elements, 266–268
 HTC-specific elements, 268
 leaf element, 165–166
 mixed data, 140, 201
 modifying, 177–178. *See also* attributes
 one use only elements, 140
 optional elements, 141
 parent element, 120–121, 172
 planning and analysis, 21–23
 repeated and optional elements, 141

 repeated and required elements, 141
 root element, 164, 166
 rules, 3–4, 192–193, 194–201
 text, 140, 173, 177, 193
 types of data, 139–141, 172–177
entities, 153–158
 declaring entities, 207–208
 defining, 156–157
 description, 153–154
 and DTD, 167, 185–186, 207–209
 external entities, 156
 general entity, 154, 207
 internal entities, 155
 minimize errors, 154
 nontext entities, 156
 parameter entity, 154, 207
 as placeholder, 155
 predefined entities, 155
 reasons for using, 154–155
 and repeated content, 154
 types of entities, 154
 updating, 154–155
 using entities, 157–158, 208–209
errors and error checking
 DTDs error checking role, 9, 170
 minimize potential errors, 154
 parsers, 129–130, 143–146
Extended Style Language, 19
extensible, 30–33
 XML document, 122
Extensible Forms Description language (XFDL), 91, 112
EXtensible Markup Language. *See* XML
Extensible Query Language (XQL), 90, 109
Extensible Style Language (XSL), 95–96, 236–237
 and CSS, 96, 238–240
 description/status/resources, 87
 transformation, 96, 237, 239
 and XQL, 109
extensions, 84
 DTD, 190
 style sheet file, 245

Index

fonts and text properties, 247, 276–280
  font-family, 276–277
  font-size, 276
  font-style, 277
  font-variant, 277
  font-weight, 277–278
  letter-spacing, 280
  line-height, 278
  text-align, 279
  text-decoration, 279
  text-indent, 278
  text-transform, 279
  word-spacing, 280
format. *See also* CSS; XSL
  vs. structure, 5–6, 7

HTC (HTML Components), 26, 97, 255
  ATTACH element, 268
  background, 97
  COMPONENT element, 266
  concepts, 260–263
  content file, 263–264
  creating, 263–266
  .css file, 264
  custom tags, 262–263
  description/status/resources, 87
  elements, 266–269
  EVENT element, 267–268
  .htc file, 264
  incorporate behavior into page, 264–266
  METHOD element, 267
  oncontentready element, 268
  ondocumentready element, 268
  PROPERTY element, 266–267
  script a style, 237–238
  separate content/display, 260–262
  separate skill sets, 262
  summary, 271
  support for behaviors, 257–259
  what a behavior does, 255–257
  working examples, 255
HTML (Hypertext Markup Language), 92
  API, 52
  attributes, 121–122
  browser support, 19

  and CSS, 239
  description/status/resources, 86
  and DOM specification, 63
  and DTD, 99, 101
  dynamic HTML. *See* DHTML
  and extensibility, 30–31, 32–33
  fixed set of elements, 121
  history of, 1–2
  and linking, 106–108
  markup, 33, 34
  roots in SGML, 6, 8, 41–42
  and searches, 19
  structural rules, 99
  tags. *See* tags, HTML
  uses, 1
  XML vs. HTML, 41–43
  and XSL, 96
HTML Components. *See* HTC
Hypertext Markup Language. *See* HTML

ICE (Information Content and Exchange Protocol), 91, 112
ID keyword, 179, 203, 204
IDREF keyword, 179, 203, 205
IE (Internet Explorer), 25, 26, 269
ignore section, 209–210
include section, 209–210
Information Content and Exchange Protocol (ICE), 91, 112
inheritance, 241
interaction, 60–62

Jade, 97
Java, 52
JavaScript, 52, 56, 58, 59

language, 37–41
  attributes are values, 38
  elements are things, 38
  syntax, 39–41
learning curve of DTD, 219–221
linking, 106
  XLink, 89, 107–108
  XPointer, 89, 106–107
location term, 106

markup, 24–25, 33–37. *See also* HTML; SGML; XML

  creating structure, 24
  description, 85, 88
  markup-related topics, 86, 89–91
  parsing a file, 143–146
  style vs. structure, 7
  types of markup, 88
Mathematical Markup Language (Math ML), 91, 112–113
Math ML, 91, 112–113
metadata, 29–30, 109–110
  RDF, 90, 110–111
  web site, 110
metalanguage, 58
metatags, 34–37
multimedia and SMIL, 112
  and SMIL, 112

namespaces, 158–160
  declaring, 159–160
  using, 160
nesting tags, 125
newspaper advertising, 112
NMTOKEN, 179, 203, 204
NOTATION, 180, 186, 205, 209
  and DTD, 167,
nontext files, 156

objects, 51–52. *See also* DOM
  and API, 52–53
outlines, expanding, 54–55, 57

parsers, 99, 129–130
  and applications, 166
  and CDATA, 150
  and comments, 150
  non-validating parsers, 130
  parsing example, 224–227
  parsing a file, 143–146
  validating parsers, 130, 166
  what a parser does, 166
pizza analogy, 50–51
placeholder, 155
planning, 21–23
  example, 213–217
  and extensibility, 31
position and visibility properties, 247, 280–282
  display, 282
  left, 281
  position, 280–281
  top, 281
  z-index, 282

Index

processing, 89, 103–104
properties, 240, 245–247
    color and background, 244, 273–276
    display property, 250–252
    fonts and text, 247, 276–280
    position and visibility, 247, 280–282
    property values, 249–250
    spacing and area, 247, 282–286
proposals under discussion, 85
    linking, 89, 106–108
    markup, 85–86, 88–92
    metadata, 90, 109–111
    processing, 89, 103–105
    query, 90, 108–109
    structure rules, 88, 98–103
    style, 87, 92–98
    XML application, 91, 111–113

querying, 108
    XML-QL, 90, 108–109
    XQL, 90, 109
quotation marks, 122, 125–126

RDF (Resource Description Framework), 110–111
    and DCD, 103
    description/status/resources, 90
repetition, and entities, 154
Resource Description Framework. *See* RDF

Saturn flying, 53–56, 64
schemas, 100
    data schema, 103
scripting, 37, 97–98
searches, 19
    querying, 90, 108–109
SGML (Standard Generalized Markup Language), 41–42, 89–91
    background, 6, 8–9
    description/status/resources, 86
    and development of XML, 43
    DTD, 9, 42, 99, 101, 167
    structural rules, 99
    style language, 97
    tag sets, 21

SMIL (Synchronized Multimedia Integration Language), 91, 112
spacing and area properties, 247, 282–286
    border properties, 284–285
    clear, 282–283
    float, 283
    height, 283
    margin properties, 285
    padding properties, 286
    width, 283–284
Standard Generalized Markup Language. *See* SGML
standards, 69–82. *See also* proposals under discussion
    how ideas become standards, 77–81, 85
    need for standards, 70–72
    people involved, 72–76
    role of standards, 69–70
    summary, 81–82
    W3C, 76–81
structure, 11. *See also* structured document
    benefits of, 19–20
    customized tags, 20–21
    vs. format, 5–6, 7
    importance of planning, 21–23
    internal structure, 16
    meaning of structure, 4–5
    rigid structure, 12–16
    and searches, 19
    structure rule sets, 98–99
    structure rules-related topics, 88
    summary, 26–27
    tying structure to display, 25–26
structured document
    creating, 21–25
    DTD writing, 23–24
    marking up documents, 24–25
    planning and analysis, 21–23
    structured model, 10–11
style, 92–93. *See also* CSS; DHTML; HTC
    cascading, 240–241
    DSSSL, 87, 97
    Extensible Style Language. *See* XSL
    options, 236–238

    style declarations, 247–249
    style properties, 245–247
    style-related topics, 87, 93–98
    style rules, 247
    style sheet. *See* CSS
    style vs. structure, 7
    what is style, 240
style sheets. *See also* CSS
    connecting XML file to, 252
    creating CSS style sheet, 244–252
    example, 227–231, 242–243
    what are style sheets?, 242
Synchronized Multimedia Integration Language (SMIL), 91, 112
syntax, 39–41, 123–126
    case sensitive, 40, 125
    empty tags, 40–41, 124–125
    nesting, 125
    and parsers, 166
    quote attribute values, 41, 125–126

tags. *See also* tags, HTML
    attribute values, 41
    beginning a tag, 123
    case sensitive, 40, 125
    closing tags, 124
    container tags, 40
    customizable tags, 20–21, 262–263
    defining and inserting, 24–25
    and elements, 124
    empty tags, 40–41, 124–125
    ending a tag, 40, 123
    extensibility, 30–33
    and HTC, 262–263
    metatags, 34–37
    and namespaces, 104–105, 158–160
    nesting, 125
    planning, 118–119
    quotes, 41
    scripting, 37
    SGML tags, 21
    syntax, 39–41, 123–125
    validating with DTD, 24
tags, HTML, 1–2, 30–31, 32, 34
    scripting, 37
    syntax, 38–41
templates, 12
    and rigid structure, 12–13

text and fonts properties, 247, 276–280
  font-family, 276–277
  font-size, 276
  font-style, 277
  font-variant, 277
  font-weight, 277–278
  letter-spacing, 280
  line-height, 278
  text-align, 279
  text-decoration, 279
  text-indent, 278
  text-transform, 279
  word-spacing, 280
tools, 126–127
tophead, 10
transformation and XSL, 96, 237, 239
tree. *See* document tree

unparsed entities, 156

validation, 99. *See also* parser; valid XML documents
valid XML documents, 132–134, 147
  attribute lists, 141–142
  creating, 134
  DOCTYPE definition, 134–139
  meaning of valid, 117, 118
  types of element data, 139–141
  validating parser, 130
  XML declaration, 134–135
vector file, 10–11
visibility and position properties, 247, 280–282
  display, 282
  left, 281
  position, 280–281
  top, 281
  z-index, 282

web site, 287–288
well-formed XML documents, 130–132, 147
  creating, 131–132
  meaning of well-formed, 117–118, 129
  non-validating parser, 130
World Wide Web Consortium. *See* W3C
W3C (World Wide Web Consortium), 76–80, 84–85
  background, 76
  director, 77
  domains, 76
  how ideas become standards, 77–81, 85
  members, 78
  proposals. *See* proposals under discussion
  web site, 76
  working group (WG), 77

XFDL (Extensible Forms Description Language), 112
  description/status/resources, 91
XLink, 107–108
  description/status/resources, 89
XML (EXtensible Markup Language), 92
  browser support, 19
  declarations. *See* XML declarations
  description, 29–41, 86, 92
  documents. *See* XML documents
  and DOM, 58–60
  and DTD, 23–24, 99–101
  editor, 126
  error checking, 129–130
  example. *See* XML example
  extensible, 30–33
  history of XML, 43–46
  vs. HTML, 41–43
  and internal structure, 16
  language, 37–41
  markup, 33–37
  proposals. *See* proposals under discussion
  queries. *See* XML–QL; XQL
  resources, 86
  schemas, 100
  and SGML, 6, 8, 9, 43
  status, 86
  structural rules, 99
  structured document model, 10–11
  tools, 126–127
  version, 132
  what XML does, 46–47
XML Data, 88, 103
XML declarations, 122
  encoding attribute, 132, 135
  standalone attribute, 132, 135
  and valid document, 134–135
  version attribute, 132, 135
  and well-formed document, 132
XML documents
  and CDATA, 150–153
  creating documents, 129, 131–132
  displaying, 227–231, 233
  editing tools, 126
  elements, 120–121
  example, 116
  know your data, 118–119
  know your DTD, 119–120
  parsing a file, 143–146
  preparation, 118–120
  syntax, 123–126
  types of documents, 117–118
  using entities, 157–158
  valid document. *See* valid XML documents
  well-formed document. *See* well-formed XML documents
  what it is, 122–123
XML example, 213
  applying DTD to documents, 223–224
  building DTD, 218–222
  displaying the document, 227–231
  parsing the document, 224–227
  summary, 231–232
  understanding your data, 213–217
XML NS (Namespace), 89, 104–105
XML-QL (XML Query Language), 108–109
  description/status/resources, 90
XPointer, 89, 106–107
XQL (Extensible Query Language), 90, 109
Xschema, 101. *See also* DDML
XSL (Extensible Style Language), 95–96, 236–237
  and CSS, 96, 238–240
  description/status/resources, 87
  transformation, 96, 237, 239
  and XQL, 109